SOURCES OF ECONOMIC AND BUSINESS STATISTICS

SOURCES OF ECONOMIC AND BUSINESS STATISTICS

BERNARD EDWARDS
M.Litt., B.Sc.(Econ.), B.Com., A.I.S., F.S.S., M.B.I.M.
Principal, Aberdeen College of Commerce

HEINEMANN : LONDON

William Heinemann Ltd
15 Queen St, Mayfair, London W1X 8BE
LONDON MELBOURNE TORONTO
JOHANNESBURG AUCKLAND

First published 1972
434 90520 8 (hardback)
434 90521 6 (limp)

Printed in Great Britain by
Willmer Brothers Limited, Birkenhead

To my Mother and Father

Preface

In a simple economy planning is relatively easy. The businessman in a small isolated community can plan successfully by maintaining close personal contact with his customers, his suppliers and his rivals. The government of a small city state can likewise respond directly to the will of its constituents without requiring any vast 'information structure' on which to base its decisions. As an economy becomes more complex, however, such direct relationship becomes progressively less satisfactory, and some more formal means of collecting and disseminating information necessary for planning becomes necessary.

In any modern economy, much of this task can only be performed by the central authority, because the government is the only body which has the power, the resources, and the freedom from sectional interests to do so. Obviously the government itself needs information for the overall planning and direction of the country's economic resources, but in addition it has the duty to make information available, in quantitative form, to the general public. This information is published in the form of official statistics, the variety and complexity of which are such as to make it very difficult for the intending user to find his way through them without a guide. It is the purpose of this book to provide a guide for all those who are concerned with planning in business or in public administration.

It covers the main economic and business statistics available in this country; their origin, possible uses, and mode of publication.

Government statisticians frequently grumble to the effect that few firms use the statistics they provide, whilst the businessmen themselves complain either that the statistics do not give them just what they require, or that they do not understand how to use those which are available.

There is substance in both points, and it is hoped that this book will help business men and others to use more effectively what is available, whilst at the same time providing them with a more informed basis from which to put forward suggestions for improvements.

Chapters 1, 2, and 3 provide the necessary background to the published statistics, and should be read first. Thereafter Chapters 4 to 9 may be read in any order—each topic standing in its own right. Chapters 10 and 11 are linked and should be read together, whilst Chapter 12 depends to a considerable extent on Chapters 5 and 8. Chapter 13, on the uses of economic statistics, may be glanced through at an early stage as an incentive to the study of the book as a whole. Its detailed study should, however, be left until the earlier chapters have been mastered.

The book is intended to be read with the official statistical publications to which it refers. It is a guide to the fruitful use of these publications, and it will not fulfil its purpose unless it is so used.

A feature of the book is the selection of exercises and topics for discussion at the end of each chapter.

The book should be useful to readers at varying levels. Whilst by no means confined to student use, it covers all that is required for the statistical sources sections of the Ordinary and Higher National Certificates, and the Diplomas in Business Studies and in Public Administration, as well as those of practically all the major professional bodies requiring the subject. It also covers the relevant parts of the R.S.A. and London Chamber of Commerce examinations in statistics, including such examinations as the Ordinary Certificate in Business Studies taken by overseas students.

The book should also be considered essential reading for all those studying economics or statistics in management courses, and in particular it includes necessary statistical source work for the Certificate in Business Administration, the Diploma in Management Studies and the Diploma in Commerce (Scotland). It may also be used as additional reading in supervisory courses.

The book also provides substantial coverage of the Economic Statistics papers for the examinations of the Institute of Statisticians, and indeed currently is the only single text to do so.

There is also substantial coverage of the material in this field required by students undertaking degree studies in economics, economic statistics, business and public administration, marketing, and distribution.

A companion volume dealing with social statistics and covering, *inter alia*, health, national insurance, housing, education, justice, crime, population, and vital statistics is in course of preparation.

Aberdeen BERNARD EDWARDS

Contents

Note

CHANGES IN THE NAMES AND RESPONSIBILITIES OF CERTAIN GOVERNMENT DEPARTMENTS

During October 1970, certain of the names of Government departments were changed. In the text, as far as practicable the new names have been used, but where reference is made to past events when the older names applied it has sometimes been more convenient to retain them.

Pre-October 1970 Department	*New Department*
Board of Trade Ministry of Technology Ministry of Fuel and Power	Department of Trade and Industry
Ministry of Local Government Ministry of Housing Ministry of Transport Ministry of Public Building and Works	Department of the Environment
Department of Employment and Productivity (previously Ministry of Labour)	Department of Employment

In 1969 the General Register Office—England and Wales, and the Social Survey were brought together under the title of the 'Office of Population Censuses & Surveys'.

CHANGES IN TITLES OF GOVERNMENT STATISTICAL PUBLICATIONS

1. The *Board of Trade Journal* became *Trade & Industry* on 16 October 1970.

2. The *Ministry of Labour Gazette* became the *Employment & Productivity Gazette* with effect from the May 1968 issue onwards and was renamed the *Department of Employment Gazette* from January 1971.

ACKNOWLEDGMENT

The reproduction of tables or parts of tables from official publications is with the kind permission of the Controller of Her Majesty's Stationery Office.

1 An Introduction to Government Statistical Sources

The government is, at one and the same time, the main compiler and the main user of statistics and it is with respect to official government sources of statistics that we shall, in the main, confine ourselves in this book. It is true that many trade associations, and the nationalized industries, publish statistics relating to their own industry, and that some of the larger local authorities such as Birmingham and the Greater London Council issue their own statistical digests. Nevertheless it is to the central government and the agencies closely linked to it that we must look first for statistical information for the country as a whole, and for most regional information.

We discuss in a fair amount of detail some of the more important fields of economic statistics. These include manpower, production, distribution, transport, overseas trade, prices, wages and the national income, and are all basic to the understanding and control of the economy. There are however, many other fields of organized human activity which are relevant to the development of the community and upon which modern government requires information in quantitative form.

Social statistics such as those dealing with housing, health, education, crime, etc. are needed not only as indices of present social conditions but also to facilitate planning. Moreover community health, housing conditions and educational standards all have an impact on the productive capacity of the economy and hence statistical information on these matters would be needed for the purposes of economic planning even if there were no social implications at all to be considered.

What should the non-specialist know about the rapidly increasing amount of statistical data becoming available from government sources? First, he should know where to find information on any major topic. Secondly, he should know broadly how the statistics have been obtained. Thirdly, the non-specialist should understand the limitations of the data and how to interpret them. Fourthly, he should understand the uses to which the data can be put by the Government and business users. This aspect is dealt with elsewhere in this book. We comment on the first three, below.

WHERE ARE THE STATISTICS?

We may conveniently divide official statistical publications into two groups:

Summary sources, which bring together statistics on many topics for easy reference, and
Primary publications, which deal with material relating to one particular topic or from one particular department.

In addition there are many publications of an *explanatory nature,* describing the organization of official statistics. We deal with these first, as if the explanatory material is not adequate the public will be unable to make full use of the published statistics.

EXPLANATORY PUBLICATIONS

GOVERNMENT STATISTICAL SERVICES (G.S.S.)

This is a short booklet which all students should read. It contains:

A description of the organization of statistical work in government departments
An outline of the methods of collection of some of the more important statistical series, and the legal powers under which they are collected
Appendixes detailing, inter alia, the data collected by each department, a classification of published statistics according to subject, the title of each publication, the frequency of issue, and the department responsible for the compilation of the statistics

LIST OF PRINCIPAL STATISTICAL SERIES AVAILABLE (L.P.S.)

This publication, complementary to the G.S.S. just mentioned, lists the principal economic and financial statistics, and the statistics available by regions of the country. Under headings for each broad topic the list gives the name of the official body or government department compiling the series, the frequency of publication, the name of the original publication in which the series appears and a short note of explanation in each case.

As reference volumes, these two publications have two major defects. Firstly they are not revised frequently enough. Annual revisions would be desirable in both cases but, at the time of writing (1971) the latest edition of G.S.S. is 1965 and L.P.S. 1967. Secondly hardly any information is provided in the growing field of social statistics. It is to be hoped that with the reorganization of official statistics now in progress steps will be taken to remedy these deficiencies. Nevertheless an acquaintance with these two publications is essential to those wishing to find their way about the maze of official statistics.

OTHER EXPLANATIONS OF OFFICIAL STATISTICS

Details of the method of collection and of analysis of a particular statistical series are often given in the publication in which the series is introduced. However, even when such explanatory notes are published, it is recognized that they are not always easily accessible, and this has led to the introduction of a series of special booklets under the general title *Studies in Official Statistics*. This series includes:

The Index of Industrial Production; Method of Compilation,—No. 7 published 1960. Now superseded by No. 17, published 1970

New Contributions to Economic Statistics,—Nos. 1, 2, 3, 4 and 5—reprints from articles in *Economic Trends*, Published 1959/1969

National Accounts Statistics—Sources and Methods,—No. 13 published 1968

Input–Output Tables for the U.K., 1963,—No. 16 published 1969

Seventeen titles had been published by early 1971. A list of the first thirteen were given in *Statistical News* No. 2 (*see* page 4).

A more general series of publications, each dealing with the historical development as well as the current methods of compilation and publication of the statistics on one broad topic, have also been published. This series is entitled *Guides to Official Sources* and the booklets *Labour Statistics* (1958)*, *Social Security Statistics* (1960), *The Census of Population, Agricultural & Food Statistics* (1957), *Local Government Statistics* (1953) and *Census of Production Reports* (1961), have already been published.

Although these booklets contain a mine of information they are subject to the criticism made earlier, in that they tend to get out of date quickly. They are by no means comprehensive, and there is much current statistical information which is not properly understood because of the lack of easily accessible explanatory material. As a result of criticism on these lines by the House of Commons Estimates Committee steps are now being taken to remedy this state of affairs. A new quarterly publication—*Statistical News,* first published in May 1968, has as its aim '. . . to provide a comprehensive account of current developments in British official statistics and to help all those who use or would like to use official statistics.' In other words, for the first time we had a publication which gave, regularly, information on the background to official statistics and described the way they were being developed.

In addition to three or four special articles dealing with particular aspects of official statistics (including descriptions of some of the major subject categories hitherto poorly documented) and surveys of matters of current importance, the *Statistical News* gives a quarterly series of notes on current developments, under some eighteen general headings classified in accordance with the major fields of official statistics. These headings range from population and vital statistics to housing, manpower, transport, national income and so on.

Alongside *Statistical News* which, in order to keep references to it up to date, has a full cumulative index printed at the end of each issue, the Central Statistical Office is planning an extension of its guides to official statistics, together with a plan for updating them as required. Another innovation stemming from the 1967 report of the Estimates Committee (see page 18) is the publication of a new *Research Series* which for the first time provides a medium for the

---

* The recently published (1971) *British Labour Statistics: Historical Abstract 1886–1968* includes a complete revision and updating of the information contained in this booklet.

regular publication of the results of departmental research on topics of academic as well as practical interest.

OTHER EXPLANATORY BOOKLETS

The Central Statistical Office in its endeavours to bring home to the businessman the importance of official statistics to his business has introduced a number of short booklets. Current titles are:

1. *Britain's Economy in Figures*—gives figures from over sixty key economic series for the three most recent years.
2. *Government Statistics for Industry*—outlines the statistical responsibilities of the main government departments and indicates the publications available.
3. *Profit from Facts*—is an endeavour to show by case studies how firms may make profitable use of official statistics.

These publications are available on request from the Central Statistical Office.

THE SUMMARY STATISTICAL SOURCES

Official statistics are published in a variety of forms. The Censuses of population, production and distribution are each published in a number of volumes devoted solely to the topic in question, whilst employment statistics are published regularly in the *Department of Employment Gazette* alongside a great deal of other material; overseas trade statistics are published in special purpose volumes, and also in less detail but with more interpretation and analysis in the journal *Trade & Industry* (*Board of Trade Journal* prior to October 1970).

Whatever the mode of publication it tends initially to be departmental in nature, but the economist or statistician frequently needs to refer to statistics from different departments in order to obtain a full picture of the particular aspect of the economy he is studying. Moreover he may be in the position of requiring information on a certain topic but be uncertain which departmental statistics are likely to be most relevant.

Statistics of personal income, for example, come from at least three different departments (the Board of Inland Revenue, the Department of Employment, and the Department of Trade and Industry) and this situation is not unusual. Publications which bring together statistics from many sources are essential if the best use is to be made of the data available.

The main summary publications are:

The Annual Abstract of Statistics. This gives a very full coverage of the more important statistics—economic and social—over the previous ten years, mainly as annual series. The categories included are:

Area and *climate*
Population and vital statistics, migration
Social conditions
Education
Labour
Production
Retail distribution and miscellaneous services
Transport and communications
External trade
Overseas finance
National income and expenditure
Home finance
Banking, insurance, etc.
Prices

The *Annual Abstract* is the publication to which a person looking for statistics on a particular topic but who is uncertain of the primary source should first look. Its plan is as follows:

Introduction—including notes on definitions and changes in contents
List of contents
Note of units of measurement used
Statistical tables (as categorized above)
Index of sources giving references to the tables in the *Abstract*, the government department or other organization responsible, and the official publication in which the statistics were originally published
Appendixes giving—
  Standard regions and conurbations for statistical purposes (transferred from 1969 onwards to the *Abstract of Regional Statistics*)
  Standard industrial classifications
Index

Similarly monthly or quarterly series for the last two or three years, with annual coverage for up to four years more on a slightly more limited basis than the Annual Abstract, are published in the *Monthly Digest of Statistics*. The *Monthly Digest* covers roughly the italicized categories given in the contents list of the *Annual Abstract* on page 6. In addition to a contents list and the tables themselves, an alphabetical index is provided.

The *Monthly Digest* gives only a limited amount of information on banking and finance. A separate monthly publication '*Financial Statistics*' covers this field in great detail. This originated in 1962 as a separate publication after the Radcliffe Committee of 1959 had strongly criticized the authorities for '... unnecessary disparity between the information at their disposal and the information released for publication'. In addition to *Financial Statistics* the Bank of England publishes a very informative *Quarterly Bulletin*, with a statistical appendix.

Detailed definitions of the items and of the statistical units employed in the *Monthly Digest* and *Financial Statistics* are issued regularly in two separate booklets. *Definitions and Explanatory Notes* relating to the *Monthly Digest* comes out annually in January whilst the corresponding notes on '*Financial Statistics*' are issued more infrequently. These publications serve a similar purpose also for the statistics contained in the '*Annual Abstract*'.

The Department of Employment* published until recently a summary quarterly publication (introduced in 1964) entitled *Statistics of Income, Prices and Employment*. This publication brought together series previously published largely in the *Employment & Productivity Gazette* and the *Board of Trade Journal* (since October 1970 called *Trade and Industry*) but it is now no longer published. It has been superseded by the *Annual Year Book of Labour Statistics* (first published in 1971, giving statistics for the year 1969.)

REGIONAL STATISTICS

The foregoing has dealt with summaries of statistics, covering the whole of the United Kingdom. A separate *Abstract of Regional Statistics*, covering the main series which are available on a regional

---

* Originally the Ministry of Labour, renamed the Department of Employment & Productivity in 1968, and the Department of Employment in October 1970. *See* page xii for changes in titles of the periodicals referred to.

basis, is published annually. Included among the topics covered are area and climate, population, education, employment, fuel and power, production, construction and investment, distribution, transport, personal income and expenditure, hospital and sickness benefit. An index of sources is given and an appendix giving a classification of standard regions, sub-regions and conurbations.

Statistics dealing with Scotland, in greater detail than found elsewhere, are published twice yearly in the *Digest of Scottish Statistics* prepared by the Scottish Statistical Office. The coverage includes:

Industrial activity
Transport and communication
Trade through Scottish ports
Labour
Population and vital statistics
Social services
Finance
Miscellaneous tables—e.g. family expenditure surveys, Scotland, and census of distribution, Scotland.

The *Annual Digest of Welsh Statistics* (published by the Welsh Office) and the semi-annual *Digest of Statistics of Northern Ireland* (Northern Ireland Cabinet Office) bring together the more important data available separately for these two countries. Whilst the Welsh and Scottish Statistics are in general compiled on the same lines as those for Great Britain as a whole, there are many ways in which the Northern Ireland statistics differ from those for the rest of the United Kingdom. On the other hand, because Welsh and English statistics are so closely identified one with another it is often difficult to separate them effectively. Effective regional planning needs a wide range and a detailed geographical break-down of statistical data; thus we can expect a considerable expansion of regional and local statistics during the next few years.

In this connection, a recent (1968) publication by Edwin Hammond of the Rowntree Research Unit, University of Durham, giving an analysis of regional economic and social statistics brings together regional statistics of population, employment, education, housing, health, environment, personal income, voting characteristics, crime and other social characteristics in a more integrated form than has hitherto been provided officially. This publication, which is a revision of one published in 1965, includes material dated up to September 1967. A commentary on, and an interpretation of the tables is also provided.

OTHER SUMMARY PUBLICATIONS

The final monthly publication of the Central Statistical Office, *Economic Trends*, summarizes a selection of economic statistics, intended to provide 'indicators' of the progress of the economy of the United Kingdom. Tables and charts are given on total domestic output and expenditure, personal income and expenditure, capital investment, stocks, production, orders on hand, employment, output, wages, price, finance, external trade and the balance of payments. Statistics are provided on a monthly or quarterly basis for a period of just over a year. In addition *charts* showing the movement of these statistics over a period of up to ten or eleven years are given. Large-scale charts show the movement of eight monthly key-indicators, namely:

Index of industrial production
Wholly unemployed (excluding school leavers) (G.B.)
Value of imports
Value of exports
Value of retail sales
New car registrations
Index of average hourly wage earnings
Index of retail prices

Unlike the summary publications so far referred to, *Economic Trends* also contains articles commenting on economic statistics. An article dealing with the current economic situation appears each month. Quarterly articles on the latest national income and expenditure statistics, on the United Kingdom balance of payments and on the balance of payments of the overseas sterling area are also published. In addition a variety of articles is included; some explaining and interpreting the results of special inquiries by particular government departments, others dealing in detail with the development of particular classes of economic statistics. Recent articles have dealt with short-term forecasting of the economy (August 1964; February and May 1967; February 1968), the incidence of taxes and social service benefits (February, July 1968, February 1969), company finance (November 1967), developments in housing statistics (November 1968), and expenditure on scientific research and development (November 1970). Selected articles of permanent value are re-issued in booklet form every two or three years in the *Studies in Official Statistics* series mentioned on page 3.

With a view to giving greater prominence to social statistics and because of 'the growing realization . . . that economic progress must be measured, in part at least, in terms of social benefits makes it the more important that the available key figures about our society should be readily accessible' (*Social Trends* No. 1.) the Central Statistical Office launched its new annual publication '*Social Trends*', in December 1970. The statistics contained therein have, in the main, been published before in diverse government publications. Their being brought together in one volume assists reference and enables trends to be examined and comparisons to be made more effectively than was possible before. In a sense *Social Trends* may be compared with *Economic Trends*. Both publications make good use of diagrammatic representation and both contain explanatory articles. However, *Social Trends* is an annual—most of the statistics it contains being produced on an annual basis—and it is aimed at a less specialized readership than *Economic Trends*. Perhaps for this latter reason it is the first government statistical publication to use colour charts regularly.

GENERAL COMMENT ON THE SUMMARY PUBLICATIONS

All the publications mentioned so far, from the *Annual Abstract* onwards, are mainly concerned with the reproduction of statistics previously published elsewhere. Nevertheless, they may be the main sources for some of the statistical data contained therein. However, as an indication of the original or primary source is always given, either at the foot of each table or at the end of the publication, it is usually easy to know if a more detailed original source exists.

PRIMARY SOURCES

To attempt to list all the statistical publications issued by government departments would be pointless in a book of this nature. As mentioned earlier, attempts have already been made officially to produce such a list on the economic side, and undoubtedly further steps will be taken in the future. In addition two lists of *Basic Statistical Sources for Community Use* have been provided by the Royal Statistical Society (J.R.S.S. Series A Part 1 1969 page 122 et seq). However, it is useful to give here an indication of some of the principal primary sources for the major divisions into which official statistics may be classified. (Page references are given where a particular topic is dealt with later in this book.)

Topic	*Publication title*
w = weekly; m = monthly; q = quarterly; a = annually; p = periodically	
Manpower and labour (page 35)	Department of Employment Gazette (previously Employment & Productivity Gazette) (m) Annual Year Book of Labour Statistics (a)
Production (page 82)	Census of Production Reports (separately for Great Britain and Northern Ireland) (p) Trade & Industry (previously Board of Trade Journal) (w) Business Monitor (p) Agricultural Statistics (separately: England and Wales, Scotland, and Northern Ireland) (a) Digest of Energy Statistics (a)
Distribution (page 119)	Census of Distribution (p) Trade & Industry (w) Business Monitor (p)
Prices (page 225)	Department of Employment Gazette (previously Employment & Productivity Gazette) (m) Trade & Industry (w) Agricultural Statistics (U.K.) (a)
Transport (road) (page 140)	Road Accidents (a) Passenger Transport in Great Britain (a) Highway Statistics (a) Survey of Road Goods Transport (p)
Transport (rail) (page 152)	British Railways Board Statistics (a)
Transport (air) (page 161)	Trade & Industry (w) Business Monitor (p)
Overseas trade & finance (trade) (page 197)	Trade & Industry (w) Annual Statement of Trade (a) Overseas Trade Statistics (m) Report on Overseas Trade (m)
(Balance of payments and finance) (page 207)	U.K. Balance of Payments 'Pink Book' (a) National Income & Balance of Payments White Paper (a) Financial Statistics (m) Bank of England Quarterly Bulletin (q) Economic Trends (quarterly figures) (m)
National income (page 165)	National Income & Expenditure ('Blue Book') (a) National Income & Balance of Payments White Paper (a) Economic Trends (quarterly articles) (m)
Home finance	Financial Statement & Budget Report (a) Financial Statistics (m) Bank of England Quarterly Bulletin (q) Report of Commissioners of H.M. Inland Revenue (a) Inland Revenue Statistics (since 1970) (a) Local Government Financial Statistics (England & Wales) (a) Local Financial Return (Scotland) (a) Local Authority Financial Return (Northern Ireland) (a)

Topic	*Publication title*
Banking & credit, insurance etc.	Bank of England Quarterly Bulletin (q)
	Financial Statistics (m)
	Trade & Industry (credit statistics) (w)
Population & vital statistics	Census Reports (separately for England & Wales, Scotland, & Northern Ireland) (p)
	Statistical Review of England and Wales (a)
	Annual Report of the Registrar General for Scotland (a)
	Annual Report of the Registrar General for Northern Ireland (a)
	Quarterly Return of Births, Deaths and Marriages (separately for England & Wales, Scotland, Northern Ireland) (q)
	Statistics of Foreigners Entering and Leaving the U.K. (a)
Health	Digest of Health Statistics (a)
	Annual Report of Department of Health & Social Security (England and Wales) (a)
	Scottish Health Statistics (Scottish Home & Health Dept.) (a)
	Health & Welfare Service in Scotland (a)
	Annual Report of Ministry of Health & Social Service (N. Ireland) (a)
	The Registrar General's Statistical Review (a)
Housing	Housing Statistics (Great Britain) (q)
	Local Housing Statistics (England and Wales) (q)
	Housing Return for Scotland (q)
	Housing Return for N. Ireland (q)
	Handbook of Statistics (Local Education Authority matters) (a)
Education	Statistics of Education (England and Wales) (a)
	Educational Statistics (N. Ireland) (a)
	Scottish Educational Statistics (a)
Personal income (pages 58, 177)	Inland Revenue Statistics (a)
	Report of the Commissioners of H.M. Inland Revenue (a)
	Department of Employment Gazette (previously Employment & Productivity Gazette) (m)

RELEASE DATES OF ECONOMIC STATISTICS

From October 1970 onwards the release dates for all major economic series has been published in advance in *Trade & Industry* and in *Economic Trends.* The first such list was issued on 29 October 1970. Lists have appeared subsequently about the middle of each month. The majority of such releases are given a Press Notice, followed by publication in one of the regular government journals, usually *Trade & Industry* or the *Department of Employment Gazette.*

HOW HAVE THE STATISTICS BEEN OBTAINED?

Official statistics are collected either as a by-product of routine administrative procedures or by means of special surveys, usually of a sample nature. Examples of statistics derived from routine administration are:

Some of our transport statistics—e.g. from vehicle registration records and the issue of bus or train tickets
Unemployment statistics—from the figures of those 'signing on' at the employment exchange
Overseas trade figures—from information collected incidentally to Customs & Excise procedures

The more complicated an economy becomes, however, the less likely is it that statistics collected as the by-product of administrative procedures will suffice. It becomes necessary to inquire of firms and persons, to obtain information solely for statistical purposes Thus we have surveys, such as family expenditure surveys and international passenger surveys, which are directed to persons, and also the censuses of distribution and of production calling for information from industry and commerce. These inquiries may involve complete enumeration or be of a sample nature.

Some of them are carried out on a regular basis, substantially the same information being supplied at monthly, quarterly or annual intervals, whilst others may be special, 'one-off', inquiries calculated to shed light on a particular topic at a given time, which it is not intended to repeat. Examples are given in subsequent chapters together with outlines of the methods involved.

Despite the greater emphasis now being placed on the integration of government statistical work and the more rational planning of the collection of data, calls upon firms to supply statistics are certain to become more frequent. This will only be tolerable if the collection of data is integrated with the way in which firms keep their records. As we see in Chapter 5 page 83 government statisticians are very much aware of this need.

LIMITATIONS AND PITFALLS

The statistical needs of the community are constantly changing. Data which were of little or no importance fifty years ago may now be vital to national or regional planning. Statistics of internal migration, of scientific manpower and of resources devoted to higher education are cases in point.

To a lesser degree the requirements for, and the compilation of, an index of retail prices now are markedly different from what they were over fifty years ago when the so-called cost of living index was first introduced.

Moreover, for purely administrative reasons, the manner in which statistics are collected may change over a period of time. Our current manpower statistics are very largely a by-product of the National Insurance Scheme introduced in June 1948, and they cannot be satisfactorily compared with the statistics produced before that date. Greater knowledge, greater understanding, or greater availability of information; all these may result in an improvement in a category of statistics over a period of time, and thus even though the definition may be unchanged the series may not be comparable throughout. Mistakes may also be made—not so much mistakes in caclulation, although these are not entirely unknown—but in basic assumptions, which may not be revealed until later. Thus prior to 1962, some transport statistics using traffic counts were calculated on the assumption of an average car occupancy of 1·5 persons. A survey in 1962 (see page 153) suggested that 1·93 persons per car would be a more valid figure, and whilst it is obviously impossible to be certain that this latter figure applied to the years prior to 1962, there was obviously no justification for continuing with the figure of 1·5 subsequently.

QUESTIONS

1. Compare and contrast the publications *Economic Trends* and *Social Trends.*
2. What should the non-specialist know about the increasing amount of statistical data from Government sources?
3. What are the summary sources of official statistics, and what are their aims?
4. Assuming that you had no knowledge of the original sources of information, how would you set about finding out what Government statistics were available on employment in the construction industry?

2 The Central Statistical Office and the development of Government Statistical Services

The Years 1941–1968

In 1941 the Central Statistical Office (C.S.O.) was established within the Cabinet Office to compile estimates of the national income and thus assist in planning the war economy. Because its work involved drawing together data from a multitude of official sources, the C.S.O. has come to acquire other functions.

The Central Statistical Office assists the central government in connection with any question involving the use of statistics. It prepares statistical reports, and assembles information for the Cabinet and Cabinet committees. It maintains a general liaison with the various government departments on statistical matters, prepares statistical series and estimates which involve the use of data collected from a number of departments, and is the main channel whereby the Government and the departments are kept in touch with international developments on statistical matters. In addition, it supplies specialist assistance to departments which have no professional statistical staff.

The C.S.O.'s functions in relationship to the various government departments are purely advisory and not mandatory. During the period 1945–68 the C.S.O. promoted inter-departmental cooperation, particularly at the planning stage, through informal contacts with the statisticians in the various government departments and through inter-departmental committees established under the chairmanship of the C.S.O. The actual production and analysis of the statistical data is still very largely in the hands of the departments.

The broad responsibilities of the various departments as regards statistical matters are given below (where Scottish or Northern

Ireland departments have responsibilities for the publication of statistics not available elsewhere these are noted in brackets.):

Department	*Statistics concerning*
Department of Trade and Industry (Ministry of Commerce) (N.I.))	Production, distribution and trade, overseas trade, energy, air transport, scientific manpower.
Department of Employment (Department of Health and Social Services, (N.I.), Ministry of Commerce, (N.I.))	Employment, unemployment, earnings, wages, trade union membership, hours worked, labour turnover, industrial disputes.
General Register Offices: England & Wales (now included in the Office of Population Censuses and Surveys) (Scotland, N.I.)	Censuses of population, births, marriages and deaths; morbidity.
Board of Inland Revenue	Personal income, profits, taxes, wealth.
Department of Customs and Excise	Overseas trade, Revenue statistics.
Department of Environment (formerly Ministry of Public Building and Works)	Construction.
Department of Environment (Local Government section). (Scottish Development Department, Ministry of Development (N.I.))	Housing, public cleansing, water supply, local government finance, planning of land use; industrial planning.
Department of Environment (Transport Industries) (Ministry of Development (N.N.))	Road and rail transport.
Department of Health & Social Security (Scottish Home & Health Department, Min. of Health & Social Services (N.I.))	Health and welfare, national insurance and social services generally; ininjuries.
Home Office (Scottish Home & Health Department, Ministry of Health and Social Services (N.I.))	Justice, crime, prisons, the electorate.
Ministry of Agriculture (Department of Agriculture and Fisheries (Scotland), Ministry of Agriculture (N.I.))	Agriculture, fishing.
Department of Education and Science (Scottish Education Department, Ministry of Education (N.I.))	Education, scientific manpower.

The Central Statistical Office has direct responsibility for the publication of annual and quarterly estimates of national income and expenditure, of data concerning the balance of payments and the index of industrial production, and of annual and quarterly estimates of the flow of funds.

In addition it is concerned with short-term forecasting in regard to national income and the balance of payments. Finally, it co-operates in providing statistical data for national planning, gives assistance to H.M. Treasury and the National Economic Development Office, and it is the recognized channel for the supply of United Kingdom statistics to the U.N.O., the O.E.C.D., and other international bodies.

The Central Statistical Office is responsible for the following publications:

Annual	Annual Abstract of Statistics
	Abstract of Regional Statistics
	National Income and Expenditure (Blue Book)
	United Kingdom Balance of Payments (Pink Book)
Quarterly	Social Trends (first published, 1970)
	Statistical News (first published, 1968)
Monthly	Monthly Digest of Statistics
	Financial Statistics
	Economic Trends.

Two of these publications, *National Income & Expenditure* and the *United Kingdom Balance of Payments,* are major planning documents containing analyses by the C.S.O. of data from various official sources. The others are convenient compendiums of statistical data reproduced direct from other sources (*see* page 5).

The foregoing gives the situation up to 1968—a Central Statistical Office with a rather weak co-ordinating role, which nevertheless had brought about significant departmental co-operation, introduced or disseminated systems of classification for universal use, and played the main part in producing statistics for national planning purposes.

1968 and later

ESTIMATES COMMITTEE'S FOURTH REPORT

At the end of 1966, however, the Fourth Report of the Estimates Committee of the House of Commons (1966–67), entitled *Government Statistical Services,* was published. (It is, perhaps, unfortunate that the title of this document is the same as that of a booklet explaining the structure of the Government Statistical services last published in 1962 and referred to in Chapter 1. When referring to the Fourth Report, however, we will always add the word 'report' in order to avoid confusion.) This Report was the result of an inquiry, extending over two parliamentary sessions, the recommendations of which have subsequently been largely accepted and implemented. The document itself is not difficult to read, and should be referred to by all who wish to gain a deeper understanding of the problems associated with the use of statistics in the national economy.

Whilst praising the departments and the C.S.O. for development in statistical information which had taken place, the Committee criticized the slowness of publication, and the lack of accuracy and detail in certain fields. They criticized also a general lack of effective integration, leading to overlapping, and insufficient publicity. These points had all been made elsewhere, but nowhere previously with such a wealth of supporting evidence.

EFFECT OF THE REPORT

The Committee made some twenty-three recommendations in all, the more important being that the status of government statisticians should be improved, that there should be more effective communication amongst all interested parties, and that steps should be taken to educate industry and commerce in the value to them of official statistics. It was further recommended that the system should be rationalized and made more efficient, with better central control and more rapid processing of the data.

In the implementation of these recommendations the C.S.O. has played a paramount part. The first fruits were seen when, in May 1968, the first issue of a new quarterly *Statistical News* (mentioned on page 4), was published.

In this issue, an article by C. A. Moser, (then newly-appointed Director of the C.S.O.) provided a starting point for a discussion of the new developments. Moser summed these up by stressing the need to produce a better integrated and planned system of official statistics, to improve the usefulness of statistics to all sections of the population which have need of them, and to enable government statisticians to contribute more effectively, along with their colleagues in the academic and research worlds, to advances in statistical methodology.

The Estimates Committee's Report called for more central control. This was accepted, Moser suggested that a completely centralized system would have the following advantages:

Priorities would be easier to determine

Overall co-ordination of the collection of data would be improved

Overlap of inquiries would be more easily avoided

Planning and phasing at all stages of an inquiry, of data processing and of publication would be more efficient

The establishment and maintenance of uniform classifications, definitions and standards would be facilitated

More efficient and economic use could be made of highly trained staff and computer facilities

Such a system would be more flexible in operation

Much of the committee work necessary under a decentralized system would be avoided

Nevertheless, a completely centralized system is not likely to be adopted in this country, in the forseeable future. A crucial point in favour of a decentralized system, as Moser pointed out, is that it gives greater opportunities for participation in policy making, than can be expected under a centralized system. On these grounds it was decided that whilst there must be a move towards greater centralization, this should proceed only so far as is compatible with maintaining the links which the individual statistical sections have with their Government Departments.

The Central Statistical Office, however, took over new responsibilities, in connection with which four new co-ordination and planning units were established:

COMPUTER AND DATA SYSTEMS UNIT

This unit has—in association with the Treasury—overall responsibility for the planning and development of computer facilities. It is consulted before any new installation is planned and it is directly implementing recommendations 4 and 9 of the Estimates Committee Report. Initially it concentrated on the computerization of business statistics.

THE STATISTICAL STANDARDS AND CLASSIFICATION UNIT

Together with the various interdepartmental committees, this unit is concerned with seeing that definitions and classifications used throughout the statistical service are compatible. The Standard Industrial classification, the Standard Regions, the Socio-Economic Groups, and the Commodity classifications are examples of major universal classifications introduced prior to the establishment of this Unit. It is unlikely that the unit will have to undertake new major tasks of this nature, but it is concerned with keeping them up to date.

THE SURVEY CONTROL UNIT

This unit was set up in 1968, to implement recommendation 3, and to some extent recommendation 11, of the Fourth Report. All government departments are asked to deposit with the unit copies of the forms they use for administrative and statistical purposes, and to give early advance notice of any planned new inquiries, or major changes in existing ones. The Survey Control Unit examines this material, endeavouring to eliminate duplication, to make sure that definitions are compatible and to review the phasing and the requirements of the inquiry from the point of view of the potential *supplier* of the data.

THE PROGRAMME DEVELOPMENT UNIT

This unit is concerned with working out the overall statistical programme and determining priorities, for as long as five years ahead. Its work involves assessing the needs of areas outside the government as well as within it. In addition it is particularly concerned with assessing the extent to which the need for rapid publication may more than compensate for any loss of precision and detail. Further attacks on delays in publication will be concerned with examining at each stage for causes of delay which might be eliminated, and seeing to what extent forecasting of final results from preliminary data is feasible.

In connection with plans for achieving better integration of the collection and storage of statistics and access thereto the C.S.O. has established the Research and Special Studies Division, (described briefly below), the Business Statistics Office and the Central Register of Businesses (*see* below) and devised a new system of industrial statistics (page 83).

Concomitant with the change over to continuous inquiries for business statistics, is the possible development of similar continuous inquiries of household and individuals. Such continuous inquiries are already a feature of North American and some European statistical programmes.

THE RESEARCH AND SPECIAL STUDIES DIVISION

This new division of the C.S.O., in addition to working on topics directly related to that body's responsibilities for certain central topics of economic and social statistics, also acts as a guide and growth point for research on matters within the sphere of the individual departments. It also acts as a central clearing house for information on research topics in general.

THE BUSINESS STATISTICS OFFICE AND THE CENTRAL REGISTER OF BUSINESSES

THE BUSINESS STATISTICS OFFICE

The Business Statistics Office came into existence on 1 January 1969, and is a development from the Census Office of the old Board of Trade. It is directed by an inter-departmental committee under the chairmanship of the Director of the Central Statistical Office, although it is staffed by the Department of Trade and Industry.

The B.S.O. is responsible for the new industrial statistics system, and for building up and maintaining the Central Register of Businesses, described below.

THE CENTRAL REGISTER OF BUSINESSES*

In 1948, when the Standard Industrial Classification was first

---

* An article on the Central Register by L. S. Berman, appeared in *Statistical News*, issue 4.

introduced, the compilation of a Central Register of Businesses was considered but was rejected, largely on grounds of cost. The suggestion was made again very forcibly by the Estimates Committee of the House of Commons in its *Report on Government Statistical Services* (1966–67). On this occasion the recommendation was accepted and the Register is currently in process of construction (1971). The decision to create a computer-held register, available for use by all government departments, arose out of the need to have mutually consistent definitions and classifications for all statistical data, no matter what department might be responsible for their compilation. Up to now the separate departments have maintained their own registers, which, although categorized in a similar manner, in practice are not always completely comparable. Moreover, it is uneconomic to maintain registers for different departments, as duplication inevitably arises.

The aims of the Register are:

To give an up-to-date list of the names and addresses of appropriate business units, classified by industry, area and size, for the use of all departments in statistical enquiries

To provide a suitable sampling frame, and to enable the Business Statistics Office to act as a central agency for addressing forms, sending out reminders, and performing other related activities

To cross-classify and relate statistics on different subjects so as to form an integrated system of business statistics. The Register will provide an index to the main statistical data held by the Business Statistics Office and by other government departments

To prevent duplication in the collection of data and to avoid the omission of information. The Register will provide a means of eliminating the duplication which can occur when inquiries are based on different registers and have different objectives

To provide a data bank. (A data bank provides a means for organizing and storing and making readily accessible a large volume of statistical data.)

It is suggested that classified lists from the Register might, with due regard to confidentiality, be made available to industry and commerce as well as to government departments. Indeed a step in this direction was made in the 1968 Census of Production where firms were asked to agree to their names and addresses being included in classified lists which the Department of Trade and Industry hope to publish.

There are (in 1971) probably over two million business establishments (excluding farms) in the United Kingdom. Whilst for manufacturing industry the compilation of a Central Register based on data from the Department of Employment and the Department of Trade and Industry may not be too difficult, the situation outside manufacturing presents a much more difficult problem. In the Retail Distributive Trade, for example, it is estimated that up to a quarter of all establishments at a given time may 'die', change hands, or be replaced within a year. This presents a formidable up-dating problem. The Census of Distribution of 1971 obviously has a very important part to play in the compilation of the Register.

THE STATISTICAL UNITS IN THE CENTRAL REGISTER

The basic statistical unit to which reference needs to be made may differ according to the purpose intended. Sometimes it may be desirable to deal in terms of an *establishment* (a unit located at a single address), sometimes in terms of a *company* (embracing one or more establishments) sometimes with a unit such as a group of companies pursuing a similar type of activity, and sometimes with an *enterprise* which includes a group of companies required by the Companies Act to file consolidated accounts, and so on.

The Common Register must have a structure which permits of selection in terms of any of these units, as may be required. Thus in addition to the actual collection of the data the planning of its file structure within the computer so as to make the optimum use of storage facilities is vital.

THE INFORMATION IN THE REGISTER

It is visualized that the Register will contain some or all of the following information for each of the basic statistical units in the Register:

A reference number to identify the unit for data processing purposes
The name and address of the unit
Its geographical location, initially on the basis of employment exchange areas

The industrial classification of the unit
The type of unit e.g. in the case of an *establishment* an indication as to whether it trades by direct sales, mail order, self service, etc.
The size-group to which the unit belongs, perhaps in terms of (*a*) net output; (*b*) turnover; (*c*) employment, and so on
A means of cross-referencing, so that the different types of basic units may be related to one another. Thus it will be necessary, for example to have a means of identifying the *establishments* belonging to a particular *company*, the *enterprise* which controls particular business units, etc.

The success or, otherwise of the project depends upon the co-operation of the business world. Businesses will not only be called upon to supply data initially but will be required to give the necessary information for the continuous up-dating of the Register. The necessary co-operation will only be forthcoming if the following conditions are fulfilled:

If fullest publicity is given to the value—to industry and commerce as well as industry—of a full and up to-to-date Register
If a means can be found whereby use can be made of the Register for its own purposes, without destroying the confidentiality that a reasonable business man would expect
If the creation of the Register is associated with the elimination of overlapping inquiries from the various departments, and by a rationalization of and a reduction in the burden of form filling required of the individual firms.

That these requirements are being taken seriously can be seen from the attention which the Central Statistical Office and the departments are giving to consultation with industry and commerce, and to re-organization of industrial statistics which is referred to in Chapter 5.

Pending the completion of the Central Register of Businesses the Business Statistics Office is currently (1971) operating for the production sector an agreed register which has been obtained by combining and rationalizing the 1968 Census of Production register of businesses with the register hitherto maintained by the Department of Employment.

The developments outlined above should provide the pattern for the evolution of our official statistical services for many years to come. Their successful implementation will depend as much upon good management and sound team work within the statistical service, as upon the technical efficiency of the data systems involved.

QUESTIONS

1. Outline briefly the main recommendations of the fourth report of the Estimates Committee 1966–67, entitled *Government Statistical Services.* To what extent have these recommendations been carried out?
2. Discuss the functions of the Central Statistical Office.
3. Consider the relative advantages of a completely centralized and of a decentralized system for the development of the Government's Statistical Services.
4. What are the aims of the Central Register of Businesses, and what obstacles are there to their full realization?
5. A fundamental prerequisite for the effective measurement of any aspect of the economy is the efficient choice and definition of the statistical units involved. Comment.

3 Some important classifications used in economic and social statistics

Since the Second World War the need to compare statistics from different sources has led to the development of a number of basic classification systems. These are outlined in the following pages.

THE STANDARD INDUSTRIAL CLASSIFICATION (S.I.C.)

The first S.I.C. was published in 1948. Its aim was to secure uniformity and comparability in statistics, relating to industry published by government statistical services. Prior to 1948, each government department decided its own industrial classifications; these naturally tended to differ from one another. For instance, the industrial categories used by the Board of Trade did not coincide with those used by the Ministry of Labour, and neither were exactly comparable with those adopted by the Registrar General for Census of Population purposes.

Useful though it was, ten years' experience of the original Standard Industrial Classification inevitably showed the need for certain changes, and a revised edition of the classification was brought out in 1958. This second edition was subject to certain relatively minor changes in 1963 and to a major revision in 1968. This latter edition, which is intended to serve until 1978, is being used in all projects involving industrial statistics. For example, it is used in connection with the 1968 Census of Production and the Index of Wholesale Prices and the Index of Industrial Production (from 1969 onwards). It was gradually introduced into Department of Employment statistics over a period of about a year from mid–1969 onwards, and is employed in the Population Census of 1971.

THE BASIS OF CLASSIFICATION IN THE S.I.C.

The classification is based on industries and not on occupations. All persons (including administrative, technical, clerical and ancillary staffs) employed in a 'unit' of industry are included, without regard to their occupations, in the employment figures for the industry into which the 'unit' falls. The classification is also based on industries irrespective of who owns or operates them. For example manufacturing 'units' owned by the Government are classified in the same way as those in private hands and not under a heading such as 'National Government Service'.

The 'unit' for classification purposes is the 'establishment'. An establishment is *normally* the whole of the premises, (such as a farm, a mine, a factory or a shop) at a particular address. Where, however, activities conducted as a single business are carried out at several addresses, each address is treated as a separate establishment unless the business is such that the information required cannot be supplied separately for the individual addresses. In such a case the whole is treated as the establishment. Usually in such cases *some* separate information will be available (e.g. numbers employed) for each address, and if this is the case the individual address may be classified as 'local units' for which some separate statistics may be produced if required.

Conversely, where at a single address two or more departments are engaged in different activities for which separate records are available, each department is treated as a separate establishment and classified accordingly. This applies even for departments whose activities are ancillary to the main activity of the business.

The 1968 classification is given in the form of twenty-seven Orders, as listed below:

ORDERS OF THE S.I.C. (1968)

I Agriculture, forestry and fishing
II Mining and quarrying
III Food, drink and tobacco
IV Coal and petroleum products
V Chemicals and allied industries
VI Metal manufacture
VII Mechanical engineering
VIII Instrument engineering

IX	Electrical engineering
X	Shipbuilding and marine engineering
XI	Vehicles
XII	Metal goods not elsewhere specified
XIII	Textiles
XIV	Leather, leather goods and fur
XV	Clothing and footwear
XVI	Bricks, pottery, glass, cement etc.
XVII	Timber, furniture etc.
XVIII	Paper, printing and publishing
XIX	Other manufacturing industries
XX	Construction
XXI	Gas, electricity and water
XXII	Transport and communications
XXIII	Distributive trades
XXIV	Insurance, banking, finance and business services
XXV	Professional and scientific services
XXVI	Miscellaneous services
XXVII	Public administration and defence

Each Order is further sub-classified into Minimum List Headings, (M.L.H.) as illustrated below for Order XIV.

M.L.H.
431 Leather (tanning and dressing) and fellmongery
432 Leather goods
433 Fur

There were 152 Minimum List Headings in the 1958 S.I.C. This has risen to 181 in S.I.C. 1968, the increase arising because of the growing importance of certain industries (e.g. a new M.L.H. 104 for Petroleum and Natural Gas extraction) or because of the need for more detailed classification in certain existing categories.

Each time a new S.I.C. is published there are a few transfers from one Order to another. In 1958 for example 'Motor vehicle repairing' was transferred from Order VII to Order XXIII. Likewise in 1968 'Vegetable and animal oils' have been moved from Order V to Order III. There is always scope for the movement of border-line cases of this nature, although such transfers are kept to a minimum as it is desirable to maintain as much continuity as possible.

The issue of the 1968 S.I.C. coincided with that of the revised

International Standard Industrial Classification published by the United Nations Organisation. Although by its very nature the I.S.I.C., which has to cater for the situation in countries with very diverse industrial structures, cannot be so detailed as the U.K. classification there is a fair measure of compatibility between the two classifications, so that statistics classified in accordance with the U.K., S.I.C., can be given in terms of the I.S.I.C. with only minor discrepancies.

CLASSIFICATION OF OCCUPATIONS

The classification of occupations used in the 1971 Census of Population, and currently employed by the Department of Employment, is based on the International Standard Classification of Occupations published by the International Labour Office in Geneva. This classification, referring as it does to the jobs done rather than to the employing industry, is complementary to the Standard Industrial Classification described above. This occupational classification, which is very lengthy and detailed, may be seen in *Classification of Occupations, 1971,* published in February 1971 by the General Register Office. It differs little from the ones issued for the Censuses of Population, 1961 and 1966.

SOCIAL CLASS—REGISTRAR GENERAL'S SOCIO-ECONOMIC GROUPS

Whether or not we agree that the grouping of human beings into social classes is desirable, it is a fact that the social scientist has found some such division desirable in his analysis of human activity. What the scientist is looking for here is some means of classifying individuals into groups which will be meaningful in terms of their social and economic activities. Some such groups are ready-made for us. We commonly distinguish between people on grounds of sex, of age, of marital status, and so on. We can also, if we wish, classify in terms of education, accent, religion, or income. However, although these latter classifications are useful in special circumstances, they do not have the sort of universal validity of being relevant to practically any type of inquiry. As long ago as the Census of 1911 the Registrar General introduced a broad classification, based largely on occupation, which stood the test of time for forty years.

The 1911 classes were:

I	Professional	(e.g. medical practitioner, clergyman, professional engineer.)
II	Intermediate	(e.g. farmer, laboratory technician, nurse.)
III	Skilled	(e.g. carpenter, printer, fitter, clerk, faceworker in coal mine.)
IV	Partly-Skilled	(e.g. gardener, textile spinner, coal miner (not at face), barmaid.)
V	Unskilled	(e.g. dock labourers, factory labourers.)

On the whole, the members of each class tend in terms of economic behaviour to be more similar to one another than to members of other classes. Nevertheless, the classification has the fault of a great many artificial classifications—namely that one of the classes contains an excessively large proportion of the whole. In fact over half of the gainfully-occupied population are in class III, which is by no means homogeneous. This fivefold classification was supplemented in 1951 by a more detailed classification into thirteen socio-economic groups, which in turn has since been expanded and revised, so that there are now seventeen such groups.

THE REGISTRAR GENERAL'S SOCIO-ECONOMIC GROUPS

1. Employers and managers in industry, commerce, central and local Government (large establishments),
2. Employers and managers; as above, but in small establishments,
3. Professional workers, self employed, work of degree standard.
4. Professional workers, employees, work of degree standard.
5. Intermediate non-manual workers, not normally requiring qualifications of university degree standard.
6. Junior non-manual workers, clerical, sales, etc.
7. Personal service workers,
8. Foremen and supervisors, manual
9. Skilled manual workers,
10. Semi-skilled manual workers,
11. Unskilled manual workers,

12. Own-account workers other than professional, not normally requiring qualifications of degree standard and having no employees except immediate family,
13. Farmers, employers and managers,
14. Farmers, own account, having no employees other than family,
15. Agricultural workers,
16. Members of armed forces,
17. Occupation inadequately described.

Three categories of economically inactive persons are also frequently used, namely:

1. Inactive residents in non-private households,
2. Students and children under compulsory school leaving age,
3. Other economically inactive persons.

Significant variations in mortality and fertility are associated with different social classifications and socio-economic groups, as are differences in habits of consumption and expenditure. Variations in the proportions of persons of different social class in different parts of the country, and of course in different areas of the same town or district, are also noticeable.

THE REGISTRAR GENERAL'S ECONOMIC PLANNING REGIONS

The Standard Industrial Classification, and the Registrar General's classification by socio-economic groups are examples of universal classifications adopted by all British government departments.

A classification designed to ensure geographical compatibility is that of the *Standard Regions* of Great Britain. There are ten such regions:

North; Yorkshire & Humberside; East Midlands; East Anglia; South East; South West; West Midlands; Wales; North West; Scotland.
(Northern Ireland may be considered an eleventh U.K. region)

The ten regions noted above coincide with the Registrar General's *Economic Planning Regions*. Prior to 1967, the Standard Regions were defined somewhat differently but, with the introduction of the new planning regions in 1966, it was decided to bring the standard region classification into line with them, as speedily as possible.

QUESTIONS

1. What led to the introduction of the Standard Industrial Classification? Trace its development from 1948 to the present day.
2. Examine critically the basis of classification for the Standard Industrial Classification and indicate any problems which arise in this connection.
3. What is the value of having standard classifications in economic and social statistical work? Discuss in some detail two of these classifications.
4. Compare and contrast the Registrar General's 'Socio-Economic Groups' and his classifications by social class. What are the purposes of these classifications, and to what extent do they fulfil their aims?
5. Discuss the statistical problems of any social classification of the population. How far are such classifications useful in statistical analysis?

4 Manpower and wages statistics

The whole of the population except for the very old and the very young can be looked upon as the source of manpower and, to this extent, population statistics provide the basis for the study of the labour force as a whole. Prior to 1948 the Census reports provided the only regular information which covered the whole of the working population, and even now the most detailed and complete occupational analysis of the labour force comes from the Population Census. The Census of Population has included questions on occupation since its inception in England and Wales in 1801, although it is true that the distinction between personal *occupation* and the *industry* in which the person is employed was only made from 1911 onwards. Nevertheless it was realized as long ago as 1893, when the Board of Trade was authorized to collect labour statistics, that more frequent, and in some respects more detailed information on manpower than was available from the Decennial Censuses ought to be provided.

The Ministry of Labour took over the collection of manpower figures when it was established in 1917. Today its successor, the Department of Employment, is responsible for the collection of statistics on all aspects of manpower. Many of these statistics are published in the *Employment and Productivity Gazette** (monthly). Broadly speaking, the statistical information available can be classified under the following headings: employment, unemployment, wages and earnings, hours of work, industrial disputes and stoppages of work, trade union membership, employment exchange placings per head, accidents at work, and output.

In 1969 the Department of Employment had three regular publications in which most of this information was published. These were the *Employment and Productivity Gazette,* (monthly) which is the major source, and *Statistics on Incomes, Prices, Employment &*

---

* Title changed to *Department of Employment Gazette* in January 1971. The earlier title is, however, retained in this chapter and elsewhere as most of the references are to the period before this most recent change.

Production, (quarterly) which brings together statistics from the *Employment and Productivity Gazette*, from *Trade and Industry*, and from the Central Statistical Office in order 'to make available in convenient form factual information which will assist those engaged in negotiation or arbitration to examine the particular cases before them in relation to the wider implication of the decisions to be made'.

This latter publication ceased publication in 1969, being superseded in 1971 by the new *Yearbook of Labour Statistics*, the first issue of which relates to 1969 and brings together all the main manpower statistics for that year.

In addition a historical outline of labour statistics covering the period 1886 to 1968, a summary of the statistics which have appeared in the *Employment and Productivity Gazette* and its predecessors over the years, has been published (*British Labour Statistics: Historical Abstract 1886–1968*). This publication also contains a set of introductory notes which, in effect replaces and brings up to date the information contained in *Guide to Official Sources, No. 1—Labour statistics* to which we referred in Chapter 1. The third regular publication by the Department of Employment is the *Time Rates of Wages and Hours of work* (annually) which gives detailed information on rates of wages and hours of work fixed by collective agreements, arbitration awards, wages regulation orders and so on.

THE EMPLOYMENT AND PRODUCTIVITY GAZETTE

Practically all the information contained in *Statistics on Income* and its successor, the *Yearbook*, has appeared previously in the *Employment and Productivity Gazette* or *Trade & Industry* (previously the *Board of Trade Journal*), and the majority of the important data in the annual *Time Rates* publication has also appeared in the *Gazette*. Thus a very good idea of the scope of our official manpower statistics can be gained from a consideration of the data appearing through the year in the *Employment and Productivity Gazette*. Before going on to consider how the major statistical series are derived, it is useful to consider the scope and timing of the material published in the *Gazette*. Since April 1966, each issue of the *Gazette* can be divided into three sections—the *statistical series*, the *monthly statistics* and the *special articles.*

THE STATISTICAL SERIES SECTION

The statistical series section of the *Gazette* is in effect a supplement which gives each month the principal statistics compiled by the Department in the form of time series, extending back over from five to fifteen years, depending on the particular series involved. The series, which include statistics of the working population, employment, unemployment, unfilled vacancies, hours worked, earnings and wage rates, retail prices, industrial stoppages, output per head and labour costs are all referred to elsewhere in the *Gazette* at various times during the year—depending on the frequency of compilation.

THE MONTHLY STATISTICS

Under the heading *Monthly Statistics* there are published a number of regular monthly series accompanied by introductory comments. Much of the information given relates only to a particular month, but in some cases comparable figures from earlier months are given. Where comparison over a longer period of time however is required reference must be made to the statistical series section mentioned above.

The current monthly statistics deal with the following topics:

1. INDUSTRIAL ANALYSES OF EMPLOYEES IN EMPLOYMENT (G.B.)

An analysis, by industry and sex, for the industries covered by the Index of Industrial Production. The figures are given for the middle of the month next but one prior to the month of publication (i.e. the March *Gazette* gives mid-January figures) and for each month back to the previous June. Mid-June is always taken as a base month because at this time a major count takes place of the National Insurance cards on which employment estimates are based. The figures for the subsequent month are derived by using ratios of change calculated from returns submitted by a large sample of manufacturing industries and from the nationalized industries and, in the case of the construction industry, from information collected by the Department of Environment (Public Buildings and Works). These monthly estimates are liable to revision in the light of the next count of insurance cards but by this time they will be appearing in the larger Statistical Series section of the *Gazette*.

2. OVERTIME AND SHORT TIME IN MANUFACTURING INDUSTRIES (G.B.)

The number and percentage of operatives involved, and the total hours of overtime or short time, analysed by industry, are given. The figures relate to the second full week in the month immediately previous to the month of publication.

3. UNEMPLOYMENT

(A) GENERAL STATISTICS OF UNEMPLOYMENT (G.B. AND U.K.)

Regional analyses by sex, type of unemployment, and duration, and a special section dealing with school leavers, are given. In addition an industrial breakdown is published covering the United Kingdom and Great Britain, separately, by sex, and by type of unemployment (i.e. temporarily stopped, and wholly unemployed). The figures are actual numbers, except that unemployment *rates* for each sex and region are also provided. All the figures relate to the second Monday of the month prior to the month of publication.

(B) AREA STATISTICS OF UNEMPLOYMENT (G.B. AND U.K.)

For certain local areas (mainly the larger towns) and for the Development areas, unemployment figures for men, women, and boys and girls together are provided. Percentage rates for these areas and an indication of the number of the unemployed who are only temporarily stopped also feature in this section. The figures relate to the second Monday in the month prior to the month of publication. Occasional explanatory articles are also given from time to time (*see* page 53).

(C) SEASONAL VARIATION IN UNEMPLOYMENT

The aim of seasonal adjustment is to remove from the series

variations which can be attributed to *normal seasonal effects* so as to enable a consistent comparison to be made between figures from one time of the year to another. It is a well-known fact, for example, that unemployment increases in the winter months.

Until April 1970 the method of seasonal adjustment used was that first introduced in September 1965. It combined the advantage of both the additive and ratio approaches, and took into account the fact that the higher the general level of unemployment the greater the seasonal fluctuations. Both actual and seasonally-adjusted figures were given for the new (post 1966) Standard Regions of Great Britain for the major industry groups and for the manufacturing industry as a whole. The method of seasonal adjustment was based on variations observed over the period June 1949 to May 1965, and the adjusted figures were extended back to the earlier date. Unfortunately, from 1967 onwards, the seasonal adjustments seemed to be over-compensating for the seasonal effects so that the winter figures *when adjusted* gave results consistently below those for the adjacent months, also seasonally adjusted. Comparable unrealistic results were observed for the seasonally-adjusted figures for months of normally low unemployment.

What appears to have happened since 1966 is a marked decline in the actual size of the seasonal variation for a given level of employment. An article in the April 1970 *Employment and Productivity Gazette*, introducing a new method of seasonal adjustment, points out that in 1958–59 and 1962–63, when unemployment was at a similar level to that in 1966–68, the difference due to seasonal variation between the winter and summer months was about 150,000 whereas in 1966–68 the difference was only about 100,000. However, although there has been this reduction in the size of the seasonal amplitude (the difference between winter peak and summer low), the way in which the seasonal pattern is distributed between the months of the year seems to have changed little, if at all.

The new method takes both these factors into account. The seasonal pattern is now being estimated from the most recent ten year period, whilst the seasonal amplitude is based primarily on figures for the last two or three years. These two estimates are used to calculate the seasonal adjustments, which are revised each quarter so that changes in the seasonal amplitude in particular will quickly be reflected in the adjustments made.

Like the earlier (September 1965) method, the new procedure

assumes that the amplitude of the seasonal variations is dependent to some extent on the general level of unemployment. Also, in calculating the seasonal amplitude, figures for months which are abnormally affected by weather conditions and other recognizable irregularities are modified so as to remove spurious influences from the adjustments. These and other technical points are dealt with in *Studies in Official Statistics,* (Research Paper No. 4) (C.S.O. Research Division). An article on this topic also appeared in *Economic Trends* in May 1970.

Seasonal adjustments have been made by the new method back to July 1966. The following table, 4.1, gives a comparison of seasonally adjusted unemployment figures, using both the old and the new method, for selected months from 1966 to 1970.

TABLE 4.1

Wholly unemployed excluding school-leavers in Great Britain (males and females)

(Thousands)

Year	*Month*	*Unadjusted series*	*Seasonally adjusted* Former series	*Seasonally adjusted* Revised series
1966	July	252	305	301
	October	367	377	375
1967	January	523	454	453
	April	517	495	491
	July	464	543	532
	October	522	541	532
1968	January	596	520	547
	April	558	535	541
	July	497	580	544
	October	532	551	539
1969	January	580	506	532
	April	542	519	525
	July	494	577	541
	October	535	555	543
1970	January	608	530	558

Source: *Employment and Productivity Gazette*, April 1970

The figures in Table 4.1 relate to the second Monday in the month prior to the month of publication.

MEASURING UNEMPLOYMENT: IMPORTANT DEFINITIONS

Three important definitions in connexion with unemployment should be noted in conjunction with the comments which follow.

Registered unemployed

Defined as: *Persons registered for employment at an employment exchange or youth employment office on the day of the monthly count who are not in employment on that day, being either wholly unemployed or temporarily stopped (certain severely disabled persons are excluded).*

Wholly unemployed

Defined as registered unemployed persons without jobs on the day of the count—and who are available for work on that day.

Temporarily stopped

Defined as registered unemployed who, on the day of the count, are suspended from work by their employers on the understanding that they will shortly resume work and are still regarded as having a job.

Unemployment statistics arise from the operation of the National Insurance Act of 1948, (prior to 1948 from the earlier Unemployment Insurance Acts). Comparison of the figures obtained over a period of time are affected by

- (i) the changing coverage of the Unemployment Insurance schemes prior to 1948
- (ii) changes in regulations regarding rights to unemployment benefit
- (iii) the introduction of the *Standard Industrial Classification* in 1948; inter-industry comparisons cannot be made satisfactorily before and after June of that year
- (iv) subsequent revisions of the S.I.C's, and of course
- (v) the extension of the National Insurance Scheme since 1948.

The numbers unemployed are obtained by totalling and analysis of the insurance cards lodged at the Employment Exchanges. Those who do not register are therefore not included in the figures. Married women not entitled to benefit (i.e. those who opted out of the scheme in 1948 or later) have less incentive to register than other persons. Consequently unemployment tends to be under-estimated in industries employing many married women.

Others who would not register (even though not working) are those who are on holiday, ill, on strike, and some who are on short-time.

The treatment of the latter category depends upon the way the short-time is being worked, and on the interpretation used by the local office as to what degree of short-time constitutes unemployment, as well as upon the wage received by the worker and generally whether or not the worker thinks 'signing on' is worth while.

Administrative changes in entitlement to benefit affect the unemployment figures. In 1932 for example, changes were introduced which meant that many married women were no longer entitled to benefit. As many of these felt that they had little chance of finding a job they ceased to register. The increase in the unemployment figures at the beginning of 1932 were thus lower than the situation merited. Since June 1948 monthly figures of unemployment have included all registered unemployed, whether they are insured or not, but the latter are very few. Before June 1948 unemployment figures referred only to the insured population, although prior to 1939 figures for both 'insured' and total registered unemployed were given.

There are certain other difficulties:

(i) *Unemployment by industry*—Prior to June 1948 the industrial classification used was that in which the person was occupied when the last exchange of cards took place. From June 1948 the industrial classification immediately prior to unemployment has been used. Where a person has only had his most recent job for a short period of time after having lost a job in his normal occupation, the figures recorded may be misleading. If it is fairly easy to get 'temporary' work in certain industries, these industries will tend to 'attract' unemployment on this basis.

(ii) *Small areas*—As employees may register at any local exchange comparative figures for small areas may be misleading. Unemployed persons tend to register at the Employment Exchange nearest their place of residence, whilst the estimates of numbers in employment are based upon the area in which they work. Thus if an area is not more or less self-contained so far as residence and workplace are concerned, the rates calculated will not be meaningful. (The employed population used as denominator will not be the true 'Population at Risk'.) In order to avoid this difficulty, unemployment rates from 1953 to 1968 were calculated for 642 relatively self-contained areas in Great Britain, several Employment Exchange areas being grouped where necessary for this purpose. Of these areas 512 were individual employment exchanges, and 130 were grouped in 'travel-to-work' areas. As time passed the number of workers living in one area and working in another, and the distances over which travel-to-work took place, increased considerably. This was recognized, and in July 1968, the areas were revised in new groupings. With effect from the count of unemployment on 8 July 1968, rates were calculated for 296 individual employment exchanges, and 170 'travel-to-work' areas. In general the 'travel-to-work' areas now embraced more individual exchanges, and the number of single-exchange areas considered to be self-contained was markedly reduced. The first rates under the new scheme were published in August 1968, an explanatory article appearing in the *Employment and Productivity Gazette* in the previous month. A further revision of the areas was published in the September 1970 *Gazette* and no doubt further changes will prove necessary from time to time.

Changes such as these obviously produce discontinuities in the series and hinder long-term comparisons. Nevertheless there is nothing which can be done to prevent this, apart from noting the areas so affected, as unemployment rates calculated for areas which are not substantially self-contained can clearly be grossly misleading.

This procedure still leaves one loophole. Certain employers having branches in several parts of the country exchange their cards at one office, irrespective of the particular workplace of any particular employee. These employers have been required, since July 1968, to supply separate figures in the June/August return for each establishment, so that their employees may be allocated correctly to their areas of employment.

(iii) *The effect of the National Insurance Scheme*—Before June 1948 the percentage unemployment rate was calculated thus

$$\frac{\text{Registered unemployed in labour force covered by Unemployment Insurance Scheme}}{\text{Labour force covered by the Unemployment Insurance Scheme}} \times 100$$

As the labour force covered by the scheme at that time was more liable to suffer from unemployment than those groups outside the scheme (e.g. professional workers) the introduction of the comprehensive National Insurance Scheme in 1948 led to an apparent fall in the percentage which was now based on

$$\frac{\text{(Unemployed registered in all occupations)}}{\text{Civilian labour force}} \times 100$$

This, in addition to the reservations noted earlier, makes comparison of the pre-and post-1948 situations very hazardous.

4. PLACING WORK AND UNFILLED VACANCIES

(A) PLACING WORK

Prior to February 1970 the tables gave monthly numbers of *persons placed in employment, and the number of vacancies unfilled,* (with separate figures for boys, girls, men and women). These figures were given for four-or-five-weekly periods ending on the first Wednesday in each month (except when that falls on a National Holiday, when the second Wednesday is taken.) Comparative figures for the first and second months immediately preceding the month of publication were given. There was also a break-down by industry, and by the four sex/age categories for the most recent months.

From February 1970, whilst the figures for unfilled vacancies continued substantially as before, those for persons placed in employment were replaced by a *quarterly* occupational analysis of placings and cancelled vacancies for adults which supplemented the existing quarterly occupational analysis of wholly unemployed adults and unfilled vacancies for adults. The introduction of this *occupational* rather than *industrial* analysis is an improvement from the point of view of economic analysis and manpower planning.

(B) INTERPRETATION OF UNFILLED-VACANCIES FIGURES

The unfilled-vacancies figure is affected by changes in the degree to which employers use the Department of Employment for obtaining employees, and the speed with which they notify the Employment Exchange of changes in their requirements. Also, if an employer asks to be informed about suitable workers, without stating the number required no addition to the unfilled-vacancies figures will be made even though vacancies exist. Changes in Government regulations have an effect, also.

From the Second World War up to March 1950 employers were compelled to engage all workers (certain categories excepted) through the appropriate Employment Exchange. This is not now the case. However, the Notification of Vacancies Order of 25 February 1952, by making it necessary that all *engagements* of workers (certain categories again excepted) should take place through Employment Exchanges, restored in some measure the degree of coverage of the statistics. Finally came the revocation of the Notification of Vacancies Order, on 7 May 1956.

As might be expected, more of the *actual* vacancies were notified prior to 1950 and between 1952 and 1956 than in the other periods.

The unfilled-vacancies figure is usually compared with the numbers unemployed to act as an indicator of changes in the economic situation.

5. STOPPAGES OF WORK (U.K.)

Figures for stoppages due to industrial disputes are published in three tables. Causes of stoppages are analysed both for numbers of stoppages and number of workers directly involved. The figures are given in respect of stoppages beginning in the month immediately prior to publication, and also cumulatively from that month back to the beginning of the calendar year. A similar cumulative comparison is made for the two most recent years, analysed by industry, number of stoppages beginning in the periods, the number of persons involved, and the number of working days lost for all stoppages in progress during the period, irrespective of when they began. Finally information is given on the length of stoppages which came to an end in the month immediately prior to the month of publication, analysed once again by number of workers directly involved and by number of working days lost.

6. BASIC WEEKLY RATES OF WAGES, NORMAL WEEKLY HOURS AND BASIC HOURLY RATES OF WAGES (U.K.)

Index Numbers (base 31 January 1956=100) are given of basic weekly rates, normal weekly hours and basic hourly rates for 'all industries', and separately for manufacturing industries only. The figures are given for the last working day of the month immediately preceding publication, and for comparative purpose the month before that, and the corresponding month a year previously.

Cumulative totals of the actual changes involved from the beginning of the calendar year are also given, analysed by industry-group as well as monthly figures for a thirteen month period, showing numbers of workers and amount of money involved.

THE SPECIAL ARTICLES

Each month the *Employment and Productivity Gazette* contains a number of special articles. Some of these refer to a specific topic, or an inquiry of a once-for-all nature. Others are regular articles dealing with statistical data which appear at approximately the same time each year. Certain of these latter articles deal with retail prices or with the family expenditure survey—both of which we comment on in another part of this book and which are not directly related to the manpower statistics we are currently concerned with. The majority of the regular special articles, however, deal with manpower and the type of information given is explained below.

It is to be regretted that up to the present the *Gazette* possesses neither an index nor a regularly published list, as in the case of the journal *Trade & Industry*, which gives the dates of publication throughout the year of each of the recurrent articles on major topics.

In general, these articles summarize and interpret the previous year's figures, already published in the *Gazette* on a (say) monthly basis, or they discuss the results of some regular annual or other periodic inquiry.

Comments on the subjects covered by the *Gazette* follow. They should be read in conjunction with the notes on the monthly series, previously referred to (page 37 et seq.).

1. EMPLOYMENT (MAINLY GREAT BRITAIN)

From mid–1948 onwards, the National Insurance scheme introduced in that year has made it possible to produce accurate estimates of size of the working population. Prior to 1948 certain classes of employees (e.g. indoor domestic servants) were outwith the existing unemployment insurance scheme, and the self-employed were very inadequately covered. With the introduction of the new scheme the opportunity was taken to use the new Standard Industrial Classification. Although, as is usual on such occasions, figures were given for 1948 on both the old and the new basis, comparison of post–1948 with pre–1948 figures is hazardous.

The main figures for employment and the working population for the previous June are given annually in the February or March *Employment and Productivity Gazette*. The information is obtained from a count of the National Insurance Cards due for exchange on the first Monday in June and actually exchanged before the first Monday in December, together with voluntary information from employers of five or more workers as to the total number of insurance cards held at the beginning of June. To this is added information on those civil servants and post office employees who do not hold insurance cards. Subsequent monthly and quarterly figures are based on these June figures, with suitable adjustments.

The March article, which is the main one, gives an analysis relating to the previous June of the number of employees (employed and unemployed) by industry, by sex, whether under-or over-18, for both Great Britain and the United Kingdom. A classification by region and industry for Great Britain is also given. Commencing with the June 1968 survey, employment statistics are available for newly defined areas. These areas are groups of Employment Exchange areas which, from Census of Population data on travel-to-work, are more or less self-contained so far as travel-to-work is concerned. Thus, in the main, area of residence and area of workplace for Employment Departments purposes is now the same. This, together with fuller information obtained in 1968 about the areas of employment of those employees whose national insurance cards are exchanged in other areas, facilitates the use of the statistics for planning purposes and make unemployment rate statistics* more reliable. The regional estimates were further improved from June 1969 onwards, as more accurate information was obtained about the location of employees in the distributive trades. The numbers of employees *actually in employment* classified by industry and sex are also given with an indication of the percentage change over the year. A further analysis of these June figures giving employees by age groups, by sex, by industry and by regions is also given regularly in the succeeding June's *Gazette*.

QUARTERLY ESTIMATES OF TOTAL EMPLOYMENT

In addition to these detailed analyses which relate only to the June figures, quarterly estimates of the size of the working population and of the civilian labour force have been published for Great Britain

---

* See page 42 for a more detailed reference to 'travel to work' areas and unemployment statistics.

on a regional basis since mid 1966.* These series were introduced so that more accurate estimates of employment could be made throughout the year than had been the case when the only figures available were the monthly (ratio) estimates referred to on page 37. The quarterly articles are published in October for the previous March and at *approximately* three monthly intervals thereafter.

TABLE 4.2

Working Population: Great Britain (March 1970)

	Males	*Females*	*Total*
Unadjusted for seasonal variations			
Working population	16,140	9,004	25,145
H.M. Forces	360	14	374
Employers and self-employed	1,383	361	1,744
Employees	14,397	8,629	23,027
Wholly unemployed	517	85	602
Total in civil employment	15,263	8,906	24,169
Employees in employment	13,880	8,545	22,425
Adjusted for normal seasonal variations			
Working population	16,202	9,015	25,217
Total in civil employment	15,359	8,921	24,280
Employees in employment	13,975	8,560	22,535

Note: Owing to rounding, the totals may differ from the sum of the components.

Source: *Employment and Productivity Gazette*, October 1970

Further breakdowns of the categories in Table 4.2 by the regions of Great Britain showing quarterly and yearly changes are given.

The working population includes all employed and registered unemployed persons. The following equations will help to an understanding of the published figures.

Working population = civilian labour force + H.M. Forces

Civilian labour force = Total in civil employment + wholly unemployed

Total in civil employment = Employees in employment + employers + self-employed

Total employees = employees in employment + wholly unemployed

* The Ministry of Labour *Gazettes*, May and June 1966, give explanatory articles on Total and Regional Employment statistics.

It should be borne in mind that our estimates of the working population are based primarily on regular returns relating to 'employees' rather than to the self-employed. Estimates of the number of self-employed persons are based primarily upon census of population figures. In 1971 for example, we were still relying on the 1966 census of population figures. Large numbers of workers, primarily in the construction industry, to avoid Selective Employment Tax payments, have since 1966 transferred to the 'self-employed' category. They have, in effect been 'lost' from the 'employee' category without reappearing fully in the 'self-employed'. Doubtless this will be corrected when the 1971 population census figures become available but similar problems may well arise in subsequent intercensal periods. In the meantime some information, on self-employed men only, is obtained annually (usually twelve months in arrears) by the Department of Health and Social Security from analyses of samples of National Insurance records. Figures given in an article *The Fall in the Working Population since 1966* (*Employment and Productivity Gazette,* June 1970) suggest that the number of self-employed men increased by at least 69,000 between June 1966 and June 1967, little further increase being shown in the succeeding two years. Because most self-employed women have opted out of the national insurance scheme no useful information on changes in this category is available.

ACTIVITY RATES

A major cause of changes in the working population is change in the size and structure of the total population of the country. It is useful, therefore, to calculate 'activity rates'; namely the ratios of the working population in each age and sex group to the total population* in that group. Changes in activity rates as a measure of working activity may then be compared over a period of time. Moreover if we apply the activity rates for one period (say 1966) to the estimated total population for another year (say 1968) we obtain estimates of what the working population in the latter year would have been had activity rates remained constant. Table 4.3 shows such comparisons for 1966 and 1968.

Thus in age group 15–19 inclusive in 1966 the working population of males was 74·45% of the total male population. The

* Sometimes the 'Resident Population' is used as denominator.

estimated total population in that age group in 1968 was 1,946,000. 74·45% of this latter figure is 1,449,000 which exceeds the actual working population in 1968 of 1,335,000 by 114,000. Similar calculations for each age group show that for males as a whole there were 345,000 fewer people in the working population in 1968 than there would have been had activity rates remained at the 1966 level. The article in the *Employment and Productivity Gazette* referred to on page 49 is an examination of the possible reasons for this decline, and is worth reading as an example of careful interpretation of figures subject to errors of estimation, which are at the same time influenced by changing economic and social conditions. Sources of error in the activity rates arise because

(*a*) the *total* population figures are intercensal estimates—based on the most recent population census and adjusted for births, deaths, and net migration. The latter estimate may be subject to considerable inaccuracy, particularly so far as movement between Great Britain and the Republic of Ireland is concerned,

TABLE 4.3

Activity rates and the working population (1966, 1968)
(Great Britain)

(Thousands)

	1966			1968			
	Total population (1)	*Working population* (2)	*Activity rate* (3)	*Total population* (4)	*Col. 3 × col. 4* (5)	*Working population* (6)	*Col. 6 minus col. 5* (7)
Males							
Age 15–19	2,110	1,571	74·45	1,946	1,449	1,335	−114
20–24	1,877	1,774	94·51	2,091	1,976	1,933	− 43
25–29	1,692	1,614	95·39	1,713	1,634	1,609	− 25
30–34	1,658	1,591	95·96	1,658	1,591	1,565	− 26
35–39	1,681	1,642	97·68	1,665	1,626	1,588	− 38
40–44	1,772	1,726	97·40	1,697	1,653	1,655	+ 2
45–49	1,653	1,587	96·01	1,785	1,714	1,705	− 9
50–54	1,672	1,656	99·04	1,552	1,537	1,521	− 16
55–59	1,621	1,551	95·68	1,609	1,539	1,537	− 2
60–64	1,390	1,276	91·80	1,424	1,307	1,301	− 6
65–69	1,009	377	37·36	1,091	408	358	− 50
70 and over	1,442	192	13·31	1,469	196	177	− 19
Total	**19,575**	**16,556**		**19,700**	**16,630**	**16,285**	**−345**
Females							
Age 15–19	2,037	1,468	72·07	1,877	1,353	1,250	−103
20–24	1,816	1,150	63·33	2,034	1,288	1,290	+ 2
25–29	1,632	663	40·63	1,660	674	652	− 22
30–34	1,570	638	40·64	1,576	640	635	− 5
35–39	1,633	800	48·99	1,598	783	772	− 11
40–44	1,773	955	53·86	1,682	906	927	+ 21
45–49	1,696	942	55·54	1,815	1,008	1,029	+ 21
50–54	1,780	954	53·60	1,645	882	889	+ 7
55–59	1,758	803	45·68	1,753	801	846	+ 45
60–64	1,613	418	25·91	1,639	425	416	− 9
65 and over	4,041	236	5·84	4,185	244	241	3
Total	**21,349**	**9,027**		**21,462**	**9,004**	**8,948**	**− 56**

Source: *Employment and Productivity Gazette*, March 1969

(*b*) the working population is estimated—probably fairly accurately except for the self-employed category—largely through counts of National Insurance cards

The influence of economic and social changes are reflected in:
(*a*) the increase in the proportion of young people in full time education,
(*b*) the trend towards earlier marriages and childbearing,
(*c*) withdrawal of older persons from the labour market as unemployment, generally, increases.

Periodic projections of the U.K. and G.B. populations are made by the Government Actuary. If we apply to each age/sex/marital status group in these projections an appropriate activity rate, we obtain projections of the working population. Such projections are used for manpower planning purposes. The latest projections of the working population, up to 1981, published in the March 1969 *Employment and Productivity Gazette*, were calculated from the mid–1967 projections of total population. These forecast an increase in the working population of the United Kingdom from about 26·2 millions in 1967 to just over 27 millions in 1981. The activity rates assume a high and constant pressure of demand for labour. Fluctuations in such pressures which are obviously occurring will have marked effects on activity from year to year, but whether the postulated activity rates continue to measure the basic long-term trend remains to be seen.

Since the 1966 Sample Census of Population a number of Department of Employment Papers have been published relating to various characteristics of the population. Paper 4 gives activity rates by sub-regions of England and Wales, and for Scotland as a whole, whilst Paper 2 gives numbers and rates for three inactive categories of the population classified by region, sex, and age group. The definitions on which the calculations were based were slightly different for Scotland on the one hand, and England and Wales on the other, but these are hardly likely to have had any major effect on the ratios. The 'economically active' are—broadly—those workers looking for work, or those who would be so if they were not ill, on holiday, temporarily stopped and so on. The 'economically inactive' are grouped in three categories,—retired, students, and others (including housewives at home) who are neither in employment nor seeking it. For Great Britain as a whole, 58% of the female population was economically inactive but only 16% of the males came into this category. Amongst the sub-regions, Coventry area had the highest activity rate (87·9%) for males, and North East Lancashire (49·6%) the highest for females, whilst the Sussex Coast (73·6% for males) and South Lindsey (32·1% for females) had the lowest activity rates. Over the regions, activity was greatest, for both males and females, in the West Midlands, and lowest in Wales and in the South West.

Some indication of the problems and pitfalls involved in the comparison of regional activity rates was given in 'Regional activity rates as a measure of potential labour reserves' (*Employment and Productivity Gazette* February 1971). This is an article which should be read by all wishing to draw conclusions about labour activity on a regional basis.

OTHER ARTICLES IN THE *EMPLOYMENT AND PRODUCTIVITY GAZETTE*

In addition to articles dealing with the total employment situation and the articles referred to above, there is a special article, usually in May, which deals with young persons entering employment in the previous year. The figures are analysed by age of entry, sex, and industry; by type of employment (i.e. by apprenticeship, clerical, professional etc.) sex, and age of entry. There are also analyses by region and industry.

The figures are obtained from Youth Employment Office records. Important reservations on the figures are usually referred to in the article and should be borne in mind when interpreting the figures. For example, young people first starting work aged over 18 are not included as they do not obtain their National Insurance cards through the Youth Employment Office. Only the first occupation is recorded, and hence young people who take a job for a few months prior to entering an apprenticeship will not be recorded when they actually enter on that apprenticeship. Moreover, young people who have obtained insurance cards for part-time work before leaving school may also be omitted.

In May or June also, and subsequently at approximately quarterly intervals, information is given by industry on the numbers of women in part-time employment in manufacturing industries. Part-time employees are not distinguished from full-timers in the general monthly employment estimates, and so this quarterly series (obtained from sample returns from employers) supplies significant additional information in a situation where part-time female employment is becoming increasingly important.

EMPLOYMENT BY REGION AND SUB-REGION

Recently, more detailed information on various aspects of employment has been published. For example, we now have information on employment in sub-divisions of regions (September 1970), and on the flow of employees between industries (April 1971). The September 1970 issue of the *Employment & Productivity Gazette* gives a comparison of the Department of Employment's and the Census of Population's estimates of employees in employment, by regions and their sub-divisions. There are marked differences between the figures from the two sources, even after allowance has been made for the known downward bias in the Population Census figures. The discrepancies appear to stem largely from the fact that students undertaking part-time employment, seasonal and irregular workers, some sick employees, and certain persons looking for work but not registered as unemployed were included in the Department of Employment totals but not in the Census of Population figures. Smaller influences affecting the discrepancies in the other direction were a number of long-term sick persons who, no longer classed as employees by the Department of Employment, nevertheless described themselves as employees in their Population Census returns, as well as some married women working in their husbands' businesses who recorded themselves as employed on their Census return but who were treated as self-employed by the Department of Employment. The comparison of the figures for the different regions and sub-regions was moreover affected by the fact that the boundaries of the Department of Employment regions and local offices do not always exactly coincide with the local authority areas used for Census purposes. There is also the continued problem of the allocation of well over one million employees with no fixed work place, whose treatment may differ in the two classifications. The reconciliation of data from these two sources and an approach to a more uniform treatment is imperative in the future, if continuity is to be maintained under the new proposals for the collection of employment statistics referred to on page 56.

OCCUPATIONS OF EMPLOYEES IN MANUFACTURING INDUSTRY

An article on this subject has been published annually, in January, since 1963, when the first survey under the Statistics of Trade Act 1947 was made. Prior to 1963, occupational information was largely limited to census data and the lack of up-to-date knowledge of the numbers in the various occupations impeded the proper planning of both industrial training and industrial development. This lack of knowledge was particularly serious so far as skilled workers were concerned. A series of annual sample inquiries into manufacturing industry was initiated in 1963 to remedy these deficiencies and has been carried out to determine the position in May of each year. In 1968, for example, inquiry schedules were sent to a sample of 9,000 establishments; this included *all* establishments with 500 or more employees, and a sample of those with 11 to 499 employees. About 92% of the sample responded adequately; this covered about 60% of all employees within the scope of the inquiry. The standard occupational classification drawn up for Census purposes by the General Register Office is not used—a simplified set of categories agreed between industrial interests and the Department has been adopted.

The occupations in each Order of the Standard Industrial Classification are first classed into four broad categories:

- A Administrative, technical and clerical occupations,
- B Those occupations generally regarded as 'skilled',
- C Production occupations involving some small degree of skill,
- D Other occupations (such as warehousemen, drivers, canteen staff, labourers etc.)

Within these categories, specific occupations for each industry are listed.

The occupational data thus collected is analysed by sex, by 'trained' or 'under-training', and by industry. Those under-training are distinguished as either apprentices or not. The only major industrial activity not covered is construction, for which the Department of Environment (Public Buildings and Works) already publishes comparable information annually. Under the scheme for the revision of industrial statistics a new earnings survey (see page 69) was introduced at the end of 1968, and because this survey as a by-product yields data on numbers employed by occupation and industry, the occupational survey was suspended in 1969, with the exception of that relating to the engineering and metal-using trades. The new scheme appears to be successful, and hence it is unlikely to be necessary to resume the suspended survey and it is probable that the separate occupational inquiry will be eliminated entirely.

In addition to the annual surveys mentioned above, semi-annual inquiries are held, in respect of the number of administrative, technical, and clerical workers in manufacturing industry. These surveys refer to the position at mid-October (published January) and mid-April (published July) and are quite independent from, but on a smaller scale to, the annual occupational survey just referred to. The October survey also calls for information on earnings, which are published in March.

OCCUPATIONS IN RETAIL DISTRIBUTION

In conjunction with an earnings inquiry—which will be commented on later (see page 62), an article on 'Occupations in Retail Distribution' has been published in the *Gazette* annually in December, since 1966. The information is obtained from a sample of retail establishments employing eleven or more people. All establishments with 100 or more workers are included. Currently about 2,500 establishments covering 15% of all Retail Distribution employers are approached—about 85% reply. It is important to note that only establishments with *selling units* are approached. This rules out most head offices and thus biases, downwards, estimates made of clerical and administrative staff. The figures are analysed by size of establishment/number of establishments, total employment, type of shop, size of shop, number of establishments, number and category of employees—making a distinction between full and part-time workers of both sexes. As with the manufacturing occupational inquiry, the retail inquiry was suspended in 1969, pending the evaluation in 1972 of the results of the new earnings surveys, and it is unlikely to be renewed.

EMPLOYMENT IN THE PUBLIC AND PRIVATE SECTORS (U.K.)

Since 1968, statistics of the numbers of persons employed in the public and private sectors of the U.K. economy have been published annually in *Economic Trends*. Figures for the years 1961 to 1967 were given in the October 1968 issue. In June 1969, figures for June 1968 and revised 1967 figures were published, and this pattern of annual publication has continued in subsequent years. Table 4.4 illustrates the type of information given.

Less detailed figures, summarizing employment by sector of the economy over the last decade, are also published in the annual *National Income & Expenditure* Blue Book. Prior to 1968, articles on this topic had appeared in *Economic Trends* in November 1960 and December 1962.

THE FUTURE OF EMPLOYMENT STATISTICS

With the possible elimination of national insurance contribution cards as envisaged in the proposals for earnings related social security a new method will need to be adopted to enable us to obtain statistics of employment.

THE EMPLOYMENT CENSUS

The employment census has hitherto been largely based upon counts of insurance cards. Proposals for an annual census of employment were first put forward in 1968. A small pilot survey by the Department of Employment in April 1970 confirmed the practicability of the procedures to be adopted, and in the summer of 1970 the first full census of employment in Great Britain was carried out under the Statistics of Trade Act 1947. The first step in the Census was to obtain from the Inland Revenue Department the addresses of all 'pay-points' from which PAYE payments are sent by employers. (Section 58 of the Finance Act permits this information to be supplied.) The census form itself went to each of these pay-points, the employer being required to give the number of his employees distinguishing between full- and part-time employees of each sex. Where employees recorded at a given pay-point are from several different employment addresses, separate information was required for each address. Farms, which are already covered under the Ministry of Agriculture, Fisheries and Food (Department of Agriculture & Fisheries in Scotland) were dealt with separately in order to avoid duplication of inquiries.

A further census planned for 1971 is intended to establish a proper linkage with the figures obtained under the existing (Insurance cards)

TABLE 4.4

Employment by sector: United Kingdom

(Thousands and percentages)

	Total	Public sector								Private sector	
		Total		Central government		Local authorities		Public corporations			
			%		%		%		%		%
At June 1968											
Total employed labour force	25,283	6,271	24·8	1,888	7·5	2,306	9·1	2,077	8·2	19,012	75·2
H.M. Forces and Women's Services	400	400	100·0	400	100·0	—	—	—	—	—	—
Employers and self-employed	1,758	—	—	—	—	—	—	—	—	1,758	100·0
Total employees in employment	23,125	5,871	25·4	1,488	6·4	2,306	10·0	2,077	9·0	17,254	74·6
At June 1969											
Total employed labour force	25,221	6,271	24·9	1,867	7·4	2,363	9·4	2,041	8·1	18,950	75·1
H.M. Forces and Women's Services	380	380	100·0	380	100·0	—	—	—	—	—	—
Employers and self-employed	1,756	—	—	—	—	—	—	—	—	1,756	100·0
Total employees in employment	23,085	5,891	25·5	1,487	6·4	2,363	10·2	2,041	8·9	17,194	74·5

Notes: Industries are classified according to the *Standard Industrial Classification*, 1958 for June 1968, and the 1968 *S.I.C.* for June 1969. A breakdown by industry groups is also given in the original table.

Source: *Economic Trends*, June 1970

scheme and with the population census also carried out in that year. From 1972 onwards the use of national insurance cards for obtaining employment statistics is likely to be discontinued. Obviously, the relationship between the population census (presumably made quinquennially) and the new employment census will require to be very close, as each will in a sense provide a means of checking on the accuracy of the other, at least so far as the employed population is concerned.

2. EARNINGS

For many years information has appeared in the *Gazette* regarding rates of wages and hours of work. In addition to the monthly series mentioned earlier, an annual article gives similar data to that given monthly, together with comparable figures for previous years and information on the method of negotiation in connexion with wage awards. Although these figures have some value as a means of comparing basic standards over a period of time, they are not very useful, on their own, as aids to economic policy and interpretation. Wage rates may differ very much from actual earnings, and normal weekly hours are not the same as actual hours worked. For this reason the Department of Employment has, over the years developed a series of inquiries into the *earnings* and *hours worked* which we will now discuss.

Information on earnings published by the Department of Employment can be considered conveniently in three sections. Firstly we have the position before 1963 when earnings statistics were restricted to two surveys; a six-monthly one relating to the earnings of manual workers in the United Kingdom and an annual one into the earnings of administrative and clerical workers. At the end of 1962, a monthly inquiry was commenced in Great Britain into the earnings of weekly- and of monthly-paid workers, making no distinction between manual and non-manual employment. In addition, annual information on occupational earnings has been obtained since 1963. In 1964, the first Survey of Total Labour Costs was introduced; a subsequent inquiry took place in 1968.

Finally, in an attempt to rationalize the collection of data on earnings, and to make most use of this information, the Department of Employment commenced a newer type of earnings-survey at the end of 1968. This it is hoped, will supersede many of the other inquiries.

EARNINGS STATISTICS BEFORE 1963

EARNINGS AND HOURS, MANUAL WORKERS

Information on the earnings of manual workers in all major employments, (excepting agriculture, coal mining, railways, London transport, shipbuilding, distribution, catering, entertainment industries, commerce, banking and domestic service) is collected by a survey of about 53,000 establishments which co-operate voluntarily and which in total employ almost 7,000,000 manual workers. In addition, information on earnings is collected separately regarding those employed in nationalized transport in the docks, agriculture and coal mining. The number of manual wage-earners at work, their total earnings and total man-hours worked is obtained from each establishment, and this is recorded separately in the four customary categories, men, women, boys and girls. Information on women working full-time and part-time is obtained separately. The figures of average weekly earnings, average hours worked, and average hourly earnings by industry are calculated for each group of worker. The average weekly earnings for men are analysed both by industry and by region. From time to time the Department publishes additional information on such topics as the distribution of earnings amongst employees, analysis of earnings by size of establishment, and so on. Some of this type of information is, of course, available from the family expenditure survey. The results of the regular inquiries referred to above are published usually in February and July of each year, and relate respectively to a particular week in the previous October and April. It is important to note that these inquiries relate to earnings by *industry* and not by occupation. These surveys like some of those which follow have been affected by the new earnings surveys to be outlined later (page 69). From the end of 1970 onwards the April survey has been very much reduced in coverage. It now relates only to a few industries where the new earnings survey cannot meet certain special needs. In October 1971 at any rate, the full manual-earnings and hours inquiry will be held as usual. Subsequently, a decision will be made as to whether or not both it and the reduced April survey will be discontinued.

THE ANNUAL SALARY INQUIRY

An annual inquiry into salaries of administrative, technical and clerical workers was carried out in October of each year, up to and including 1970, the results being published in the succeeding March *Gazette*. Up to 1959, whilst the then Ministry of Labour obtained information on this topic from the public authorities, banking, insurance and the nationalized industries, the Board of Trade (as it was then) was responsible for obtaining information on salary earnings in manufacturing and other production industries. From 1959 to 1971, however, the March (or occasionally, the April) *Gazette* has given figures, analysed by industry, of average earnings, distinguishing between males and females and between monthly-paid and weekly-paid persons. Comparisons were made with previous years, and there were separate analyses for full-time and part-time females. Separate figures were given for public administration, the public corporations and banking/insurance, as well as all the various manufacturing and production industry groups. More recently indices of average salary earnings, as well as absolute monetary figures, have been given. No regional or area analysis, was given, partly because of the smaller scale of this inquiry compared with the manual earnings inquiry, but more particularly because the centralized methods of payment adopted by many firms made it impracticable for them to supply information on which a regional analysis could be based. The new earnings survey now supplies information in this field on a more comprehensive basis, and this has led to the decision to discontinue the separate survey, mentioned above, after 1970.

IMPROVED EARNINGS STATISTICS—1963 ONWARDS

There were three main defects of the earnings data existing at this time. The significance of earnings as an economic indicator is such that six-monthly or annual inquiries do not produce information early enough. Information on earnings by occupation or degree of skill was lacking. Finally, as wages and salaries form only a part of the total cost of labour to an employer, it was felt desirable that some estimate of total labour costs including such things as national insurance payments, selective employment tax, social welfare schemes, expenditure on recruitment and training, and so on, were needed.

THE MONTHLY EARNINGS SURVEY (G.B.)

In November, 1962, a monthly earnings inquiry set up under the Statistics of Trade Act 1967 (which means that it was a compulsory and not a voluntary inquiry) was introduced. The inquiry covered about 8,000 firms, employing about 7,000,000 persons, and covered the manufacturing, extractive, and construction industries as well as gas, electricity and water supply and the nationalized transport industry. A series of monthly earning indices for the main industrial groups has been published regularly in the statistical series section of the *Employment and Productivity Gazette* since April, 1963. Currently, the indices are based on January 1966 = 100.

All firms with more than 500 employees in the industries mentioned are included; 50% of the establishments with 100–249 and 10% of those with 25–99 employees are also covered. The figures are published within about six weeks of the month to which they relate. In this inquiry no distinction is made between manual and salaried workers, although information on numbers of weekly-paid and of monthly-paid employees are required, together with aggregate earnings for the calendar month in question. It is obvious that direct comparison between these indices and the six-monthly and annual surveys referred to previously cannot be made, although so far as weekly-paid workers are concerned this is not considered to be a handicap, as whatever evidence there is suggests that earnings of weekly-paid salaried workers tend to be similar to, and march in step with, those of weekly-paid manual workers. The results of this inquiry, in addition to providing up to date information for the purposes of economic planning and control, also provides a useful additional check on the estimates of the total annual wage bill in various sectors of the economy.

OCCUPATIONAL ANALYSIS OF EARNINGS (G.B.)

(a) *Manufacturing industry*

Since the beginning of 1963 an inquiry has been carried out under the Statistics of Trade Act 1947, in January and June of each year, into the weekly and hourly earnings and weekly hours of work for adult male manual workers in certain occupations in engineering and other metal using industries. In 1970, about 2,700 establishments employing 250 or more persons provided details on various occupational headings of numbers of employed, number of hours worked (distinguishing overtime separately), and of total earnings. A distinction is made between time workers and those on a payment-by-results basis. The breakdown of the sample is much the same in principle as that used for the monthly earnings enquiry. There are in addition separate surveys of firms in the construction industry, forms being sent to all firms with 100 or more employees and to a sample of those who have fewer.

Both surveys refer to a specified week in January and June of each year.

Recently the engineering and allied survey has been expanded to include the chemical and the iron and steel industries. The results of the January survey are published in May of each year; earnings are analysed by occupation, industry, method of payment and degree of skill. There are also regional analyses, by skill, for each occupation. Some tables also provide information on overtime hours and overtime earnings. Similar data for June is published in the October *Gazette*.

In construction, the information on which is published one month later than the engineering survey, similar information is given, with the addition of data on 'make-up' payments, where special compensation is given for inclement weather or other hindrances to production. From 1970 onwards some of these inquiries were discontinued or reduced, in view of the introduction of the new earnings survey. It is possible that there will be further reduction after 1972.

(b) *Distribution*

It is obviously desirable to collect occupational information for categories other than those for which it is already available, and a first step was made, based on the results of a pilot enquiry held in May 1965, into the earnings and hours of work of selling staff in retail distribution. A regular annual survey has been conducted since this date, in May of each year up to 1969, the results being published in the December *Gazette*. The survey related to shops with eleven or more employees, all known establishments employing 100 or more workers being included, whilst a sample of the smaller ones supplied information. The information obtained and published relates to the average earnings and average hours for selling staff, distinguishing between full-time, part-time (except Saturday) and Saturday-only workers. There are analyses by four types of store: (*a*) supermarket; (*b*) other grocery or provision shop, and other food shop; (*c*) department and variety stores; (*d*) other non-food store. The definitions used are those employed in the census of distribution. Four categories of selling staff are identified—managers, shop assistants, store warehouse staff, and shop cashiers. As bonus payments often play a large part in the wages of selling staff, the information which is required for a particular week in May includes not only actual payments made during that week but a proportion of any bonus which may in fact be paid in respect of a longer period. As mentioned previously, this particular survey was carried out in conjunction with the survey of occupations in retail distribution. Pending a review in 1972 of the new earnings surveys previously mentioned, it has been discontinued. It is unlikely to be resumed.

TOTAL LABOUR COSTS

In 1964 and again in 1968 the Department of Employment carried out an inquiry into total labour costs. Wages and salaries are at present time inadequate as a measure either of total labour costs to the employer, or of the total income of the employee. The first inquiry, the results of which were published in the *Gazette* in December 1966 and in March 1967, covered mining, manufacturing, construction, gas and electricity, water, banks, insurance, public administration and nationalized transport. In manufacturing, all firms employing 1,000 persons or more were covered, with a sample of the rest. So far as non-manufacturing firms were concerned, a great deal was available from central sources but in addition over 1,200 employers were approached for information.

When we refer to total labour costs, we mean in addition to wages and salaries all payments, either voluntary or compulsory, which the employer makes in connexion with his labour force. In the 1964 survey national insurance payments, private social welfare payments, payments in kind, subsidized services (e.g. canteen), recruitment and training expenditure and a series of other minor categories were included. For each industrial category, an average total labour cost per employee was calculated. In manufacturing and in construction a further analysis was carried out by size of establishment, but this was not possible for the other categories because of the way in which the data had been collected. Because of the desirability of comparing this information with that relating to other countries, classifications were prepared in terms of the

Standard Industrial Classification and of a classification comparable with that employed in the European Economic Community.

In October, 1968, the *Gazette* for the first time published a series of indices of labour costs per unit of output for the various industries for each quarter, going back to 1960. Data for these indices came in part from the total labour costs enquiry. It should be noted that since the 1964 inquiry the introduction of redundancy payment, industrial training and the selective employment tax have added other dimensions to total labour costs. Estimates of the effect of these have been included in the indices just mentioned, and also feature in the new total labour cost enquiry of 1968, the results of which were published in the *Employment and Productivity Gazette* in August and October, 1970. The 1968 inquiry, unlike the 1964 survey which was confined to Great Britain, covered Great Britain and Northern Ireland. The sampling method for Great Britain was similar to that in 1964, but in Northern Ireland all enterprises employing over twenty-five employees were included.

Information on labour costs in nine categories was requested.

For operatives. and for administrative, technical and clerical workers separately.	1. Wages and salaries 2. National insurance contributions 3. Selective employment tax 4. Redundancy provision 5. Private and social welfare payments 6. Payments in kind
For all workers combined.	7. Subsidized services to employees 8. Vocational training 9. Other labour costs

Some particulars of total hours worked were also asked for.

Various analyses for Great Britain, by industry and by type of labour cost, both on an annual basis and by hourly amounts including some comparable figures for 1964, were given in the August 1970 *Gazette*. A more detailed breakdown of the types of labour cost in Great Britain was given in the October 1970 *Gazette*, along with a report on the Northern Ireland inquiry.

The figures revealed that labour costs in manufacturing industry were about 25% lower in Northern Ireland than in Great Britain as a whole. In the financial and professional area however the two countries had closely similar labour costs.

A later article appeared in the January 1971 *Gazette*.

FURTHER REGIONAL EMPLOYMENT FIGURES

Some further information on the regional distribution of earnings becomes available when Pay-As-You-Earn returns under the graduated contribution scheme are matched with the March insurance card exchange. From the beginning of the graduated pensions scheme, the Department of Health and Social Security was able to obtain information about the gross earnings of persons covered by the P.A.Y.E. scheme through which the graduated contributions are collected. This information has been used to derive figures showing the pattern of earnings in the standard regions. The data are obtained from a sample of the population of persons registered for national insurance. For general purposes the department maintains a 2% sample of people with contribution cards requiring to be exchanged in March, June, September and December. From the March exchange sample (equal to ½% of the total number of persons covered by national insurance) the records of employed persons in the age ranges 18–64 (males) and 18–59 (females) inclusive are selected. These form the basis of the published statistics referred to below. It should be noted that allocation to region is based on each person's home address—not his place of work (Table 4·5).

The series do *not* cover the following classes of people:

Employees aged under 18, men 65 and over, and women 60 years and over

Members of the armed forces

Employees who never come within the scope of P.A.Y.E. because their weekly or monthly incomes fall below the exemption limits

Employees who have paid or been credited with less than forty-eight contributions in the insurance year (except for 1967/8 as mentioned below).

Those in the latter two categories are mainly married women who work part-time or for part of the year only.

The statistics are published in *Abstract of Regional Statistics* each September, and are provided for the immediately-preceding tax year and for the four preceding years. Average annual earnings are shown separately for men, all women, and spinsters only, in three age groups. Because the coverage is known to be inadequate separate regional analyses are not given for married, divorced or widowed women. Separate tables are given, classified as mentioned above, for:

(i) Persons with at least forty-eight contributions actually paid (i.e. those who had had a full year's employment, and
(ii) Persons with at least one contribution actually paid *but* at least forty-eight contributions either credited or paid (i.e. those in the employment field throughout the year, who may have been sick or unemployed). (Group (ii) includes group (i).)

Persons unemployed, or sick throughout the year, are excluded from all tables.
For 1967–68, a further table relating to those persons who had at least one, but less than forty-eight contributions paid or credited was given. This was an attempt to give some information on the average earnings of workers who were not full-year workers. However, this table was not repeated in the following year, probably because of unreliability suspected in some of the categories where the numbers sampled were small, and also because of the lack of information on the actual earnings of the 15% or so of the sample who fell below the minimum P.A.Y.E. level.

As is the case with all samples the figures are subject to sampling errors, although the size of these are not given with the published tables. It may be suspected that in some cases these standard errors are quite large, relatively speaking, and when interpreting the figures this, and the restricted population under study should be borne in mind.

An article in the *Employment and Productivity Gazette* of March 1969 gave an interesting analysis by region of average weekly and hourly earnings of full-time male manual workers. The average earnings figures for each region were given in two forms, namely, the actual averages based on the employment structures in each particular region, and a figure showing what the average would have been for that region had the number of men in the individual industries in that region been distributed between those industries in the same proportion as for the United Kingdom as a whole. A comparison of the actual with the standardized figures suggests that less than a quarter of the observed difference between the actual averages can be accounted for by differences in employment structure (Table 4·6).

TABLE 4.5

Average gross annual earnings of men in civil employment according to age* and region of residence
New Standard Regions

	Income tax year								
	1964–65	1965–66	1966–67	1967–68	1968–69				
	Average earnings (£)					*Average earnings* (£)			
	Men 18–64				*Number of records analyzed*	*Men* 18–64	18–24	25–44	*Men* 45–64
Persons with at least 48 contributions actually paid: Men									
Great Britain†	1,033	1,104	1,165	1,249	49,908	1,328	956	1,409	1,391
North	968	1,032	1,082	1,158	2,612	1,232	895	1,319	1,278
Yorkshire and Humberside	969	1,042	1,088	1,159	4,230	1,227	913	1,297	1,280
East Midlands	983	1,050	1,104	1,171	3,146	1,237	969	1,312	1,273
East Anglia	944	1,007	1,058	1,128	1,471	1,227	939	1,297	1,262
G.L.C. area	1,135	1,204	1,272	1,362	6,974	1,443	1,030	1,519	1,535
Rest of South East	1,112	1,188	1,258	1,349	8,726	1,433	975	1,530	1,506
South West	961	1,014	1,070	1,155	3,103	1,220	867	1,301	1,271
Wales	1,002	1,060	1,107	1,189	2,136	1,245	924	1,326	1,283
West Midlands	1,054	1,129	1,182	1,252	4,951	1,335	1,000	1,408	1,391
North West	1,000	1,074	1,143	1,219	5,831	1,294	941	1,391	1,338
Scotland	937	1,019	1,082	1,163	4,168	1,248	910	1,330	1,305
Northern Ireland	—	—	—	1,057	9,644	1,106	734	1,174	1,196

* Age on last birthday, at 30 September.
† Including persons whose region of residence is not known.

Source: *Abstract of Regional Statistics* 1970

TABLE 4.6

Average weekly earnings of full-time men manual workers, by region, April 1967 (Industries covered by six-monthly inquiry)

Region	*Regional average earnings*			
	Based on actual employment structures		*Based on national employment structures*	
	(1)		(2)	
	s.	d.	s.	d.
London and South Eastern	432	3	428	4
Eastern and Southern	412	5	410	0
South Western	382	11	385	11
Midlands	421	2	413	2
Yorkshire and Humberside	392	0	392	1
North Western	401	0	402	5
Northern	401	5	398	8
Wales	408	3	392	11
Scotland	394	4	395	10
Northern Ireland	351	0	361	2

Source: *Employment and Productivity Gazette*

In addition to earnings surveys conducted by the Department of Employment and data from the Department of Health and Social Security, information on the earnings of employees comes from the tax records of the Inland Revenue Department, from the family expenditure survey, from the censuses of production and of distribution, and from various unofficial inquiries (e.g. the Office Management Association's publication *Salaries of Clerical Workers*).

THE DISTRIBUTION OF EARNINGS

The regular earnings statistics published by the Department of Employment had not up to 1969 been able to provide us with frequency distributions, although the new survey (page 69) now does this and much more. Earlier however, a Ministry of Labour (now Department of Employment) inquiry into the earnings of full-time manual workers did provide detailed information on this for the various industries of the standard industrial classification. Since then the family expenditure Survey has provided sample information of this nature which may be analysed by region, industry and occupation, whilst, for those covered by the graduated pension scheme only, the Department of Health and Social Security provides information of the distribution of earnings on a regional basis (see page 65). Finally, in its annual 'Inland Revenue Statistics' the

Board of Inland Revenue publishes its comprehensive *Survey of Personal Incomes.* (The time lag is such that the survey for 1968–69 appeared in the 1971 issue of *Inland Revenue Statistics.*)

Very detailed distributions of earnings and investment income analysed by sex and types of income are given, but without regional, industrial or occupational breakdown. In addition there are details of personal income by ranges of type of income, and by regions. A separate table cross-classifies family iircumstances by income size. Standard errors have been calculated for some of the data. Comparative figures for as far back as 1954 are given in some cases.

A recent paper bringing together much of this type of information, *The Distribution of Earnings of Employees* (A. R. Thatcher, J.R.S.S. Vol. 131 Part 2, 1968) suggests a remarkable stability in the relative dispersion of earnings particularly for adult males over the last eighty years.

THE NEW EARNINGS SURVEY

It will be obvious from the above that there has been some tendency in the past for surveys to behave like Topsy—they have just growed. The new earnings survey first carried out in 1968 is a part of the scheme for rationalizing the collection of statistical data in one particular field. In addition to cutting out many of the existing inquiries, the new survey is intended to provide much additional information which has not been regularly available up to now. It covers all industries, all occupations and all sizes of establishments.

Some of the additional information available from the new survey is given below:

- Distribution of earnings of wage and salary earners by industry, by occupation, by each collective agreement, (including wages council agreements) by region, by age, by sex, and by degree of skill
- Distribution of hourly earnings on a similar pattern
- Breakdown of earnings in more detail than hitherto in terms of basic rates, overtime, bonuses and so on
- The proportion of wage and salary earners who are not subject to collective agreements

The regional, occupational and industrial distribution of low-paid workers
Variations in earnings between sub-regions
The ratio of the earnings of men to those of women in the occupations affected or likely to be affected by equal pay
Various aspects of conditions of service i.e., length of working week, holidays, length of service and so on
Aspects of migration, occupational mobility, absenteeism and labour turnover

The survey of earnings was carried out on a relatively small scale, using an effectively random sample selected through employee's National Insurance numbers. A pre-test of the survey was held in September 1967, and the success of this led to a full-scale sample inquiry on the occasion of the September/December 1968 exchange of national insurance cards. Special arrangements were made to include in the sample Civil Servants, and certain other public employees who have National Insurance numbers but no cards.

In all, 92,500 employees of all categories were selected and their employers asked to complete returns. Of these employers satisfactorily completed forms for about 84,000, representing about 1 in 270 of the total number of employees in Great Britain, were received. The main definitions employed in the survey were noted in the *Employment and Productivity Gazette* for May 1969, and an article also appeared in *Statistical News* (No. 8 February 1970.) The results were published in the May 1969 *Gazette*, and in the five subsequent issues. A separate comprehensive report has since been issued.

The survey revealed some interesting facts. The disparity between the earnings of men and women is highlighted by the revelation that in September 1968 over 2,000,000 women, but only about 200,000 men, earned under £12 per week. At the other end of the scale, only 100,000 women earned over £40 per week, whilst 1,000,000 men came in this category. A comparison of the earnings of skilled maual workers with those of the unskilled show that the distribution of earnings in each of the two groups had a similar shape. Skilled men's earnings tended to be about 25% greater than those of the unskilled throughout the range.

Surprisingly, perhaps, regional variations in earnings were small compared with the variations at different age levels. Manual workers, tend to earn more in their 30's and 40's than at earlier or later ages.

The importance of overtime and other 'premiums' in the earnings of manual workers—particularly the men—is illustrated by the following figures taken from the results of the survey.

TABLE 4.7

Basic pay and earnings premiums (September 1968)

	Percentage of earnings	
Manual workers	*Men*	*Women*
Basic pay	67	79
Overtime	16	4
Payment by results	9	12
Shift premium	2	
Bonus	2	5
Miscellaneous	4	
	100%	100%
Non-manual workers		
Basic pay	91	96
Overtime	2	1
Bonus	2	1
Commission	3	
Miscellaneous	2	2
	100%	100%

Source: *Employment and Productivity Gazette*, August 1969

During the week of the survey only 85% of men and 78% of women on full-time received their full basic pay. The reasons for loss of pay are analysed by industry, occupation, age group and region. The number of workers stated not to be affected by national collective agreements was much larger than expected. The earnings of those which were stated not to be so affected differed little, nevertheless, from those subject to such agreements.

The survey has justified itself to such an extent that the expert group set up to appraise the results recommended that an annual survey, using a matched sample design, which should provide information on the movement of workers between industries, on about twice the scale of the 1968 one, should be held each April. The first such survey was carried out in April 1970, with the intention of covering 1% of all employees.

Satisfactory data was obtained for 170,601 employees, representing about 1 in 130 of the total number of employees in Great Britain. Similar information to that obtained in the 1968 inquiry was asked for, with the addition of questions on membership of occupational pension schemes and on sick pay agreements. Reports on this survey, which related to the pay period which included 15 April 1970, have appeared in issues of the *Employment and Productivity Gazette* commencing with the November 1970 issue. This issue, in addition to analysing earnings by industry and by wage agreement, also outlined the survey method employed and listed in some detail the various categories of information obtained.

Analyses of earnings by occupation and details of the make-up of weekly earnings were given in December 1970, whilst the January 1971 issue provided information on regional earnings. A variety of miscellaneous matters were covered in February 1971. As previously, a comprehensive report drawing largely from these articles was also published in 1971. In general, the data obtained was similar to that published for the 1968 survey, but was more detailed. A feature of both surveys is the emphasis laid upon providing earnings distributions.

Table 4.8. gives a breakdown by sex, age and full-time or part-time of the numbers in the sample. Figures in column 'Basis A' include all employees in the sample; 'Basis B' excludes employees not receiving any pay in the period, 'Basis C' excludes *in addition* those who received only holiday or sick pay during the period, and 'Basis D' excludes, further, those whose pay was affected by absence in the period.

These four categories are used in subsequent tabulations of weekly earnings, classified in various ways. As might be expected 'D' is the most useful basis, and it is the one used most often. Where hourly (as distinct from weekly) earnings are given they are stated to be on 'Basis Y'.

Although the results of the surveys from year to year are intended to be generally comparable, there will always be some differences, and hence some limitation on the comparisons which can be made. When comparing the 1968 and the 1970 survey results the following points should be noted:

> The surveys were carried out at different times of the year. Hence seasonal variations in earnings are significant in certain types of employment

TABLE 4.8

Composition of the sample, April 1970: Numbers of employees on various bases used for analyses of weekly earnings

		Manual workers				*Non-manual workers*				*All workers*			
		Basis A	*Basis B*	*Basis C*	*Basis D*	*Basis A*	*Basis B*	*Basis C*	*Basis D*	*Basis A*	*Basis B*	*Basis C*	*Basis D*
Full-time workers													
Males:	21 and over	65,260	63,844	62,675	54,756	31,924	31,863	31,747	31,109	97,184	95,707	94,422	85,865
	under 21	7,025	6,928	6,870	5,525	2,514	2,497	2,490	2,367	9,539	9,425	9,360	7,892
	total	72,285	70,772	69,545	60,281	34,438	34,360	34,237	33,476	106,723	105,132	103,782	93,757
Females:	18 and over	15,347	15,027	14,810	11,668	24,113	24,021	32,898	22,993	39,460	39,048	38,708	34,661
	under 18	1,207	1,193	1,188	855	2,071	2,062	2,054	1,955	3,278	3,255	3,242	2,810
	total	16,554	16,220	15,998	12,523	26,184	26,083	25,952	24,948	42,738	42,303	41,950	37,471
Part-time workers													
Males:	21 and over	1,483	1,457	1,449	1,371	623	612	611	591	2,106	2,069	2,060	1,962
	under 21	105	100	100	92	169	166	166	160	274	266	266	252
	total	1,588	1,557	1,549	1,463	792	778	777	751	2,380	2,335	2,326	2,214
Females:	18 and over	11,539	11,302	11,204	9,915	6,650	6,555	6,530	6,200	18,189	17,857	17,734	16,115
	under 18	71	71	71	67	500	494	494	473	571	565	565	540
	total	11,610	11,373	11,275	9,982	7,150	7,049	7,024	6,673	18,760	18,422	18,299	16,655
All workers													
Males	21 and over	66,743	65,301	64,124	56,127	32,547	32,475	32,358	31,700	99,290	97,776	96,482	87,827
	under 21	7,130	7,028	6,970	5,617	2,683	2,663	2,656	2,527	9,813	9,691	9,626	8,144
	total	73,873	72,329	71,094	61,744	35,230	35,138	35,014	34,227	109,103	107,467	106,108	95,971
Females:	18 and over	26,886	26,329	26,014	21,583	30,763	30,576	30,428	29,193	57,649	56,905	56,442	50,776
	under 18	1,278	1,264	1,259	922	2,571	2,556	2,548	2,428	3,849	3,820	3,807	3,350
	total	28,164	27,593	27,273	22,505	33,334	33,132	32,976	31,621	61,498	60,725	60,249	54,126
Males and females:	total	102,037	99,922	98,367	84,249	68,564	68,270	67,990	65,848	170,601	168,192	166,357	150,097

Source: *Employment and Productivity Gazette*, November 1970

The questionnaires and the occupational classifications used differed somewhat between the two years

The 1970 survey used the 1968 Standard Industrial Classification whilst that for 1968 used the 1958 S.I.C.

The treatment of shift pay and of sick pay differed from 1968 to 1970

Members of police and fire services, shop assistants, some other sales staff and some foremen and supervisors which had been classified as manual workers in 1968 were transferred to the non-manual category in 1970.

These new surveys replace the earlier April series of surveys of earnings of manual workers and the October series covering *salaries* (see page 59). The October surveys of manual workers earnings will, however, continue for the time being. The whole situation is due to be reviewed once again after the 1971 Earnings Survey has been completed.

The 1971 survey is on lines closely similar to those of 1970. The main difference is that whilst the sampling fraction, 1% remains the same, a shorter questionnaire which it is hoped will encourage response was used.

EARNINGS OF QUALIFIED MANPOWER

In 1966–67 the Department of Education & Science approached a sample of 15,000 'qualified' and 5,000 unqualified persons in an attempt to calculate a 'rate of return' on investment in higher education. Comparisons of earnings using the net present value method were made. Some of the results, along with earnings distributions classified by age, sex and qualifications, were published in *Statistics of Education* (*Special Series* No. 3) and in the 1971 issue of *Economic Trends.*

3. HOURS WORKED

Just as earnings often differ from basic wage rates, so hours actually worked differ from the length of the standard working week. The half-yearly earnings inquiries for manual workers also yields information on numbers of hours worked as do the new earnings surveys. The monthly employment returns sent in by a large sample of employers yield information on hours of overtime and of short-time working. From these latter, supplemented by other information obtained at the same time, the Department of Employment prepares monthly, an index number series giving total hours worked by manual workers in manufacturing industry. These indices, first published in August 1962, have been calculated back to 1956. In addition, an index of average hours worked per operative in manufacturing is calculated. More recently, an index of output per operative hour has been calculated by dividing the index of industrial production by the index of total weekly hours worked. Obviously this is just one of many measures of productivity which may be calculated. The index of total hours worked also serves as a measure of the exposure to risk so far as accidents are concerned, and as such is used in the Factory Inspectorate's *Reports*.

4. INDUSTRIAL DISPUTES (U.K.)

In addition to regular monthly publications an article summarizing the previous year's figures appears each May in the *Employment and Productivity Gazette*. The information for the series and for the yearly article comes from the Local Employment Exchanges and the Department's Industrial Relations Advisers. The main tabulations are:

An analysis by industry group, giving number of stoppages beginning in the year, number of workers involved in all stoppages in progress during the year, and the number of working days lost together with the days lost per 1,000 employees

An analysis on similar lines to the above, classified by cause but with broader industrial groups

Actual location and detailed cause of the principal stoppages in the year

Frequency distributions of stoppages classified by
(*a*) duration in working days
(*b*) aggregate working days lost
(*c*) total of workers directly and indirectly involved

Regional analyses

Yearly time series over the past twenty years

TABLE 4.9

Stoppages in years 1950–70

Year	*Number of stoppages beginning in year*	*Number of workers involved in stoppages**			*Aggregate number of working days lost in stoppages*		
		Beginning in year		*In progress in year*	*Beginning in year*		*In progress in year*
		Directly	*Indirectly*		(*a*)	(*b*)	
		000's	000's	000's	000's	000's	000's
1950	1,339	269	33	303	1,375	1,382	1,389
1951	1,719	336	43	379	1,687	1,710	1,694
1952	1,714	303	112	416	1,769	1,797	1,792
1953	1,746	1,329	41	1,374	2,157	2,173	2,184
1954	1,989	402	46	450	2,441	2,480	2,457
1955	2,419	599	60	671	3,741	3,788	3,781
1956	2,648	464	43	508	2,036	2,051	2,083
1957	2,859	1,275	81	1,359	8,398	8,399	8,412
1958	2,629	456	67	524	3,461	3,474	3,462
1959	2,093	522	123	646	5,257	5,280	5,270
1960	2,832	698†	116	819†	3,001	3,049	3,024
1961	2,686	673	98	779	2,998	3,038	3,046
1962	2,449	4,297	123	4,423	5,757	5,778	5,798
1963	2,068	455	135	593	1,731	1,997	1,755
1964	2,524	700†	172	883†	2,011	2,030	2,277
1965	2,354	673	195	876	2,906	2,932	2,925
1966	1,937	414†	116	544†	2,372	2,395	2,398
1967	2,116	551†	180	734†	2,765	2,783	2,787
1968	2,378	2,073†	182	2,258†	4,672	4,719	4,690
1969	3,116	1,426	228†	1,665†	6,799	6,925	6,846
1970	3,906	1,460	333	1,801	10,854	10,908	10,980

(a) The figures in this column include days lost only in the year in which the stoppages began.
(b) The figures in this column include days lost both in the year in which the stoppages began and also in the following year.
* Workers involved in more than one stoppage in any year are counted more than once in the year's total. Workers involved in a stoppage beginning in the year and continuing into another are counted in both years in the column showing the number of workers involved in stoppages in progress.
† Figures exclude workers becoming involved after the end of the year in which the stoppage began.

Source: *Department of Employment Gazette*, May 1971

When referring to these statistics the following points should be noted:

Stoppages involving less than ten workers and those lasting for less than one day are excluded unless, in aggregate, the number of man days lost exceeds one hundred

Time lost due to shortages of material, restrictions on transport and so on in establishments other than those in which the stoppages are taking place are not included

The figures given include workers both directly and indirectly involved at the establishments concerned, unless otherwise stated. When comparing 'rates per 1,000 employees', it should be borne in mind that similar rates in different industries could conceal quite different tendencies for employees to become directly involved. This is particularly important where there are markedly different proportions of clerical and administrative workers in the industries concerned, as these categories are not normally prone to stoppages. (It is, in any case, often difficult to distinguish between direct and indirect involvement)

The precise number of days lost is not always easy to determine, as in many instances there is a gradual return to work

5. ACCIDENTS AT WORK

Industrial accidents notified to the Factories Inspectorate are analysed in the *Gazette* in a short quarterly article. A distinction is made between fatal accidents and all accidents, the analyses being given by area (using the divisions of the inspectorate—not the Standard Regions) and by the process involved. To require to be reported, an accident must either be a fatal one, or disable a person for more than three days.

6. LABOUR TURNOVER

Figures for the number of engagements, discharges and other losses during a four- or five-week period, per 100 employed at the beginning of the period, are published quarterly for each manufacturing industry. A distinction is made between males and females. The figures tend to underestimate the total amount of labour wastage, as persons who were engaged and who left *within* the period are not included. This could have quite a significant effect in those few industries which employ a large amount of unskilled labour in rather unpleasant conditions. In these circumstances a considerable proportion of 'drifters' is employed. Apart from these industries, however, it is reckoned that the published figures permit valid comparisons to be made between industries, and also over periods of time. There are, however, many limitations on the validity of labour turnover ratios calculated in this manner. Those who are interested in this rather complex problem of measuring labour wastage may wish to refer to the following:

The Phenomenon of Labour Turnover—H. Silcock (Journal of the Royal Statistical Society Vol. 117 Part 4, 1954)

A Method of Labour Turnover Analyses—K. F. Lane and J. E. Andrews (Journal, Royal Statistical Society 1953 Vol. 118 Part 3)

The Problem of Labour Turnover—B. Edwards (Unpublished Thesis, University of Newcastle-upon-Tyne, 1959)

7. TRADE UNION MEMBERSHIP

Each year in November the *Gazette* contains an article on trade union membership for the United Kingdom in the previous calendar year. The distribution by size of the trade unions is given as shown below:

TABLE 4.10

Size distribution of Trade Unions (1969)

Number of members	*Number of unions*	*Total membership**	*Percentage of Total number of all unions*	*Percentage of Total membership of all unions*
Under 500	212	33,000	41·7	0·3
500 and under 1,000	60	42,000	11·8	0·4
1,000 and under 2,500	67	110,000	13·2	1·0
2,500 and under 5,000	53	194,000	10·4	1·9
5,000 and under 10,000	28	192,000	5·5	1·9
10,000 and under 15,000	11	134,000	2·2	1·3
15,000 and under 25,000	23	430,000	4·5	4·2
25,000 and under 50,000	14	492,000	2·8	4·8
50,000 and under 100,000	16	1,116,000	3·1	10·8
100,000 and under 250,000	15	1,875,000	3·0	18·2
250,000 and more	9	5,684,000	1·8	55·2
Totals	508	10,302,000	100·0	100·0

* The figures have been rounded to the nearest 1,000.

Source: *Employment and Productivity Gazette*, November 1970

In addition there are analyses of membership, classified by sex and by industry group, as well as a comparison of union membership by sex over the previous ten or eleven years. Total membership has not varied significantly since 1960, but, as might be expected, there has been a progressive decline in the number of unions (685 in 1957, 664 in 1960 and 555 in 1967)

The figures include organizations of salaried and professional, as well as manual, workers, where these include in their charter negotiation with employer on wages and working conditions.

MANPOWER STUDIES

Enough has been said to indicate the complexity of the manpower statistics currently published on a regular basis. There are in addition the figures put out by nationalized industries, other public authorities and services, and by some industries outside the public sector. Furthermore, from time to time special manpower surveys outwith the regular scheme are produced by the Department of

Employment. An example is the *Labour Mobility Survey* of 1963, published in 1967 and referred to in the July 1966, April 1967 and August 1967 issues of the *Gazette*. This survey dealt largely with industrial and occupational mobility, and movement from one firm to another in the same industry, as well as with some aspects of geographical mobility.

More recently we have the series of *Manpower Studies*. Largely of a statistical nature, these are published in booklet form by the Manpower Research Unit (part of the Department of Employment). These studies, originally planned in connexion with the Industrial Training Scheme, have proved to be valuable in a very much wider planning field.

SPECIAL GROUPS AND MANPOWER STATISTICS

From time to time special statistical studies of particular occupational groups are undertaken, and it is obviously impracticable to comment upon most of them here. However, it is worthwhile to draw attention to recent inquiries into technological manpower.

When the Ministry of Technology (now part of the Department of Trade & Industry) was formed in October 1964 one of its statutory duties was a special responsibility for professional engineers. In order to obtain more detailed information than had hitherto been available, the Ministry of Technology and the Council of Engineering Institutions (C.E.I.) conducted a sample survey in 1966. A sample of 25,000 U.K. members of the fourteen engineering institutions was taken, and 80% of these supplied usable questionnaires. Data from this survey were published in *The Survey of Professional Engineers* (1966), and in the occasional paper *Statistics of Science & Technology*, published 1968.

A further survey was carried out in 1968, and its results have been published in the 1970 issue of *Statistics of Science & Technology*.

SURVEY OF SCIENTISTS

In 1968, in conjunction with the Ministry of Technology and the C.E.I., the five British Scientific Societies conducted a survey on lines similar to that for engineers. This was published in *Statistics of Science & Technology* (1970 issue).

In addition, the Ministry of Technology annually prepares estimates of the numbers of persons with qualifications in engineering, technology and science, who enter or leave the U.K. for a period of a year or more. Some of this data, for periods prior to 1967, provided statistical source material for the inquiry by Dr. F. E. Jones into the migration of persons with scientific and technological skills, published under the title *The Brain Drain* (H.M.S.O. 1967).

With the growing emphasis on manpower planning, such surveys are likely to become regular features.

The next inquiry in engineering, science and technology will be confined to firms employing 200 or more persons.

An article on *Science Manpower Statistics* by H. E. Bishop (*Statistical News* No. 2), illustrates in one particular field the importance of detailed statistical information for manpower planning.

FORECASTING AND ECONOMIC PLANNING

Manpower forecasts are essential for planning purposes. Some indication of the extent to which the Department of Employment's figures are used to produce forecasts is given on page 149 of the *Estimates Committee Report* of 1966–67, and many of these have been referred to earlier in this chapter. One most important aspect of this is found in the regular projections or forecasts of the size and compositions of the working population, based on estimates of the population as a whole prepared by the Government Actuary and published periodically. The most recent projection at the time of writing relates to the period 1967–81. It should be clearly understood that planning can be no better than the statistics on which it is based. This in itself must be an incentive to the improvement in the timeliness of accuracy of the basic data, and in the forecasting methods employed. Hitherto these have been, at best, only moderately successful.

QUESTIONS

1. Examine the statistics available on trade unions, and comment on any notable changes which have taken place since the Second World War.
2. Discuss the developments in statistics of earnings since 1963.
3. Outline the development in earnings statistics which have taken place since 1968, paying special attention to the new earnings surveys.
4. Give details of the source and nature of employment statistics in the United Kingdom, and comment on any problems involved in their interpretation.
5. Discuss the problems that arise in formulating estimates of changes in the regional distribution of the working population in the United Kingdom. To what extent is the calculation of activity rates helpful in connection with the regional development plans?
6. What are the main features of the Department of Employment's indices of wage rates and of earnings? Why do the movements of these indices differ? To what extent is the concept of 'wage drift' valuable in this connection?
7. Your firm is considering a wages claim from a group of employees. What statistics would you provide your Managing Director with in order to help him consider such a claim, and how would you suggest he uses these statistics?
8. It is often suggested that statistics of earnings and employment should be presented by occupation rather than by industry. Discuss this point of view.
9. What statistics would you need and how would you use them, if you were asked to construct a series of average wages-per-head and average salaries-per-head for all industries on an annual basis for the United Kingdom over a period 1958–1971?
10. Discuss the problem of measuring unemployment, and consider how far statistics available in this country are adequate.
11. In January 1971, it was stated that there were three unemployed men for every vacancy. To what extent do the statistics available support such a statement?
12. What do you understand by the term 'travel to work areas'? Why were they developed and to what extent do they achieve their aim?
13. Examine and compare the different ways in which labour turnover can be measured.

5 Production and industrial statistics

A knowledge of the level of output (both in aggregate and per head), of holdings of stocks of finished products, materials and fuels, of work in progress, and of capital expenditure in the different industries of this country is essential to governmental planning and forecasting. Moreover, information of this nature is increasingly used, particularly by the larger and the more progressive firms, as a basis for their own production and marketing plans, and as a means of enabling them to judge their market position as compared with the industry as a whole.

It is nevertheless true that there is as yet only a very small proportion of firms who use the industrial statistics prepared by governmental agencies as effectively as they might. Whatever the reason for this, there is little doubt that as management comes to adopt more sophisticated production, planning and marketing techniques, and as computers, with their facilities to process rapidly large masses of figures, become universally available, more and more firms will have recourse to statistics for planning purposes. These considerations make it essential that statistics collected and published by government departments be properly integrated, as comprehensive as possible, and prepared without wasteful duplication of effort.

To this end, on 1 January 1969 a Business Statistics Office was set up. It is administered by the Department of Trade and Industry, but directed by an Interdepartmental Committee with the Director of the Central Statistical Office as Chairman. The Business Statistics Office succeeds the Board of Trade Census Office but has a much wider field of activitiy. It is charged with implementing the new system of industrial statistics which will be described below, and, as another necessary part of the rationalization process, with constructing and maintaining a Central Register of Businesses as explained on page 22.

Even though individual firms may be tending to use official

sources of statistics more, there is still a marked lack of enthusiasm in many firms for the work of supplying the raw data. When basically similar information is demanded, at different times and in slightly different forms, by several government departments this lack of enthusiasm may become positive irritation, and lead to a reduction in co-operation. The need to avoid such difficulties, which had existed in the past, was recognized in the setting up by the Central Statistics Office of a Survey Control Unit to examine all statistical forms sent out by government departments and other public bodies, so as to eliminate duplication and to make sure that the definitions and categories used are consistent throughout the government statistical services.

1. THE NEW SYSTEM OF INDUSTRIAL STATISTICS

The creation of the new system of industrial statistics, foreshadowed by the report of the Estimates Committee on Government Statistical Services (1966–67), and outlined in an article by J. Stafford in *Statistical News,* No. 1, is intimately linked with the creation of the Common Register of Businesses. The idea is to replace large-scale Production Censuses by a system of more frequent inquiries reporting on a more comprehensive basis than hitherto.

A system of quarterly (or in a few cases monthly) reports of production, orders and sales is being introduced industry by industry, after consultation with those involved. The closest co-operation is being sought with representatives of the industries selected, the intention being to help industry to see the need for this information from a national point of view, to encourage firms to use the data for their own purposes, and to collect the figure in a form which gives the least inconvenience to the firms concerned. Furthermore, because production statistics can only be used effectively if they are properly related to manpower and trade figures, the intention is to bring the classifications for these various sections as closely into line as possible. The fact that both production and employment statistics will both be based on the Common Register will greatly help.

Each reporting unit (firm, establishment, etc. as the case may be) under the new system makes a return of its output on one form.

Previously many of the inter-censal short-period inquiries were concerned with a particular group of products, so that a firm which was a substantial producer of several types of goods might have to complete several forms, at different times, relating to different sections of its output. This is both uneconomic and irritating. The success of the new system, which will undoubtedly call for more data from many firms, is dependent upon the elimination of unnecessary work of the type referred to. The comprehensive type of reporting mentioned also has the advantage that it overcomes the difficulties, experienced under the earlier system, of maintaining correct lists of firms making any given set of products, and of ensuring that the classification of industrial establishments is kept up to date.

The quarterly or monthly figures of output and sales are supplemented by data from annual surveys into aggregated data such as totals of sales and purchases, capital investment, stocks and work in progress, employment, wages and salaries.* From these, estimates of net output can be made (see page 97) and regional and industry investment levels calculated. The results will also provide benchmarks for the short-period statistics as well as being used in national income calculations.

At varying intervals of time it is also intended to have a variety of ad hoc inquiries on such topics as types and quantities of materials, services and components used, transport facilities and costs, research and development, expenditure, marketing channels, and so on. Throughout all these inquiries it is intended to use the same reporting units in order to maintain continuity and ensure comparability.

Whilst it is realized that the new system imposes an additional burden on industry, the intention is to ensure that the value of the information becoming newly available to industry will more than offset the cost. Indeed because the new system will be largely of a regular nature and on a uniform basis, agreed with the industry concerned, it is hoped that once firms have adapted their record-keeping procedures to the new system, the provision of the required figures will become largely a matter of routine.

Already (1972) a large number of inquiries have been initiated under the new system.

---

* See *New Earnings Survey*, page 69.

QUARTERLY SALES INQUIRIES

The quarterly sales inquiries form the backbone of the short-period inquiries in the new system, and it is therefore worthwhile to consider the problems involved in planning them, as they are typical of those involved in all such surveys of this nature. The information obtained consists basically of sales by value of products for each industry. Such information is normally more easily obtained from firms' records than are production figures. However, where the industries themselves desire it, production figures are also collected, and there are instances where figures in physical terms, e.g. quantity, volume, etc., are used.

In the discussions that take place with a selected industry the emphasis is on the list of products for which the information is to be collected. Obviously, not all products can be covered, but the list has to be as well balanced and comprehensive as possible, although not too long.

Definitions, which should be as clear and unambiguous as possible, have presented some difficulty. The suppliers and the users of the commodities concerned are often in conflict about them. Suppliers wish to define product categories in terms which are related to their production methods, whilst the users often wish a product to be defined in terms of the end-use. As apparently similar commodities from the producers' point of view may have markedly different end-uses, there may be a considerable problem of reconciliation here. Furthermore, suppliers do not often maintain sales records classified by the type of use, or by the user industry. In these cases, classification by end-use is obviously not practicable.

Because the statistics derived from these enquiries need to be related to import and export statistics, product definitions in the sales enquiries need to be compatible—at least so far as groups of commodities are concerned—with those in the external trade classification. Very detailed discussions between the appropriate Government Departments and Industrial or Trade Association representatives are held before the arrangements for each particular industry are agreed, but the difficulties outlined above have been overcome in a considerable number of cases. It is hoped that when the reorganization is completed, quarterly information will be available in respect of at least 5,000 product categories as compared with the situation prior to the introduction of the new system, when less than half this number of products was covered.

When the Central Register of Businesses is available it will provide the basis for the collection of the data required. The reporting unit is the *establishment,* as defined in the standard industrial classification. In order to reduce the burden on industry as a whole, quarterly inquiries will usually be limited to establishments with twenty-five or more employees. Although this excludes about 60% of all industrial establishments, it is nevertheless expected that the inquiries will cover at least 95% of total ouput. There are one or two exceptions where existing short-period statistics have a more comprehensive coverage than that referred to above. In such circumstances, where the industry concerned wishes the more comprehensive coverage to be maintained, quarterly inquiries will be extended to involve establishments with eleven or more employees. Subsequent changes in the cut-off limit in other industries, where small firms contribute a substantial proportion of output is not, of course, precluded.

The quarterly inquiries are industry-based as is the case with the censuses of production, not product-based as had previously been the case with most short-period production inquiries. This is most important; it should be borne in mind that an industry-based inquiry embraces the total sales of establishments in that industry, and that these figures include sales of products which may more typically be related to other industries. A product-based inquiry, on the other hand, merely covers the total sales of a particular product, or range of products, by establishments in a particular industry. It is theoretically possible to get the same information by either procedure, but industry-based figures are easier to collect and easier to convert to product-totals than is the reverse. Moreover, as has already been mentioned, an industry-based inquiry involves less form-completion than a product-based inquiry. Each establishment in the industry receives one quarterly form only. This form, in addition to including the headings of products characteristic of the industry, includes other headings under which products not typical of that industry may be included. These latter are combined in due course with the data received from establishments in other industries. For an inquiry of this nature to be successful, a considerable amount of co-ordination in the conduct of inquiries is necessary in order to ensure that related industry and product-totals are obtained at the same time. For similar reasons, it is desirable that the publication of results for related industries is simultaneous.

Of the approximately 170 industries covered by the Standard Industrial Classification, new quarterly inquiries were arranged to be initiated before the end of 1971 in respect of between one half and two thirds. The data is published, at present, in the extended *Business Monitor Series.*

The index of industrial production is compiled monthly, and it is likely that extant monthly inquiries (requesting relatively simple information for this and other Government purposes) will continue, for the time being at least, alongside the quarterly surveys, although ultimately some form of rationalization is inevitable.

Despite the overall advantages of the new system, the very real difficulties to be overcome should not be minimized. They were brought out clearly—and possibly with a little over-emphasis—in the evidence by the Board of Trade to the Parliamentary Committee on Government Statistical Services. (see page 102 of *Report on Government Statistical Services, Session 1966–67, H.M.S.O.*). These comments were made in 1966. Obviously, in the period which elapsed between these comments being made and the implementation of the new proposals the feasibility as well as the desirability of the change-over has been sufficiently demonstrated. Nevertheless, the success or otherwise of the new system cannot properly be judged for several years, although it appears to have made a good start.

2. CENSUSES OF PRODUCTION

The main purposes of the censuses of production are:

- To ascertain the structure of industry, the size of its various parts and their relative importance
- To provide information for the construction of input-output tables, and for the estimates of national income and expenditure
- To provide bench-marks against which short-term statistics of output, sales, etc., may be measured
- To provide a weighting system for index numbers of production and of wholesale prices
- To provide information for regional planning, marketing research, industrial development, and general economic analyses

To provide information on industrial characteristics which will assist in other subsequent inquiries by providing a basis for more efficient sampling designs for more specific inquiries.

The Statistics of Trade Act 1947 was passed by Parliament in order to give general powers for the collection of statistics from business organizations outside the public sector. Under the Act, the Board of Trade (now the Department of Trade and Industry) is obliged to take an annual census of production, and powers are also given to enable it to take a census of distribution in any year which may be prescribed. Annual production censuses, on a sample basis, have been carried out since the date of the Act, with fully detailed censuses taking place quinquennially.

The 1968 Census of Production was intended to be the last of the five-yearly full censuses, their place being taken by more frequent inquiries under the new system, as mentioned earlier.

The new system calls for more information than that hitherto required at the annual sample censuses of production (which hitherto have been held during the years between the main censuses), together with a considerable increase in the number of monthly and quarterly inquiries into sales output for individual industries. Although the detailed coverage of the censuses has varied from year to year, it has in general included mining and quarrying, manufacturing (under both public and private ownership) and construction; agriculture has been excluded. Repairs for the trade are included, but repairs for the public are covered by censuses of distribution, as are all garage firms, when they are covered at all. Laundering was included under production until 1966, when it was included in the distribution census for that year.

The first census of production covering the whole of the British Isles was held in 1907 under the authorization of an Act of 1906. Subsequent censuses, prior to 1947, were held as under:

Census year	*Area covered*	*Establishment coverage*
1912	British Isles	Firms having five or fewer employees exempted.
1924	U.K.	All covered.
1930	U.K.	Firms having ten or fewer (G.B.) and firms having five or fewer (Northern Ireland) employees exempted.
1935	U.K.	Firms having ten or fewer (G.B.) and firms having five or fewer (Northern Ireland) employees exempted.
1946	G.B.	On a restricted scale; only certain industries covered.

Even when exempted from filling in the main returns, all firms had to supply particulars of the numbers employed, (including proprietors).

The first post-war census was carried out in 1949 and covered the year 1948. Firms were permitted, in this Census as in others, to submit returns either for the calendar year or for any twelve-month period ending between 5 April 1948 and 5 April 1949. This was a full census, carried out by post; its coverage being indicated below:

All firms engaged in film production, coal, gas, electricity production, and mineral oil refining were required to complete *all* particulars irrespective of size

Some businesses employing ten or under (where the production from such firms was high in relation to total output) had to supply more particulars than other small firms

Other firms employing ten or under furnished information only on number employed and nature of business

In the building trade, firms of eleven to twenty-four employees completed a special form in more detail than those firms in category (*c*)

The *establishment* was the basis of collection of data, and where one firm had more than one establishment separate returns were made—except where, for accounting reasons, it was difficult; in which case one return sufficed—plus summaries for each establishment

This census related to Great Britain only, as the necessary legal powers were not taken in Northern Ireland until 1949. (Since then censuses have been held annually in both Great Britain and Northern Ireland). In general, the full censuses are conducted and published on a United Kingdom basis, whilst the restricted censuses are published separately in Great Britain and Northern Ireland, and have not always been entirely compatible. The censuses for 1949 and 1950 required calling for rather less information than in 1948, whilst in 1951, a full census, requiring somewhat greater information than in 1948, was carried out. 1952 and 1953 saw restricted censuses once again, but 1954 was a full census year. The reports on this census were not all available until 1958, when the data was used to provide a new weighting system for the Index of Industrial Production.

THE VERDON SMITH COMMITTEE

1954 also saw the publication of the *Report of the Verdon Smith Committee* (October 1954). This committee made certain suggestions regarding both the censuses of production and of distribution. These were:

A full census of production should be held every three years, with a sample census annually at other times
A full census of distribution should be held every ten years, with sample censuses every three or four years

It was also recommended that:

The censuses and sample surveys should be recognized as necessary—despite much trade opposition—both for the checking of current statistics collected on a sample basis (e.g. weekly, monthly, quarterly statistics), and the maintenance and improvement in accuracy of national income statistics
Advance copies of the forms should be sent to industry before the start of the census year, and the census forms should be sent out early in the year of collection
The calendar year and not the firm's business year should be used in all cases
Electronic computers should be used to hasten publication of results (the results of the 1948 census were not finally completed and published until 1953)
Sampling, for certain returns, should be used even when a full census is taken
The Board of Trade (now the Department of Trade & Industry) should liaise more closely with industry, (i) to encourage the use of census data, and (ii) to decrease the difficulties which firms had in completing the forms
The exemption limit should be raised from firms of eleven to firms of twenty-five employees

A number of other minor recommendations, regarding inclusion or exclusion of various questions, were also made.

The Government accepted the Verdon Smith recommendations. Subsequently, the Department of Trade & Industry announced the postponement of the next full census until 1958 (to be taken in 1959). This was partly due to the desire not to trouble industrialists, (who on the whole showed little understanding of the value of the statistics to them) and partly to the desire to create a favourable climate by 'educating' industry by better public relations, and by up-to-date publication of data from the sample surveys.

In fact, with the exception of the recommendation regarding the calendar year (see (c) above) (which, had it been adopted would have probably aroused widespread resistance) the recommendations have been largely put into practice. Full censuses of production have been carried out every five (not three) years since 1958, and each inter-censal year has seen a limited census or sample survey.

The subsequent full census was carried out for 1958, when the decision was taken to raise the exemption level for the completion of the full detailed questionnaire from under eleven to under twenty-five employees. This change coincided with the revision of the Standard Industrial Classification first introduced in 1948.

The 1955, 1956 and 1957 censuses covered approximately one in every nine or ten establishments in Great Britain, including all the largest establishments, although somewhat different arrangements applied in Northern Ireland. Similar procedures were adopted for 1960, 1961, and 1962, although the 1959 Census covered a much wider range and can be looked upon more as a limited census, in that a few questions were asked of many firms, rather than more detail being required from a few.

THE 1963 FULL CENSUS

The 1963 full census had a similar scope and coverage to that of 1958, and indeed as that of the 1968 Census, with which we shall deal in more detail later. In the meantime, it is of some concern to note that despite (or perhaps in this instance because of) the introduction of electronic data processing systems, the delay in publishing census results is still excessive. For the 1958 Census, provisional results were published in January 1960, the complete series of reports being issued between June 1960, and March 1963. The whole process took about 4½ years. Provisional results for 1963 appeared in *Board of Trade Journal* for 24 December 1965. Although the first of the final reports appeared in 1966, they were not completed until mid 1970.* Thus the 1968 census was actually undertaken before the 1963 census information had been fully processed. The delay in producing the results is serious, and

* The publication of the 129 separate 'industry' reports was completed in 1969. The index and three summary volumes did not appear until 1970.

although it is probable that the slowness in producing the 1963 census figures arose from special circumstances which may not repeat themselves, the proposals for the development of the new system of industrial statistics have come none too soon.

The results of the 1963 census of production were used for the first time to calculate operating ratios, relating to certain important business variables. The intention was to enable individual firms to compare the more easily their own performances with that of their industry. The ratios chosen were:

Total stocks, as a percentage of total sales
Stocks of good on hand for sale, as a percentage of total sales
Work-in-progress, as a percentage of total sales
Stocks of materials and fuel, as a percentage of total sales
Materials and fuel consumed, as a percentage of total sales
Salaries, as a percentage of total wages and salaries
Wages, as a percentage of net output
Wages per £ of total sales
Salaries per £ of total sales
Net output per head

The ratios were given in an article in the *Board of Trade Journal* of 16 February 1968. They related, of course, to firms employing twenty-five or more persons. A typical set of figures for ratio 1 (total stocks as a percentage of total sales is):

TABLE 5.1

Total stocks as a percentage of total sales in the bread and flour confectionery industry

Lower quartile	*Median*	*Upper quartile*	*Number of firms*
2·1%	2·8%	4·0%	524

Thus out of 524 firms, a quarter had a ratio of 2·1% or less, half a ratio of 2·8% or less, and only one quarter had a ratio exceeding 4·0%

By comparing its own ratio with these, a given firm would know whether its stocks were relatively low or high compared with the industry as a whole. Although there might be special reasons why a firm had (say) a high stock ratio, the guide lines given by the industry ratios would assist it in making a decision as to whether or not to alter its existing practices.

Similar remarks of course apply to the comparisons of other ratios.

THE 1964–67 SAMPLE-CENSUSES

Since 1963 there have been four annual inquiries of a very simple character on a sample basis. In these inquiries, information on capital expenditure and stocks in manufacturing industry only were required, except in 1966, when firms in the construction industry were required to supply information on employment. The annual sample-censuses are on a 'business-unit' basis, returns being called for in respect of the business as a whole—i.e. a company, or group of companies—rather than for individual establishments, as is the case in the quinquennial censuses. The first business-unit census was held in 1959 and, as has been remarked, covered all businesses employing twenty-five or more. The 1960 to 1962 sample-censuses had a more restricted coverage, including those firms supplying information on a voluntary basis for the Board of Trade quarterly industrial inquiries, plus a stratified sample of all other firms employing twenty-five or more persons. In 1962 for example, the inquiry covered some 10,000 firms additional to the 2,000 large ones participating in the voluntary scheme. Results appeared to indicate that the extra costs associated with the 10,000 additional firms were hardly worth while. Consequently in 1964 and subsequent years, only 1,500 of the larger manufacturing firms, additional to the 2,000 voluntary contributors, were approached. It is estimated that these 3,500 firms accounted for some 80% of the stocks and capital expenditure in all manufacturing industry.

The construction industry was included in the survey for 1966 and 1967. Because the coverage of the voluntary quarterly inquiry is poorer for construction than for manufacturing, an additional sample of 3,200 construction firms employing twenty-five or more persons was taken. In addition to answering the general questions on stock and capital expenditure, these firms were required to give information about employment.

The data collected was used to make estimates of stock, work in progress, and fixed capital expenditure by industry-group for all manufacturing firms in the United Kingdom. The grossing up-from the sample values was accomplished by linking them to the 1963 (full census) results, after converting the latter to a business unit basis. In the grossing-up, allowance was made for firms having fewer than twenty-five employees.

Articles on the 1963, 1964, 1965 and 1966 sample censuses were published in the *Board of Trade Journal* of 14 April 1967 and 29 December 1967, to which anyone requiring further details should refer. Comparisons over the whole period from 1963 are given in these articles, and in the separately published *Report on the Censuses of Production* for 1964, 1965, 1966 and 1967 (H.M.S.O.) which also gives full details of the sampling and estimation procedures.

THE CENSUS OF PRODUCTION 1968

In view of the introduction of the new system of industrial statistics it is intended that the Census of Production for 1968 will be the last of the quinquennial censuses.

In its evidence to the Estimates Committee of the House of Commons (*Government Statistical Services,* 1966–67) the Board of Trade explained how preparations for a full census of production begins about two years before the start of the census year. At this time the content and form of the census is agreed. The questions included in the 1968 census, which was taken in 1969, cover:

- Details of the business
- Working proprietors
- Employment
- Wages and salaries
- Stocks
- Capital expenditure
- Work given out to be done by other firms
- Transport costs and certain other expenses
- Details of purchases, (quantity and value)
- Details of sales and output, (quantity and value)

The information requested was much the same as for the 1963 census excepting that questions previously asked regarding employers' contributions to Pensions and National Insurance Funds were omitted in 1968, the information being obtained in another way. Also, in 1968, firms were asked if they would agree to having their names included, as appropriate, in lists showing the firms which contributed to the sales of the main products of each census industry. It was felt that this would be of help to those engaged in market research and would not involve any breach of confidence. As a means of improving the government's statistics on distribution, and the Central Statistical Office's estimates of consumer expenditure, information was sought on the amount of sales made by each firm direct to the general public.

There are over 10,000 detailed headings in the purchases, sales and output sections, and for each full census these are discussed with the trade associations, before the forms—which differ from industry to industry—are designed and printed. In 1968, 154 different industries were separately defined, compared with 128 in 1963. Of the 90,000 manufacturing establishments in the United Kingdom, less than half have twenty-five or more employees. Full particulars were required from all firms emplying twenty-five or more, and these accounted for about 94% of total employment. Most small firms employing under twenty-five persons were in 1968, as in earlier censuses, required to state only the number employed and the type of business. Where however such small firms produced a large part of an industry's total output a sample of such firms was asked to supply additonal particulars. As with other quinquennial censuses, the 1968 census was conducted on an establishment basis and not on a 'business unit' or 'enterprise' basis, this facilitating a more detailed analysis.

Advance copies of the census forms were sent out to industry in 1967. This was to enable firms to be informed, before the Census year stated, just what particulars they would be required to supply. On 1 January 1969 the census forms proper were issued, and three months allowed for their completion and return. In fact, in 1969 as in previous years, there was much delay, some returns being still outstanding at the end of the year.

An article *The Census of Production* by H. E. Browning (*Statistical News, No. 5*) explains in some detail the procedures involved in preparing for the 1963 and 1968 censuses, in collecting the data, and in processing it.

Provisional information appeared first in the *Board of Trade Journal,* and this is followed by the serial publication of the separate parts (one for each census industry)—153 in total in 1968—together with a number of volumes of summary tables, a commodity index and a volume of introductory notes. These introductory notes are essential as a guide to the report as a whole, for they include definitions of the terms used, and general explanations of the tables published in the other parts.

Up to the time of writing four articles have appeared in *Board of Trade Journal* (31 December 1969, 28 January, 29 April and

2 September 1970) giving preliminary results of the 1968 Census together with comparable figures for 1963. The December article gave brief details of the census procedure and preliminary estimates of the larger aggregates. Its main purpose was, however, to explain some of the limitations of these preliminary estimates, and to act as a guide to the interpretation of the provisional results. The January 1970 article compared 1963 and 1968 figures for employment, wages and salaries, and net output, (the latter two both in aggregate and per head) for each of the orders II to XXI of the Standard Industrial Classification (1968 Revision). An analysis of employment and net output by sizes of establishment was given in April 1970, whilst the September 1970 article was concerned largely with area analyses of employment and net output for each of the manufacturing Orders of the Standard Industrial Classification Orders III to XIX. It should be noted that comparisons between 1963 and 1968 Census figures require to be handled with caution in view of the fact that the 1963 S.I.C., differed in several major respects from the 1968 S.I.C. (see page 28). Whilst the general description of the Census appeared in July 1971 the first of the 'industry' parts of the 1968 Census scheduled to appear in mid-1971 had not actually been issued by October of that year largely due to delays in response from some of the industry group. The publications are unlikely to be completed before mid-1973. There will be 171 parts in all, 153 devoted to the separate industries and 12 to a Directory of Businesses which have contributed to the Census and which have agreed to have their names published.

Table 5.2 illustrates one of the principal tabulations found in each industry report in the censuses of production. The tabulation is that adopted for the 1963 Census, and it is likely that the 1968 results will be cast in a similar form. Most of the categories are self-explanatory. The difference between 'enterprise' and 'establishment' has been explained on page 24.

MERCHANTED GOODS

Merchanted goods and those *for merchanting* are those purchased for sale without processing by the firm concerned.

GROSS OUTPUT

This is defined as the aggregate value of goods made and other work done during the year by the establishments classified to the industry, and is calculated as follows:

Value of sales work done

less value of stocks and work in progress at beginning of year

plus value of stocks and work in progress at end of year

TABLE 5.2

Industry summary: United Kingdom (Industry 'X')
Estimates for all firms (1958 and 1963)

		Unit	1958	1963
Number of enterprises		No.	48	53
Number of establishments		No.	55	66
Gross output		£'000	20,123	28,774
Net output		£'000	10,328	15,804
Net output per head		£	1,331	1,889
Sales and work done	goods produced and work done			
	merchanted goods and canteen takings	Specimen figures have been given above. The remainder of the figures in this table have been omitted as their inclusion would add nothing to the exposition.		
Purchases	materials for processing and packaging, and fuel			
	goods for merchanting and canteen purchases			
Payments to other organizations	for work done on materials given out			
	for transport			
Stocks and work in progress				
Total stocks and work in progress	change during year			
	at end of year			
of which Goods on hand for sale	change during year			
	at end of year			
Work in progress	change during year			
	at end of year			
Materials, stores and fuel	change during year			
	at end of year			
Average number employed	total, including working proprietors			
	operatives			
	other employees			
Wages and salaries	of operatives			
	of other employees			
Employers' contributions to National Insurance and private pension schemes, etc.				
Capital expenditure (excludes expenditure for establishments not yet producing)				
Total capital expenditure				
New building work				
Land and existing buildings (acquisitions *less* disposals)				
Plant and machinery	,, ,, ,,			
Vehicles	,, ,, ,,			

Source: *Census of Production*, 1963

NET OUTPUT

The net output of a firm, according to the census of production, is obtained by estimating the gross output, (i.e. sales adjusted for any changes in stock) and subtracting the cost of materials, once again adjusted for stock changes, and also subtracting any payments to other organizations for transport, and work subcontracted as well as Customs and Excise duties paid. The net output does not take into account any payments which may have been made to other industries for advertising, insurance and certain other services. Therefore the net output for any given industry is actually in excess of the value added by that industry, by the amount of payments for services just mentioned. However in 1963 and again in 1968, an attempt was made to collect either entire, or in some cases sample, information on some of these payments for services which had not previously been available. It has, therefore, proved possible in the 1963 census figures to eliminate from the census net output figures for some of the broad categories much of the value of the inputs of services so as to give a truer estimate of the value added. Even for individual industries where such estimates are not available changes in net output may be a useful indicator of changes in value added provided the services not eliminated bear a fairly constant relationship to calculated net output.

NET OUTPUT PER HEAD

From the figures of net output for each industry is calculated the net output per head,

$$\frac{\text{Net output}}{\text{Average number of persons of all categories employed (full-time and part-time)}}$$

This is another useful ratio for comparison purposes, although its use as a measure of productivity is severely limited in view of the different degrees of capitalization from industry to industry. In the coal and petroleum products Order, for example, net output per head was provisionally estimated as £4,229 in 1968, whilst in clothing and footwear it was only £1,102. The greater amount of physical capital necessarily used in the former industry prevents, however, any facile direct comparison of the efficiency—or productivity—of the two industrial groups on the basis of net output per head alone.

In the National Income and Expenditure Blue Book the figures of value of net output are obtained by adding together estimates of income from employment, income from self-employment and gross trading profits of firms. This avoids the double-counting entailed in the conventional census net output mentioned above. The additional information available on service costs in the 1963 and 1968 censuses mean that the final *overall* net output figures in the Censuses can be brought quite close to the figures derived in another manner for the national income and expenditure estimates.

PROBLEMS INVOLVED IN MEASURING NET OUTPUT FROM THE CENSUS OF PRODUCTION

Difficulties occur in measuring net output and net output per head and comparing the latter, from industry to industry or over periods of time, because the aggregates for which the net output figures are given are never completely homogeneous. For example, figures for the net output of a particular industry group are made up of data from individual units which are not producing exactly the same things. An industry group, even at the minimum list heading level, may consist of several sub-industries which differ slightly from one another. If the proportionate importance of the sub-industries change, it is quite conceivable that net output per head for the industry group as a whole may change, even if there has been no change in the net output per head of the sub-industries. Furthermore, as different firms within even the most closely defined sub-industry will not be producing exactly the same product mix, which may vary from time to time, net output per head for their industry group may vary simply because of changes in the structure of firms within that industry, and not because of any changes in real productivity.

The foregoing problems are completely unavoidable, and all that can be hoped for is to provide net output figures for groups as homogeneous as possible.

A quite distinct problem arises because of the way in which information is collected from firms. Firms return statistics of their total sales, including both the output which is typical of the industry of which they are a member, and any other subsidiary output which may be the main products of some other industry groups. For example, the 'sugar industry' as defined in the standard industrial classification contains firms which produce, in addition to sugar, chocolates and sweets. Firms which specialize in chocolate and sweet production are however allocated to a separate industry group called the 'Cocoa, Chocolate and Sugar Confectionery Group'. Part of the output of the sugar industry firms ought, ideally, to be attributed to the 'Cocoa, Chocolate and Confectionery Industry Group'. Thus, when we think we are measuring net output of the sugar industry, we are actually measuring to some extent a little of the net output of another industry. Obviously variations in the degree to which an industry produces goods which are the typical products of another industry can affect comparisons of net output per head over a period of time. This problem is not confined solely to manufacturing. There are some firms, classified to a particular manufacturing industry group which at the same time are providing certain services e.g. manufacturers who have their own transport fleets. The same remarks apply here as above.

Where firms have establishments in several geographical locations they may, because of the way in which their accounts are made up, need to make a single output return. If the establishments are in different regions, there is the problem of allocating the net output recorded for the firm as a whole over the various regions, and this is by no means an easy task, although obviously attempts must be made to make such an allocation.

Finally it should be borne in mind that net output, as defined for the censuses of production, does not eliminate the cost of certain services purchased by firms. Hence to the extent that some industries make less use of these external services than others, their net output figure will be a truer reflection of value added.

CENSUSES SINCE 1968

The 1969 census of production, an outline of the plans for which was given in the *Board of Trade Journal,* 24 December 1969, was carried out in 1970. It provided information on capital expenditure, stocks and work-in-progress, its coverage being similar to that of the 1967 census. An article on this 1969 Census appeared in *Trade & Industry* on 30 December 1970.

CENSUS OF PRODUCTION FOR 1970

This was the first census held under the scheme for the new system of industrial statistics. It covered mining, manufacturing, gas, electricity and water industries (Orders II to XIX and XXI of the S.I.C.) but excluded the construction industry. All firms with twenty-five or more employees were included, and in industries where small businesses are particularly numerous, firms with eleven or more employees were covered; 128 industry groups were covered.

The following are the main categories on which information was obtained:

Persons engaged (working proprietors, operatives, technical, administrative, and clerical employees)
Wages/salaries paid
Stocks at beginning and end of year
Capital expenditure
Payments for work given out
Payments for transport
Total purchases
Sales and work done
Duties paid

Details of commodities sold and purchased were not required, as these are currently collected under the new quarterly inquiries. As in 1968, firms were asked to allow the publication of their names and addresses, as contributing to the sales of the major products of their industry.

NORTHERN IRELAND CENSUSES OF PRODUCTION

When detailed censuses of production are taken in Great Britain, the Ministry of Commerce undertakes a comparable one in Northern Ireland, so that the whole may be incorporated in the censuses for the United Kingdom.

In those years where a *full* census in Great Britain has not been taken, the Ministry of Commerce takes a less detailed one in Northern Ireland, calling for information on output, employment, wages and salaries, capital expenditure, and the value of purchases and sales, the latter without the commodity-analyses of the full censuses. Value of sales and work done are analysed into those to customers in Northern Ireland, in Great Britain and elsewhere. Exports outside the United Kingdom are analysed by geographical area and industrial grouping, and also by country of destination. The figures are restricted to firms employing twenty-five or more persons.

3. REGULARLY PRODUCED STATISTICS

The censuses of production—particularly the five-yearly ones—give us comprehensive information in detail at long intervals. They are supplemented by less comprehensive but more frequent information on key aspects of the industrial economy. The change-over to the new system of industrial statistics referred to earlier means an increasing emphasis on such statistics, on a much expanded basis. Nevertheless, until the new system is in full operation, the full census of production will continue to provide a means of maintaining a check on the accuracy of the more frequently published series. In addition the full census will, as in the past, provide the base date and weighting system for any such series which is expressed in index number form.

In addition to the indices of wholesale prices and of industrial production some of the supplementary industrial series currently published in *Trade & Industry* are:

	Figures in	*Frequency of publication*
1. Capital expenditure (by type of industry)	£m	quarterly
2. Electronic capital equipment deliveries	£m	quarterly
3. Investment intentions	article with figures	thrice yearly
4. United Kingdom computer market	article with figures	quarterly
5. Deliveries of certain engineering and electrical products	£m	quarterly
6. Engineering and electrical industry; production, exports and orders	index numbers	monthly
7. Footwear industry; orders and deliveries	million pairs	monthly
8. Industrial building	million square feet	quarterly
9. Industrial development;		
a. approvals	million	a. quarterly
b. certificates refused	square feet	b. annually
10. Machine tools; deliveries and orders		monthly
11. Man-made fibres;	million lb	a. quarterly and annually
11. Man-made fibres;		
a. analyses of production	million lb	a. quarterly and annually
b. total production	million lb	b. monthly
c. deliveries	thousand lb	c. quarterly
12. Car and commercial vehicle production	number of vehicles	monthly
13. Manufacturers' stocks	million lb and index numbers	quarterly
14. Clothing and textiles; orders and deliveries	index numbers	monthly
15. Cotton production	million lb and million yards	monthly
16. Wool textile exports and wool textile production	million lb and million square yards	quarterly and monthly
17. Hosiery production	index numbers	monthly

	Figures in	*Frequency of publication*
18. Chemical industry; production, prices, employment, capital expenditure, import expenditure	index numbers	quarterly

Figures are obtained from samples covering the larger firms in the relevant industrial groups. As an example of the procedure adopted, the statistics in categories 5 and 6 above are taken from firms employing more than twenty-five persons. Each month all firms with annual turnovers over £1 million are asked to supply information, and figures are also called for from a sample one-fifth of medium-sized and one-tenth of small firms. Every quarter, firms who have not been approached for the monthly survey are asked to supply information. About a thousand firms supply the monthly data, and an additional four thousand give information quarterly. In order to check the effectiveness of the monthly sampling, the quarterly figures are compared with the aggregates (suitably grossed-up) of the monthly figures.

4. BUSINESS MONITOR

In 1962 (*Board of Trade Journal*, 9 March 1962) the Board of Trade introduced its business monitor series, published monthly or quarterly. This consists of monthly or quarterly reports on output and related matters for some ninety different industries; for example, *Boxes, cartons and fibre board, packing cases,* (published monthly), *Perambulators, bed folders and push chairs,* (published quarterly), *Home-grown timber,* (monthly), *salt,* (monthly), and so on. These publications, providing as they do a much more detailed breakdown of production and related figures than can be publishtd generally, have proved very popular with business firms. It is suggested that a main use is to enable firms to estimate their share of the market. As the new quarterly inquiries to which reference has been made on page 85 become established, it is likely that much of the detail will be published in the *Business Monitor* series, which will increase considerably in number, supplying short-term data for the first time for some industries. For example, in 1970, five new *Monitors,* dealing with sales of metal furniture, wooden furniture and upholstery, bedding and soft furnishing, shop and office fittings and wall coverings, stemming directly from the new quarterly inquiries, were published. Except for domestic furniture and bedding, no short-term figures had previously been available for these products.

At present the *Business Monitor* series is divided into four categories:

I. Production Series, giving figures of output, sales, exports, consumption of raw materials, stocks and prices in various industry groups. This series is being expanded to include also figures of imports and employment.

II. Civil Aviation Series (referred to in more detail on page 162).

III. Service and Distribution Services Series (referred to in more detail on page 121).

IV. Miscellaneous Series, dealing with motor vehicle registrations, cinemas, company finance, overseas transactions, insurance companies, overseas travel etc.

MISCELLANEOUS INDUSTRIAL STATISTICS

From time to time, statistical articles of particular concern to industry are published in *Economic Trends,* in *Statistical News,* or in separate government publications.

INPUT-OUTPUT ANALYSIS

The structure of industrial output is revealed by the censuses of production, and by the short-term statistics for which the census provides a bench-mark. However, for the purposes of planning and forecasting on a national basis, not only the output of individual industries, but also the inter-relationships between the various industries, the demands which one industry makes upon others as suppliers, and the extent to which given commodities are used as input into each industry, are required. Such information, in the form of input-output tables, is now produced by Government statistical agencies in most developed countries. The first official summary table for this country was published in *National Income and Expenditure*, 1952. (It related to 1948). Information from a census of production, covering in detail purchases, sales and business expenses, is necessary if soundly-based input-output tables are to be produced. Thus, although a variety of summary input-output tables have appeared from time to time (unofficial ones being published as long ago as 1935), it is only in respect of the very detailed production census years of 1954 and 1963 that comprehensive tables, giving considerable detail, have been constructed officially. Published in 1961, *Input-output Tables for the United Kingdom, 1954* provided tables and matrices for forty-six industry groups. A table consisting of thirty-one industry groups for 1960, based on an updating of the 1954 tables, was produced by the Department of Applied Economics, Cambridge, under Professor Stone, and this table was used as part of the statistical basis for the 1965 National Plan. The provisional results of the 1963 census of production permitted of further updating of the 1954 tables, a restricted table of fourteen industry groups for 1963 being published in the August 1966 issue of *Economic Trends.* Subsequently (in 1968) this updating was carried further, tables for twenty-eight industrial groups for 1963 being published in *Economic Trends* in August 1968. Updating relies very heavily on the structure of the base year from which the new figures are calculated, and is only carried out when there is not sufficient information for the current year on which to produce detailed original tables. Thus, once the final figures for the 1963 Census of production were ready, work on producing input-output tables for that year, in its own right so to speak, went ahead. The result published in 1970 is *Input-output tables for the United Kingdom 1963* (*Studies in official statistics,* No. 16. H.M.S.O.)

THE 1963 INPUT-OUTPUT TABLES

Up to now, only a brief idea of the general purpose of input-output analysis has been given. Using the 1963 tables as examples, we can now explain in rather more detail the type of information, typical of input-output tables generally, which is available.

Firstly, about seventy industry and commodity groups, each embracing one or more of the 'Minimum List' headings of the 1958 S.I.C. are identified.

There are three basic tables. *Table A* provides a classification by commodity group of the output of each industry group. An extract from this table is given below (Table 5.3).

Let us consider, as an example, the industry group whose principal product is sugar (M.L.H. 216 of the S.I.C.). The total of

TABLE 5.3

Commodity analysis of domestic output in 1963

	Sales by industry group	Agriculture	Forestry and fishing	Coal mining	Other mining and quarrying	Grain milling	Other cereal foodstuffs	Sugar	Cocoa, chocolate, and sugar confectionery	Other food
	Sales by commodity group	1	2	3	4	5	6	7	8	9
1	Agriculture	1844·9	—	—	—	—	—	—	—	—
2	Forestry and fishing	1·5	89·0	—	—	—	—	—	—	—
3	Coal mining	—	—	905·3	—	—	—	—	—	—
4	Other mining and quarrying	—	—	0·3	176·7	—	—	—	—	—
5	Grain milling	—	—	—	—	241·8	8·9	—	—	—
6	Other cereal foodstuffs	—	—	—	—	53·8	751·8	—	5·6	4·1
7	Sugar	—	—	—	—	—	—	225·2	0·6	1·3
8	Cocoa, chocolate, and sugar confectionery	—	—	—	—	—	1·5	0·2	239·4	3·6
9	Other food	—	—	—	2·9	10·5	9·4	0·3	5·5	841·0
10	Drink	—	—	—	—	0·7	0·3	0·3	0·1	4·4
11	Tobacco	—	—	—	—	—	—	—	—	—
12	Mineral oil refining	—	—	—	—	—	—	—	—	—
13	Paint and printing ink	—	—	—	—	—	—	—	—	—
14	Coke ovens	—	—	—	—	—	—	—	—	—
15	Pharmaceutical and toilet preparations	—	—	—	—	—	0·1	—	1·7	0·6
16	Soap, oils and fats	—	—	—	—	—	5·2	—	—	6·7
17	Synthetic resin and plastic materials	—	—	—	—	—	—	—	—	—
18	Other chemicals and allied industries	—	—	—	—	0·2	1·0	0·1	0·1	1·2
	....									
48	Other textiles							0·1		
	....									
70	Miscellaneous services							−0·1		
71	Total goods and services							226·1		

Source: Extract from Table A, *Input-Output Tables for the U.K.* (H.M.S.O., 1963)

column 7 represents the value (in £m) of the sales of this industry group. We see that the sugar industry sold £226·1m of commodities in 1963. Of this, £225·2m was sugar (*row 7*), £0·2m chocolates, cocoa and sugar confectionery, (*row 8*), £0·3m other foods, (*row 9*), £0·3m drink, (*row 10*), £0·1m other chemicals and similar products, (*row 18*,) and £0·1m other textiles (*row 48*), whilst there was a *loss* of £0·1m on the supply of services, (*row 70*). (This was due mainly to the loss on subsidized canteen services for staff.) In other words, the sugar industry sold £225·2m of its principal product and £0·9m (net) of other commodities, the principal products of other industries. The table can be used also to ascertain the extent to which other industries were subsidiary producers of sugar. Consider *row 7*, which shows the sales of sugar by different industries. As is to be expected, the sugar industry (i.e. the one whose principal product is sugar) sold £225·2m of sugar but the cocoa, chocolate etc. industry also sold £0·6m of sugar, and 'other food' industries sold £1·32m. Thus of the total sales of sugar, only $\frac{1 \cdot 9}{227 \cdot 1} \times 100\% = 0 \cdot 84\%$ came from outwith the sugar industry as such.

The whole table, seventy columns by seventy rows, is called the 'make matrix'.

Table B

This is conventionally called the 'absorption matrix'. It classifies, by commodity group, the purchase or other intake of domestically-produced (rather than imported) goods and services used for current production or sold to 'final buyer'. 'Final buyers' are consumers, public authorities and—the conventional categories—'fixed capital', 'Stocks unused', and 'Exports'. A short extract from the table overleaf.

Table C

Table B gives the analysis of the purchase of *domestic* output. Table C is constructed on similar lines, but shows the industries (and final buyers) who purchase imported goods.

Table D

The other tables are derived from the three basic tables. Table D is an industry-by-industry matrix showing the amount of the sales of each industry which are taken up by each industry.

TABLE 5.4

Commodity analysis of purchases from domestic production in 1963

Sales by commodity group	Purchases by industry group	Office machinery	Other non-electric machinery	Industrial plant and steel work	Other mechanical engineering	Scientific instruments, etc.	Electrical machinery	Insulated wires and cables	Radio and telecommunications
		28	29	30	31	32	33	34	35
28	Office machinery	2·0	—	—	0·1	—	—	—	—
29	Other non-electrical machinery	0·2	46·3	14·4	1·9	0·1	0·9	0·5	0·4
30	Industrial plant and steel work	—	3·4	27·2	0·5	0·1	5·7	—	0·2

Source: Extract from Table B, *Input-Output Tables for the U.K.* (H.M.S.O., 1963)

Table 5.5 shows some of the data given in Table D. In order to reduce the amount of space required for displaying it, several of the industry groups have been combined, the inter-industry transactions still being included in the combined totals however. Thus, in 1963 £277·5m of goods produced by the agricultural industry (see *row 1*) were taken up by sales to firms within that industry £44m went to the grain milling industry, £60·3m to the other cereal food-stuffs industry, £979·9m to consumers, and so on.

The table shows, too, that the agricultural industry purchased £790·0m from all the other industries, (*row 2, column 1*) £30·7m of imports, and £2·9m of goods from 'consumers' (*column 1*). It also *received* subsidies (net) of £239·9m, and paid £320m to employees. Profits accruing to the owners of agricultural undertakings were £574m. The term 'gross profit' here is gross only in the sense that no allowance for capital consumption or depreciation is made. The economist's 'gross profit' is roughly equivalent to the accountant's 'net profit'.

From the information in the industry-by-industry matrix, (Table D—5.5), tables showing the total of goods and services from each industry required to provide £1,000s worth of output (in both gross and net terms) for a given industry have been produced, and also a table on similar lines, giving the various commodities required to produce £1,000s worth of output of a given commodity.

These tables may be used for estimating the relationship between the outputs and the inputs of the various industry groups, for calculating the primary input content (i.e. import, plus labour-cost content) of the output of the different industries, and for tracing the effect of price and manpower changes.

They may also be used to show the degree to which each industry is dependent on each 'class' of final demand. An article, *The dependence of industry on final demand and on imports in 1963* in *Economic Trends* (May 1970), by L. S. Berman gives the result of an analysis on these lines. The extract below contrasts two quite different industries (Table 5.6, page 112).

Industry A sells 92·6% of its output direct to final use—mostly direct consumers. Only 7·4% of its output (intermediate output) goes to other industries for processing, and then, as indirect output, to final use. On the other hand, 92% of all output of Industry B goes to other industries before it passes to final users.

This sort of information can be a major guide to marketing and production policy for firms in the industries concerned. There is

T

Industry-by-ind

Sales by industry / Purchases by industry	1 Agriculture	2 to 4 Other groups	5 Grain milling	6 Other cereal foodstuffs	7 Sugar	8 Cocoa, chocolate, etc.	9 Other food	10 Drink	11 to 70
1 Agriculture	(277·5)		44·0	60·3	31·3	3·2	212·9	32·2	
2–70 Other industry groups	790·0	274·3	93·3	379·8	36·5	108·1	335·9	146·7	13,
71 Public admin., defence, health, education	—	—	—	—	—	—	—	—	
72 Domestic services, etc., to households	—	—	—	—	—	—	—	—	
73 Ownership of dwellings	—	—	—	—	—	—	—	—	
74 Imports of goods	30·7	11·1	119·0	96·6	128·5	46·2	85·2	22·1	2
75 Imports of services	—	2·0	0·4	1·2	1·5	1·2	3·3	6·1	
76 Sales by final buyers	2·9	0·4	0·3	1·1	−6·0	0·4	1·2	1·5	
77 Taxes on expenditure *less* subsidies	−239·9	10·7	3·8	17·7	3·0	3·5	14·2	12·6	
78 Income from employment	320·0	615·0	28·5	159·6	16·5	57·8	130·8	115·6	1
79 Gross profits and other trading income	574·0	178·0	26·9	68·7	14·3	29·8	73·1	160·3	
80 Total input	1,577·7	1,091·5	306·2	784·0	225·6	250·2	856·6	497·1	3

growing evidence that the larger firms are already using this and other input-output data in their planning.

The commodity/commodity tables are by some felt to be most suitable for detailed forecasting work, because the technical coefficients (e.g. the total requirements to produce unit output of the various commodities) are assumed to be more stable than are the comparable industry/industry coefficients.

Although input-output tables may be used in a variety of ways to show the structure of production, they are only of real value if in addition to describing the situation at a given time they can show changes which are taking place over time. Consequently the production of input-output tables at regular intervals of time, at least quinquennially, and without inordinate delay, is essential if they are to be used as a guide to planning. Professor Stone, in his

x 1963

education	72 Domestic services to households	73 Ownership of dwellings	74 Total intermediate output	75 Consumers' current expenses	76 Public authorities' current expenditure	77 Gross fixed capital formation	78 Stocks	79 Exports	80 Total final output	81 Total output
	—	—	434·9	979·9	98·7	8·8	7·8	47·6	1,142·8	1,577·7
	—	—	15,932·8	13,220·6	2,428·1	4,746·4	198·6	5,389·1	25,981·8	41,914·6
	—	—	—	—	2,736·0	—	—	—	2,736·0	2,736·0
	—	—	—	343·0	—	—	—	—	343·0	343·0
	—	—	—	1,149·0	—	—	—	—	1,149·0	1,149·0
	—	—	2,781·1	1,236·6	16·5	237·2	12·6	273·0	1,775·9	4,557·0
	—	—	872·0	348·0	168·0	—	—	—	517·0	1,389·0
	—	—	179·0	263·0	353·3	−177·0	—	88·3	−179·0	—
	—	—	694·5	2,584·9	90·0	100·6	—	17·0	2,792·5	3,487·0
·6	343·0	—	18,191·0	—	—	—	—	—	—	18,191·0
	—	1,149·0	8,635·0	—	—	—	—	—	—	8,635·0
·6	343·0	1,149·0	47,720·3	20,125·0	5,184·0	4,916·0	219·0	5,815	36,259·0	83,979·3

Source: Modified from Table D, *Input-Output Tables for the U.K.* (H.M.S.O., 1963)

evidence to the Sub-Committee on Economic Affairs (*4th Report of the Estimates Committee Session 1966–67, Government Statistical Services*) puts the matter clearly,

> Building economic models for planning purposes requires not only statistical data relating to the past, but also a forward look at the coefficients derived from such data, so as to see how they are likely to change over the next five or ten years. To take as an example the estimation of input-output coefficients, everyone realizes in a general way that in most branches of industry the use of coal per unit of output has been falling and that its place has largely been taken by oil. What determines how much further this process will go and the speed at which it will go?

TABLE 5.6

Allocation of output and use of imports in 1963

(Percentages)

	Total intermediate output	*Total final output*			*Final output:* *Consumers' expenditure*			*Public authorities' current expenditure on goods and services*			*Gross domestic fixed capital formation*			*Additions to stocks and work in progress*			*Exports of goods and services*			*Import content of output*		
		Dir.	*Ind.*	*Total*	*Dir.*	*Ind.*	*Total*	*Dir.*	*Ind.*	*Total*	*Dir.*	*Ind.*	*Total*	*Dir.*	*Ind.*	*Total*	*Dir.*	*Ind.*	*Total*	*Dir.*	*Ind.*	*Total*
8 Cocoa, chocolate, and sugar confectionery (Industry A)	7·4	92·6	7·4	100·0	81·8	6·4	88·2	0·4	0·3	0·7	—	0·1	0·1	1·4	—	1·4	9·0	0·6	9·6	19·0	10·5	29·0
37 Cans and metal boxes (Industry B)	92·0	8·0	92·0	100·0	0·7	66·3	67·0	0·1	5·8	5·9	0·2	5·3	5·5	0·2	1·8	2·0	6·8	12·8	19·6	2·7	9·5	12·2

Note: Dir. = direct; Ind. = indirect

Source: 'The dependence of industry on final demand and on imports in 1963', *Economic Trends*, May 1970

The new system of industrial statistics is expected to facilitate the calculation of input-output tables for subsequent years up-dated from the 1963 ones.

The figures from the new quarterly inquiries will make this up-dating more efficient than hitherto. Moreover, in addition to the annual census dealing with sales, stocks, and capital expenditure, every three or four years detailed information on goods and services purchased will be collected. This will mean that new firmly-based tables will be available at frequent and regular intervals. Whilst the interval between the collection of the data and the publication of these tables may still be of the order of five or more years the programme now envisaged, of regular intermediate up-dating, should go a long way to improving the planning outlook.

An article in *Statistical News* issue No. 3 (*Developments in Input-Output Statistics,* L. S. Berman) discusses some of the problems involved in comparing input-output data over time. The 1963 input-output tables provided the basis on which up-dating exercises for 1968 could be undertaken. The necessary analyses were commenced as soon as the provisional results for the 1968 census of production, published in the 20 December 1969 issue of the *Board of Trade Journal* were available. A complication arose during this up-dating, because the 1963 tables had been based on the 1958 Standard Industrial Classification, whilst the 1968 Census used the revised 1963 S.I.C. So, before up-dating could commence, the 1963 tables had to be re-classified according to the 1963 S.I.C.

The 1968, up-dated tables in summary form were published in *Economic Trends* in January 1971. More detailed tables—not published nationally—are available from the Central Statistical Office.

Investment matrices for 1963 and 1968 (up-dated) providing an analysis of capital expenditure by thirty commodity/industry groups were published in *Economic Trends* in August 1971.

Input-output tables for 1968, firmly based on the data from the 1968 Census of Production, are expected to be published in 1972. There will be a breakdown into ninety-two industry groups compared with fifty-seven in the 1963 tables.

ENERGY STATISTICS

Because of the vital importance of energy-production to industry, analyses of energy output have a special annual publication to themselves, in addition to being well documented in the annual reports of the public corporations concerned and the oil companies. An outline of the basic statistics available is given below.

THE DIGEST OF ENERGY STATISTICS

Since 1944, the Ministry of Power, and latterly the Ministry of Technology (superseded in 1970 by the Department of Trade & Industry) has published statistics of fuel and power, and of energy consumption. Some of the series now available extend back to 1939, but it is only since 1950, when the first Ministry of Power *Statistical Digest* (for the years 1948 and 1949) was published, that a comprehensive coverage has been obtained. Since 1969 (for the years 1968 and 1969) the *Digest* has been published annually in the summer, under the title of *The Digest of Energy Statistics.*

The *Digest* currently, (1971), contains in its first part a general summary of energy production and consumption, both in physical units and in terms of the thermal content of the fuels involved. There are also charts showing trends in fuel consumption over upwards of a decade. In this part, the section giving key energy statistics for the latest available year is of particular interest. For each type of fuel, coal, gas, petroleum and electricity, a set of key figures and ratios is given, together with the ratios of the value of fuels exported to total exports, a similar ratio for imports, the proportion of consumers' expenditure going on fuel and light, and so on.

Particular attention may be drawn to two tables in the *Digest.* Table 1 deals with inland energy consumption in terms of primary fuel 'input'. Details regarding coal, petroleum, natural gas, nuclear electricity and hydro-electricity, (these being the only primary fuels others being derived from them), are given in terms of common measure. The common measure is 'coal equivalent', conversion factors being used to relate the units of the other types of fuel to coal. This table gives details of actual consumption for each of the categories and, at the same time, seasonally-adjusted and temperature-adjusted data for coal consumption, petroleum consumption, and total inland consumption. The consumption of fuels varies in accordance with the season of the year, but, in addition, it is thought necessary to allow for variations in annual consumption arising out of variations in the average annual temperature. The correction for temperature is that for each 1°C temperature deviation from the temperature average of the years 1931 to 1960 there is assumed to be a change in consumption, in the reverse direction, of 1·8%.

Details of estimated transactions in the energy section, for the calendar year ending approximately eighteen months prior to publication, are given in Table 3 of the *Digest*. This analyses the expenditure on the various types of fuel by the various final consumers (domestic and industrial); also by the secondary fuel industry and by primary fuel users such as power stations, gasworks, coke ovens, and so on.

The remainder of the *Digest* deals with the following topics:

Coal—production, consumption, stocks, manpower, productivity and costs, together with certain analyses on a geographical basis, and by types of output and end-use. The figures given are for Great Britain, except for consumption, where they cover the United Kingdom

Petroleum—refinery capacity and output, inland deliveries by type of product, by end-use, by area and by manpower. Figures given relate to United Kingdom, and to overseas operations

Natural gas—areas, licences issued, supply

Gas—fuel used, production and availability, consumption and sales of gas, coke made, load factors, plant employed. Figures are given for Great Britain and the United Kingdom

Electricity—fuels used, production, availability, costs and sales. Figures are given for Great Britain and the United Kingdom

Coke and manufactured fuel—the supply and consumption of coke and the various types of manufactured fuel, together with details of the operation of coke ovens. Figures are given for Great Britain and the United Kingdom

Prices and values—details of consumer expenditure on fuel and light analysed by type, representative retail prices of domestic fuels in the various towns, and the retail price index for fuel and light. Figures are given for Great Britain and the United Kingdom

Industrial return of fuels used—the consumption of coal and liquid fuels by the larger industrial consumers in Great Britain, analysed by industry group, region and type of fuel used

Annual census results—the following industries are not included in the regular censuses of production, but make annual returns similar in scope to those supplied by other industries in the full census of production:

Deep-mine coal production, gas supply, electricity supply, petroleum refining, petroleum and natural gas production

Information on the value of output, capital expenditure, wages and salaries for each industrial category are given. The figures for petroleum refining and petroleum and natural gas production refer to the United Kingdom, others to Great Britain only

Foreign trade in fuel—details are given, for all fuels, of the value of imports and exports to the United Kingdom, and separately for the exports of coal or coke and manufactured fuels and for imports and exports of petroleum

Minerals other than coal—the statistics here refer primarily to solid minerals (not fuels) other than coal, analysed by type, produced in the United Kingdom, together with details of employment at the mines and quarries producing them.

The statistical information on gas, electricity and coal stems almost entirely either from regular returns made by these nationalized industries, or from their annual reports, which themselves contain a wealth of statistical material.

QUESTIONS

1. Discuss the extent to which the results of the Census of Production can be used to meet the requirements of: (*a*) Government economic planning, (*b*) Private industry.
2. What were the reasons for setting up the Business Statistics Office, and what is its job?
3. What do you understand by input-output analysis? Describe the main tabulation given in the most recent set of firmly based tables for the United Kingdom, and consider their practical applications.
4. 'Input output tables provide the fundamental plan of the operation of the economy.' Comment on this statement in general terms, and discuss more specifically the structure of one of the main tabulations usually found.
5. Regular surveys of investment *intentions* in the main fields of British industry are made by the Department of Trade and Industry. It is sometimes suggested that such information provides a more useful guide to the future level of economic activity than do figures on current investment *expenditure*. Do you agree? Justify your answer.
6. What are the main problems met with in compiling an industry-by-industry input-output matrix? How is such a table used?
7. Discuss the value of enquiries into business men's assessments of the scale of their future activities as a basis for Government economic forecasting.
8. What is meant by net output, so far as the Census of Production is concerned? How does this differ from 'value added'?
9. Discuss some of the problems associated with the calculation of net output and net output per head, for individual industry groups and for the nation as a whole.
10. Explain the purpose of and describe the information collected in connection with the 1968 Census of Production.
11. It has been said that the 1968 Census of Production will be the last of the full quinquennial Censuses. Why is this and what is intended to take its place? Discuss some of the implications of this change.
12. Describe the development of the Census of Production from the 1930's until the present day.
13. Describe in general terms the new system of industrial

statistics introduced subsequent to the report on *Government Statistical Services* of 1966. What improvements does this system promise?

14. 'The recently developed system of quarterly sales enquiries is the fundamental core of the new system of industrial statistics.' Comment on this statement, describing the new quarterly enquiries to which reference has been made.
15. During the next few years considerable expansion in the number and range of *Business Monitors* is likely to take place. Explain the reasons for this, and comment in general terms on the newly developed inquiries from which this expansion of statistical data will stem.

6 Distribution statistics

Prior to the 1951 census of distribution—the first such census ever to be held in Great Britain—information on the distributive trades in this country was very limited. The distributive trades, for the purpose of the census, include all retail and wholesale trade, together with certain service trades such as hairdressing, garages, boot and shoe repairing, etc. Retailing is by far and away the most important, whether judged by numbers employed, by value of turnover or of number of trading units.

STATISTICS OF DISTRIBUTION

The census of distribution aims to give up-to-date information on the structure of the distributive trades. This is of vital importance for national planning, and amongst other things highlights areas of greater or lesser efficiency. In addition, a census provides a bench mark, or new starting point, for the various short-term statistics which, over the years since the previous census, may have become less and less accurate. Weights and bases for index numbers of retail sales, retail and wholesale stocks, turnover in the service trades and so on are all derived from the latest census data, and are published regularly in *Trade & Industry*, or in *Business Monitors*. At present, short-term statistics in the following categories are regularly published in *Trade & Industry*, or in the new *Service and Distributive Trade Monitors*:

TRADE AND INDUSTRY STATISTICS ON DISTRIBUTION AND ALLIED TRADES

Captial expenditure, and stocks in distribution and service trades (annually)

Catering trades; index numbers of turnover (monthly)
(transferred to *Business Monitor* series in 1971)

TABLE 6.1

Establishments, turnover, and persons engaged by form of organization and kind of business (broad), 1957, 1966

Form of organization and kind of business	1957			1966		
	Establishments	*Turnover*	*Persons engaged*	*Establishments*	*Turnover*	*Persons engaged*
	Number	£'000	*Number*	*Number*	£'000	*Number*
Total retail trade	577,405	7,587,154	2,529,602	504,412	11,131,816	2,555,737
Co-operative societies	28,945	904,796	197,625	26,684	1,015,938	173,458
Multiples	59,105	1,883,809	531,160	73,852	3,837,244	741,833
Independents	489,355	4,798,548	1,800,817	403,876	6,278,634	1,640,446
Grocers and provision dealers	151,859	2,038,374	556,796	123,385	2,907,655	522,343
Other food retailers	123,295	1,544,703	490,866	104,359	2,081,314	459,358
Confectioners, tobacconists, newsagents	77,437	702,996	285,163	63,333	1,045,572	297,762
Clothing and footwear shops	97,656	1,180,212	411,631	83,199	1,741,141	417,135
Household goods shops	62,115	795,566	259,603	69,761	1,327,252	299,871
Other non-food retailers	61,360	563,050	237,597	57,540	988,131	260,248
General stores	3,683	762,253	287,946	2,835	1,040,751	299,020
	Percentages between forms of organization					
	%	%	%	%	%	%
Total retail trade	100	100	100	100	100	100
Co-operatives	5·0	11·9	7·8	5·3	9·1	6·8
Multiples	10·2	24·8	21·0	14·7	34·5	29·0
Independents	84·8	63·2	71·2	80·0	56·4	64·2

Source: *Report on the Census of Distribution* 1966 (main volume) (H.M.S.O.)

Hairdressing trades; index numbers of turnover (monthly)
Laundries and dry-cleaners; index numbers of turnover (monthly)
Retail stocks; index numbers (monthly)
Wholesale textile houses; value of sales and stock (monthly)
Retail trade*; index numbers of sales by value & volume, for food shops and various categories of non-food shops. The index numbers are seasonally adjusted (monthly)

Indices are published separately for Great Britain and Northern Ireland.

From time to time, also, special articles appear in *Trade & Industry*. Of particular interest (issue dated 14 October 1971) is a 'Commodity analysis of the turnover of large retailers' based on information from the new annual inquiries in the distributive and service trades and from the 1966 Census of Distribution.

BUSINESS MONITORS FOR THE RETAIL TRADE

On 11 March 1970, four new monthly *Business Monitors* were published, giving detailed index numbers for retail sales starting with January 1970. The *Monitors* are: *S.D.1.*, foodshops, *S.D.2.*, clothing and footwear shops, *S.D.3.*, durable-goods shops, and *S.D.4.*, miscellaneous non-food shops. Each contains monthly and quarterly index numbers, covering at least two years, for the different kinds of business and forms of organization within the group with which the monitor is concerned. Summary figures for the other three groups of shops are also given in each monitor, as well as separately classified information for department stores and mail-order houses.

OTHER BUSINESS MONITORS

Subsequently, in 1971, figures on the service trades and on instalment credit which had previously appeared regularly in *Trade & Industry* were transferred to the *Business Monitor* series. The monitors are:

S.D.5. Catering Trades;
S.D.6. Instalment credit business of finance houses;

---

* Where sudden but persistent changes in retail sales are taking place, weekly indices may be calculated for a limited period of time—(see *Statistical News*, No. 1).

S.D.7. Assets and liabilities of finance houses;
S.D.8. Instalment credit business or retailer.

'DISTRIBUTIVE TRADES STATISTICS—A GUIDE TO OFFICIAL SOURCES'(H.M.S.O.)

This comprehensive guide to government statistics on distribution was prepared by the Distributive Trades' Economic Development Committee and published in April 1970.

THE CENSUSES OF DISTRIBUTION

PURPOSE OF THE CENSUS

At present the distributive industry, and particularly its retail section, is the fastest changing industry in Britain. The government need to know how quickly, and in what direction, these changes are taking place.

It must not be forgotten however that the results of the census are intended to be of value to the industry as well as to the government. Market researchers, for instance, use the census reports as a principal source of information when advising manufacturers and advertising agencies. Wholesalers and those who control nation-wide retail chains should be particularly concerned, in their planning, with the area analyses provided, which show the regional pattern of retailing. Town-planners and property developers should also find this information invaluable.

Operational ratios and other key data, such as the following, are published:

Turnover per square-foot of selling area
Turnover per establishment, by kind of business and form of organization
Turnover per employee
Wages as a proportion of turnover
Ratio of stocks to turnover
Turnover per head of population in given areas
Capital expenditure, by size and type of shop
Breakdown of sales, by different commodities and by kind of business

Value of sales and percentage share of sale in various product categories according to type of retail outlet
Gross margin* and gross margin as a percentage of turnover.

The extent to which detailed ratios can be calculated depends, of course, on the coverage of each particular census. Only on the occasion of a full census (in Great Britain, in 1950, 1961, and 1971) will all the information be available. Sample censuses for example have not hitherto yielded 'area' information, and there are other analyses which because of the small numbers involved cannot be undertaken in such circumstances.

Individual retailers can compare these aspects of their businesses on a national, regional and even—in many cases—a town or shopping-centre level. Moreover, special analyses may in future be commissioned from the new Business Statistics Office at a small charge. These would of course not be published.

THE FIRST CENSUS OF DISTRIBUTION—1950

As in the case of many other governmental statistical inquiries, powers for holding censuses of distribution were given by the *Statistics of Trade Act of 1947*. The first census was conducted by the Board of Trade, as have been all subsequent ones. It took place in 1951 and referred nominally to the trading year 1950. Firms were, however, allowed to give information in respect of their financial years ending at any time within the period of April 1950 to April 1951 instead of the calendar year 1950, if the former was more convenient.

As no suitable list of establishments was available, the first step was to employ a large body of enumerators who by external inspection of the premises, listed the names and addresses of distributive traders.

The enumerators were required to distinguish between various types of premises, such as shops, yards, stalls, and so on. This list was compiled during the period May—October 1950.

The details of this pre-census enumeration and its results are given in the publication 'British Shops' (H.M.S.O. 1951), which is particularly useful for the insight it gives into the methods employed in building up a sampling frame from scratch.

* Gross margin is defined as the difference between turnover (i.e. trading receipts) and purchases, including purchase tax, less stocks at the beginning of the year, plus stocks at the end. The gross margin can be regarded as the fund out of which came the expenses of running the business and the trading profit.

The census itself was intended to provide:

Information about the number and size of wholesale and retail outlets and other establishments providing consumer services

Information regarding the value of the services rendered, to enable more accurate estimates of the national product to be made

A measure of the relative efficiency of the distributive system as between different regions in the country, (e.g. which areas have the most shops of certain kinds per head of the population, and what is their turnover?)

Information on wages, stock levels, turnover and methods of delivery used.

Firms were given three months in which to reply, but many forms were returned late and there were several prosecutions for failure to supply proper returns. Although efforts had been made—following a pilot survey—to simplify the returns and to ensure co-operation, the survey was very unpopular, particularly amongst the smaller retailers. This was partly due to the natural reaction of any firm finding itself called upon to supply information, at the cost of considerable extra work without any obvious benefit, but undoubtedly to a large extent due to the fear that the information given might be revealed in identifiable form to competitors, or to the Inland Revenue authorities. In view of the safeguards contained in the Act and the rules governing the census, no such breach of confidence should be possible, but it is difficult to convince people of this. In the end, 91% of all establishments (accounting for 95% of total turnover) made satisfactory returns. However, it is fair to say that several thousand forms had to be heavily edited before inclusion in the analysis, and there is no positive guarantee that they were, in the end, completely accurate. Only very limited checks can be imposed on the accuracy of the statements in census forms which, prima facie, have been correctly completed.

The Verdon Smith Committee, reporting in 1954, (H.M.S.O. Cmd 9276) suggested that full distribution censuses should be held decennially, with sample inquiries at intermediate stages—say, every three or four years. In the event postal surveys have been carried out in respect of the years 1957, 1959, 1961 (full census), 1965 and 1966. The recommendations of this Committee are more fully discussed in the section dealing with the census of production (page 90).

SAMPLE SURVEY OF RETAILING FOR 1957

This survey covered retailing only and was intended to cover all retailers with an annual turnover of £100,000 and over, together with a sample of smaller traders. The enumeration of the larger firms presented no special problem. For the smaller firms, however, the population was stratified on a geographical basis, certain areas only being selected. All the shops in the selected areas were enumerated initially in a manner similar to that employed in the 1950 Census, but only a proportion in each area was required to supply information.

About 57,000 establishments, out of a total of perhaps 480,000, were covered. The overall response was good; 95% of the multiples and larger retailers, 89% of the independents and even 75% of itinerant and street traders completed the forms.

Data for both 1950 and 1957 were obtained from the sampled firms. Ratios of the 1957 to 1950 figures for equivalent samples were calculated, and these ratios were used to gross up the 1950 census figures to give 1957 estimates for the industry as a whole.

The information was tabulated initially by type of organization and by type of business, both these being classified in terms of number of establishments, number of people employed, annual turnover, to mention some of the main categories.

Results of the survey were published in the *Board of Trade Journal,* on 2 January 1959.

TABLE 6.2

Distribution of retail establishments by number of persons engaged (1961)

	Establishments	*Turnover*	*Persons engaged* Full-time	*Persons engaged* Part-time
	Number	*£'000*	*Number*	*Number*
Total retail trade	508,529	8,297,949	1,722,285	616,530
Establishments with:				
0 or 1 person engaged*	113,384	367,301	94,448	12,731
2 persons engaged	140,349	965,256	208,174	72,524
3 ,, ,,	84,236	888,878	176,317	76,391
4 ,, ,,	52,599	746,069	145,383	65,013
5– 6 ,, ,,	52,425	1,022,047	197,264	85,541
7– 9 ,, ,,	30,447	872,708	167,361	69,449
10–19 ,, ,,	23,985	1,103,007	220,152	88,894
20–49 ,, ,,	8,006	846,380	179,181	52,731
50–99 ,, ,,	1,905	479,734	101,780	27,388
100 and over persons engaged	1,193	1,006,570	232,225	65,868

* Where one person operates more than one shop or stall on different days of the week the excess establishments are given as having 0 persons engaged in order to avoid fractions.

Source: *Report on Census of Distribution and other Services—1961* (H.M.S.O.)

THE WHOLESALE SAMPLE SURVEY OF 1959

The main aim of this survey was to obtain reliable figures of stocks and capital expenditure to provide a base for regular quarterly and annual estimates which have been published since that time. The survey was not preceded by a comprehensive enumeration as in the case of the 1950 and 1957 survey, but this was hardly necessary. The intention was to include all wholesalers having over five employees, practically all of whom might be expected to be recorded in the register of companies, trade directories and records kept locally by government departments. In the event, and allowing for a 1·7% failure to respond, it was estimated that at least 93% of the total trading activity was covered. Information was called for on stocks, receipts, capital expenditure, and type of business.

THE SECOND FULL CENSUS OF DISTRIBUTION 1961

This census was conducted in 1962. The necessary enumeration of shop premises (whether empty or occupied) was carried out in conjunction with the 1961 population census. As in earlier inquiries, the respondents could supply information in respect of any twelve-month period ending between April 1961 and April 1962.

The coverage of the 1961 census was similar to that of 1950, except that information was collected from laundries, laundrettes and dry cleaners, whilst wholesalers were excluded.

A return of the turnover in the year and the number of persons engaged, together with a description of the business, was required for every separately identified establishment wholly or mainly engaged in retailing or the other trades within the scope of the census. All large retail organizations (defined as co-operative societies, multiple retailers with five or more branches, and other retailers with twenty-five or more persons engaged) and a sample of smaller organizations were also required to complete a return in respect of the whole of their business, for certain additional items (e.g. purchases, stocks, capital expenditure and sales of certain selected commodities).

In fact, only about 5% of the respondents were required to answer the whole range of questions. There was considerable delay in the completion of the census, some of the firms not having made proper returns by the latter end of 1963. Even then, the necessary editing and checking of doubtful replies with the respondents caused further delay. Ultimately 88% of the establishments (representing about 93% of total turnover) responded. This was rather lower than the corresponding response in 1950. Differences in the stringency of checking for acceptance, however, makes comparison difficult.

The results of this census of distribution were published by the end of 1963 in fourteen parts plus a supplement:

Part 1.—establishment tables

Part 2 to 13.—area tables, including a general introductory part and separate parts for each of the eleven Standard Regions in Great Britain

Part 14.—organization tables, distinguishing between co-operatives, multiples (ten or more branches) and independents

Supplement—a reprint of a number of explanatory articles which appeared in the *Board of Trade Journal.*

The first thirteen parts give information classified in terms of the establishment i.e. separate place of business. In part fourteen, however, the classifications are in terms of the organization, i.e. the firms, and gives analyses in terms of purchases, stocks, capital expenditure, gross margins.

In the census, classification by *kind of business* means classification in accordance with the main type of goods sold. (Table 6.1 is, for example, classified in this way). There are seven broad classifications (including the category 'General Stores') which correspond to the *Minimum List Headings 820 and 821* of the *Standard Industrial Classification.* These headings are broken down into over fifty-five different categories of retail business.

The form of organization classification refers to the way in which the firm is organized:

Co-operative stores
Multiple stores (five or more branches)*
Independent (four or fewer branches)†

Information collected for the first time in this census includes counts of the numbers of outlets selling particular commodities (see Table 6.3, page 128).

---

* For some of the analyses multiples having ten or more branches are identified.
† Independents may be divided into 'large' and 'others'.

TABLE 6.3

Number of retail outlets selling certain commodities, 1961
Commodity—china and earthenware

Kind of business	*Total*	*Co-operative societies*	*Multiple retailers*	*Large independent retailers*	*Other Independent retailers having turnover of* Over £20,000	£5,001 to £20,000	£5,000 and under
	Number	*Number*	*Number*	*Number*	*Number*	*Number*	*Number*
Total retail trade	40,138	4,834	6,249	945	2,653	14,467	10,990
Grocers and provision dealers	12,843	3,225	1,407	45	1,009	5,536	1,621
Other food retailers	428	31	11	4	33	216	133
Confectioners, tobacconists, newsagents	2,067	1	49	11	192	1,383	431
Clothing and footwear shops	1,936	381	289	126	114	467	559
Household goods shops	15,787	587	1,971	343	903	5,451	6,532
Other non-food retailers	4,060	24	627	72	274	1,349	1,714
General stores	3,017	585	1,895	344	128	65	—
Department stores	655	194	201	260	—	—	—
Variety stores	1,113	—	1,113	—	—	—	—
Other general stores	1,249	391	581	84	128	65	—

Source: *Report on Census of Distribution and other Services* (H.M.S.O.), 1961

THE WHOLESALE SAMPLE CENSUS OF 1965

This second survey of the wholesale trade, which covered Great Britain only, was based primarily on the original register of wholesalers compiled for the 1959 survey with additional information supplied by the (then) Ministry of Labour. The survey itself covered all wholesalers whose 1959 turnover exceeded £50,000 whilst a one in three sample, stratified by kind of business, was taken of the smaller wholesalers. Every wholesaler with turnover of £500,000 or more (in 1959) was followed up to ensure 100% response. Businesses with a turnover of between £50,000 and £500,000 (1959) were stratified in size groups for each kind of business and any trader who did not respond was allotted figures equal to the average of the responding traders in that particular stratum. For businesses with a turnover less than £50,000 (and new traders not covered in 1959), the figures obtained were grossed-up (multiplied by the reciprocal of the actual sampling fraction. That is, if one-third of the traders were approached and replied, the figures obtained were multiplied by three).

Information was asked for on goods sold, commission received, receipts and purchases, capital expenditure, value of stocks, cost of operating transport vehicles and amount paid out for transport, together with number of persons engaged. The results of the survey were published in the *Board of Trade Journal,* 26 July 1968. Figures were given for the actual firms replying, as well as estimated 'grossed-up' figures for the industry as a whole. Tabulations showing capital expenditure by kind of business, transport cost by kind of business, total receipts by size and kind of business, trading accounts by kind of business and method of trading were also provided.

Table 6.4 below shows one of the latter tabulations.

Gross margin as given in the table is defined as the value of goods sold on own account, minus the value of purchases, adjusted in each case for stock changes during the year. The gross margin figure as a percentage of sales is one of the key ratios for making comparisons. It must however be treated with considerable care. As an example, the gross margin ratio in 1965 for beer, wines and spirits at 31% is very high, both in relation to the other kinds of business and to the figure for the same group in 1950 which was about 16%. It is suggested that this may be due to the variation in the amount of purchased stock laid down to mature in any given year.

TABLE 6.4

Analysis by method of trading within each kind of business trading with stock
For businesses which made satisfactory returns: Great Britain

(£'000)

Kind of business	*Business units*	*Persons engaged*	*Receipts* *Amounts for services and commissions*	*Receipts* *Goods sold on own account*	*Purchases*	*Stocks* *Beginning year*	*Stocks* *End year*	*Stocks as a percentage of sales*	*Gross margin*	*Gross margin as a percentage of sales*	*Net capital expenditure*
Total, including Marketing Boards	28,735	685,291	105,335	12,404,982	10,844,629	1,051,417	1,119,252	%	1,628,188	%	122,980
Wholesale distribution	16,162	403,061	56,711	7,454,609	6,490,106	661,718	693,094		995,879		75,965
Grocery and provisions	1,263	52,419	7,046	1,279,584	1,194,467	95,241	98,614	8	88,490	7	6,830
Beer, wines and spirits	576	20,277	2,233	386,183	272,673	84,656	91,294	24	120,148	31	3,637
Chocolate and sugar confectionery	359	4,143	157	51,578	46,175	3,436	3,757	7	5,724	11	338
Tea and coffee	164	9,955	308	169,799	136,542	36,468	36,980	22	33,769	20	1,885
			(16 other categories are identified separately)								
Dealing in coal, builders' materials, grain and agricultural supplies (wholesale or retail)	6,107	132,893	18,620	1,827,928	1,569,026	107,775	115,177		266,304		21,216
			(4 categories are identified separately)								
Dealing in other industrial materials and machinery	6,459	145,390	29,724	2,665,512	2,341,816	267,553	296,610		352,753		24,832
			(8 categories are identified separately)								
Marketing boards	7	3,947	280	456,933	443,681	14,371	14,371	3	13,252	3	967

Source: *Board of Trade Journal*, 26 July 1968 (H.M.S.O.)

THE SAMPLE CENSUS OF 1966

This census covered mainly retailing, automatic vending-machine operators, shoe repairing, hairdressing, laundering and dry cleaning, radio and T.V. relay services—the latter group for the first time. An article in the *Board of Trade Journal* of 30 December 1966 introduced the census, which for the first time included questions on transport costs.

THE SAMPLING SCHEME

Eighty-five thousand shopkeepers were included in the sample which, as in 1957, covered all large organizations and some specialist types of firms in full, together with a sample of small independent retail and shoe repairing establishments and hairdressers. The sample taken was a sample of areas.

Some areas were enumerated in full. In some of these areas all the shops were included; in other areas, only a sample.

GREATER LONDON (G.L.C.) AREA

Central London was enumerated in full; a sample of shops listed were covered. Thirty-three out of seventy-six other shopping centres were enumerated in full, and all shops there were covered. The remainder were covered by a sample of the wards; stratified, and selected systematically, with a random start within each stratum:

LARGE TOWNS

Sixty large towns were covered by a sample of streets. Within any one town, these streets or segments of streets were sampled systematically with a random start in four strata.

SPECIAL AREAS

Thirty-two special areas where there had been rapid development since 1961 were enumerated in full, and a sample of the shops listed there was covered.

LOCAL AUTHORITY AREA SAMPLE

The remainder of Great Britain is made up of 1,687 local authority areas, of which 168 were selected as a sample. In each area selected, all shops were covered. The sample was stratified by standard regions and by a number of other criteria.

The traders covered in full were those who were either known to be large, or who formed groups of limited size but special interest, for which registers could be compiled by desk research. They comprised:

ENTIRE ORGANIZATIONS

co-operative societies,
multiple retailers and shoe repairers with ten or more establishments,
mail order businesses,
radio and television relay firms with 500 or more subscribers,
automatic vending machine operators,
laundries, launderettes, and dry cleaners.

INDIVIDUAL ESTABLISHMENTS

large independents i.e.—retail establishments not belonging to a co-operative society or to a multiple retailer, with a turnover in 1961 of more than £50,000 (more than £20,000 for booksellers/stationers and off-licences),
Credit traders calling on customers.

Those sampled were small or new independent retail establishments:

Independent shoe repair establishments
Hairdressing establishments
Launderettes and dry cleaners not already on the register.

The *sample* data was collected in respect of individual establishments and not of whole organizations, because this considerably simplified the linking of the sampled data with that collected for the categories which were surveyed one hundred per cent.

The form sent to most independent traders asked for information on legal status and a description of the business (both in words and by indicating, in order of importance, which of a list of commodities and services accounted for more than a fifth of turnover). Questions were also asked about turnover, and the number of persons engaged, whether the shop was operated by self service methods, and whether the trader was a credit trader calling on customers for orders. The form included questions on membership of retailer or wholesaler-sponsored buying groups. For traders with a turnover of £5,000 or more, further information was asked for on:

Wages and salaries
Trading purchases
Stocks
Capital expenditure
Sales on hire purchase or instalment credit terms
Book debts
Sales, analysed by commodity groups, and the number of goods vehicles operated.

The form sent to the larger independent traders also included questions on transport costs.* Independent traders situated in shopping centres only were asked to provide floor space figures for the first time.† Multiple traders and co-operative societies, in addition to answering the questions mentioned above (except for those to do with floor space) for the organization as a whole, were asked to give for each of their branches the kind of business, turnover and number of persons engaged. They were also asked to indicate which branches traded by self-service methods, and if any were mobile shops. For branches reporting self-service, those showing a turnover of £100,000 or more and branches situated within selected shopping centres, the floor space was required. For independent traders not in shopping centres, those who had reported self-service or turnovers of £100,000 or more were asked to supply information on floor space. A post-census inquiry went to about 50% of the independent traders in the sample field to obtain transport costs information, to supplement that already obtained for the larger independents, multiples and co-operative societies. For the service trades and automatic vending machine operators, special forms were used.

An article describing the method of conducting the census and dealing with the planning, the selection of the sample, the method

* Questions on transport were also asked in the Census of Production for 1963 and in the Inquiry into Wholesaling for 1965.
† Floor space information had previously been collected for self-service establishments only.

of data collection, the processing of the results and the preparation of the reports appeared in *Statistical News, No. 7* (November 1969) and should be read by all interested in the problems involved. (*Census of Distribution for 1966*—J. R. L. Schneider and J. C. Suich).

THE CENSUS REPORTS

Preliminary reports of the census appeared in the *Board of Trade Journal* on 23 February 1968. Four tabulations were given, with figures for 1966 and comparable data for 1950, 1957 and 1961.

Table 1—'Establishments & Turnover by Broad Kind of Business 1950–1966', (e.g. grocers, other food retailers, confectioners, etc., clothing and footwear shops, and so on). (Actual amounts, and percentage changes from one census to another).

Table 2—Establishments Turnover and Persons engaged by Food/Non-food and by form of Organization'.
(Actual amounts, and percentage changes from one census to another).

Table 3—'Percentage Change in Retail Turnover by Form of Organization'.
(Changes from one census to another).

Table 4—'Establishments, Turnover, and Persons engaged by Kind of Business'.
(Actual amounts, and percentage changes 1957, 1961 and 1966).

Table 6.1 (page 120) illustrates some of the data given in Table 2 of the *Preliminary Report,* as up-dated from the main report. A glance shows significant changes in the relative positions of co-operatives, multiples, and independents. This and other evidence of rapid economic change brought out in the report point to the need for more frequent censuses of distribution than have hitherto been thought necessary.

A further article, introducing the *Main Volume* (*Census of Distribution and other Services, 1966*—Vol. I) appeared in the *Board of Trade Journal,* 18 March 1970. Some of the tables published with this article were amended in the *Board of Trade Journal* of 8 July 1970.

The final results were published in two parts—a *Main Volume* and a *Supplementary Volume*. The following list of main tabulations gives an indication of the information supplied.

MAIN VOLUME

Establishment tables*

1. totals (establishments, turnover, persons engaged), by form of organization by kind of business,
2. size analysis according to turnover, for each kind of business,
3. totals, by form of organization by kind of business (broad groups) for standard regions.

Organization tables*

4. totals (organizations, establishments, turnover, purchases, stocks, gross margin and capital expenditure), by kind of business by form of organization,
5. totals for large enterprises, by kind of business (broad groups) by size according to turnover,
6. totals for independent retailers, by membership of voluntary buying groups,
7. persons engaged and wages and salaries, by kind of business by form of organization,
8. analysis of turnover, by (group of) commodity or service supplied, separately by form of organization and by kind of business,
9. instalment credit trade, by kind of business by form of organization,
10. book debts, by kind of business by form of organization,
11. capital expenditure in detail, by kind of business by form of business.

Service Trades

(hairdressers & manicure, boot and shoe repairers, laundries etc.)

1. totals and detailed analyses of establishments, turnover and persons engaged, by kind of business and by amount of turnover,
2. establishments and commodities, by turnover by kind of business,
3. capital expenditure.

---

* See page 127 for definitions.

SUPPLEMENTARY VOLUME

The tables in the *Supplementary Volume* are based partly on the main census returns, and partly on further data obtained after the census from samples of shops on the census register. The topics covered are:

- self-service trading,
- mail-order trading,
- mobile shops of co-operative societies and multiple retailers,
- goods vehicles used and transport costs (distinguishing costs of running the trader's own vehicles and payments made for carriage by other organizations),
- floor space of shops in central shopping areas,
- sampling errors of the published estimates.

There has been delay in publishing these reports, the *Main Volume* not being published until *mid* 1970, and the *Supplementary Volume* not until 1971.

THE CENSUS OF DISTRIBUTION—1971

1971 was selected as the year for which a full census of distribution would be taken. The enumerators for the census of population of that year were charged with listing the addresses of retail and other premises, which list would provide the basic frame for the census of distribution. The scope of the latter census will cover retail trades (as defined by *Minimum List Headings 820 and 821* of the *Standard Industrial Classification)*, check trading, hairdressing, laundering and dry cleaning, pawnbroking and shoe repairing. The installation, maintenance and repair of consumer goods, towel and other linen hire, and radio and T.V. relay services are also included. About 400,000 firms were to be asked to make returns, covering some 600,000 establishments.

THE INFORMATION REQUIRED

Most firms were asked to give information about their business such as if they run a *sub-post office*, if they operate mainly as credit traders calling on customers, if they are members of a retailers' buying group or a wholesaler-sponsored voluntary group, if they purchase goods on cash-and-carry, and if they give trading stamps.

Self-service trading and the selling of goods by mail order were to be covered.

In addition, the following was required,

(*a*) From traders with a total turnover of less than £10,000 in 1971:

(i) Total turnover (£)
(ii) Total purchases (£)
(iii) Number of persons working in the business
(iv) An indication of the kind of goods sold (by means of a list which retailer will 'tick').

(*b*) From traders with a total turnover of £10,000 or more in 1971:

(v) Items (i) to (iv) above, plus
(vi) Wages and salaries paid
(vii) Stocks of goods for sale or processing at the beginning, and at the end of the year
(viii) Capital expenditure on land and buildings, on vehicles and on plant, machinery and other capital equipment
(ix) Sales on hire purchases and other instalment credit terms
(x) Book debts at the end of the year
(xi) An analysis of turnover by specified classes of goods sold and services provided
(xii) Certain costs of operating the traders' own goods, vehicles and other transport costs
(xiii) Selling space.

Reasonable estimates were accepted where exact figures were not available.

This was the first full census for ten years. Planning commenced in 1969, and the Business Statistics Office, which controls the operation, has made considerable efforts to obtain co-operation from the trade at all levels, as well as from manufacturers and from the academic field. If the publicity and educational effort* which the Business Statistics Office put into this—perhaps the most difficult field so far as response is concerned—is rewarded

---

* For example, an article in *Trade & Industry*, 25 November 1970, *How the 1971 Retail Census can help Industry and retailer*—M. C. Fessey, Director, B.S.O.

by prompt returns from retailers, the preliminary report should be published before the end of 1972 and the final report in 1973–74.

THE NORTHERN IRELAND RETAIL DISTRIBUTION CENSUS

The first census of distribution for Northern Ireland was taken in respect of 1965. A preliminary report was published in March 1967, and the final one was issued in mid–1970.

The census covered retail establishments, and the motor, hairdressing, catering, laundering, and shoe-repairing trades. Fifteen thousand six hundred retail and 6,700 service establishments were covered. The pre-census list of establishments was compiled by the Royal Ulster Constabulary during mid–1965. A single type of form was employed, irrespective of the nature of the establishment, largely because the pre-census list did not provide the exact description of the establishments included. In future censuses this difficulty is less likely to arise, as the completed census forms will supply this information for the future in respect of existing shops. Unlike the experience in Great Britain, a very high level of response was obtained—largely due to the intensive personal visitation which was employed.

QUESTIONS

1. Distinguish between 'Gross Margin' in the Census of Distribution, and 'Net Output' in the Census of Production. What is the economic importance of these two concepts, and how are they used?
2. Outline the official statistics available on retail trade, and comment on their limitations and reliability.
3. Give an account of the methods employed in collecting data for the 1966 Census of Distribution.
4. What is the value of a Census of Distribution to: (*a*) the private sector of the economy, and (*b*) Government planners?
5. Write an account of the planning for and methods of collection employed in the 1971 Census of Distribution.
6. Compare and contrast the information collected in connection with the Census of Distribution for 1961 and 1971. Comment on any fundamental changes which have taken place.
7. Comment on and discuss the present statistics relating to hire purchase and other instalment credit arrangements, and their limitations.

7 Transport statistics

Statistical information in considerable detail has been available regularly on rail transport since 1920. This information is currently published in the *Annual Reports of the British Rail and the Transport Holding Company,* and also in *British Railways Board Statistics,* a monthly issued by the British Railways Board. In addition both the *Monthly Digest* and the *Annual Abstract of Statistics* contain long series of less detailed information, mainly of freight carried and the number of passenger journeys.

SITUATION PRIOR TO 1957

Information on road transport prior to 1957 was not comprehensive, and the statistics published arose largely as a by-product of the working of the administrative system (e.g. motor vehicle taxation and licence records; counts of the number of tickets issued for passenger journeys). Quarterly analyses were published for the country as a whole, giving information on licences current, and new vehicle registrations, both classified by type of motor vehicle and unladen weight. Annual figures of the number and type of motor vehicles in use, classified by area, were also provided. Additional information relating to public road passenger transport obtained under the 1930 Road Traffic Act was summarized annually in *Public Passenger Transport Statistics—Great Britain* by the Ministry of Transport.

Details of expenditure on roads and the mileage of public highway in Great Britain, together with other related topics, were given in the *Road Fund Annual Report.*

The data from official sources was then, as it is today, summarized in the *Monthly Digest* and the *Annual Abstract.* Such bodies as the Society of Motor Manufacturers and Traders and the British Road Federation also supplemented the official statistics by data obtained from their own members. (e.g. the annual, *British Road Statistics,* published by the British Road Federation.)

SITUATION SINCE 1957

Ten years after the end of the Second World War it was increasingly recognized that something must be done to remedy the uncoordinated and incomplete nature of our transport statistics. In particular the following deficiencies were noted:

> There was no information on the type of work road goods vehicles were doing, nor on the amount of goods they carried. Only a very limited amount of information was available on passenger mileage and on passenger movement generally, so far as public service road transport was concerned. Even less was known on these topics so far as private cars were concerned. What information there was was not properly co-ordinated. Road, rail, and air transport statistics tended to be kept in isolated compartments which limited their effective use for overall national planning.

GOODS TRANSPORT BY ROAD

In 1958 the Ministry of Transport carried out its first official sample survey of road goods transport. An earlier inquiry in 1952, which included details of road, rail and coastal shipping, had been conducted. In 1958, operators of selected vehicles were required to give information on the work performed by those vehicles in respect of one week in April 1958, and a corresponding week in 1952. The sample was stratified by

(*a*) type of licence, and
(*b*) unladen weight of the vehicles.

The results were published in *The Transport of Goods by Road—April 1958* (H.M.S.O. July 1959). Methodological and other details of these smaller-scale inquiries in 1952 and 1958 were published in *The Outline of the Road Goods Transport Industry,* (Glover and Miller, Journal of the Royal Statistical Society (Series A) Vol. 117 Part 3, 1954), and *The Transport of Goods by Road,* (Glover, Journal of the Royal Statistical Society (Series A) Vol. 123 Part 2, 1960).

In conjunction with information on vehicle mileages obtained from traffic counts inaugurated on 1 January, 1958, using both personal and automatic counting methods, the survey results were used to estimate trends in road transport in subsequent years.

Monthly estimates of the volume of road transport have been published regularly since then. This information permits the calculation of a monthly index of inland goods transport, relating to both road and rail, which is published regularly in the *Monthly Digest of Statistics.*

Additionally, statistics of road goods transport (by tons-carried and ton-miles) and of road goods vehicles—by type of carriers licence, unladen weight and class of licence—are published annually in *Highway Statistics* (see page 158) and in the *Annual Abstract of Statistics.*

Obviously the monthly estimates are subject to the possibility of errors, notably in assuming that the characteristics of the loads carried have not changed, so that the changes in mileage obtained from the traffic counts may be applied direct to the 1958 figures to obtain valid estimates of ton mileage. Over a few years this assumption is unlikely to give rise to much error, but it points to the necessity of regular sample surveys on the 1958 lines to provide, periodically, a new base line so to speak. In 1962 a further survey, on a larger scale, was carried out. This survey revealed, inter alia, that the estimates to which we have just referred underestimated the growth of road ton-mileage by about 2½% per annum.

THE 1962 SURVEY OF ROAD GOODS TRANSPORT

In preparation for this survey, the Ministry of Transport began in 1961 to build up a new list or index of road goods vehicles, to supersede an earlier list which was known to contain many errors. One-and-a-half million vehicles were involved, but in view of the magnitude of the task, the new list was restricted to all Public Haulage Vehicles (A and B licences), and C licence vehicles having an unladen weight of over three tons. Unfortunately this new index (i.e. list) of goods vehicles was not completed, so far as 'C' licence vehicles were concerned, until 1963. Hence, although the new list provided a suitable sampling frame for A and B licensed vehicles, an older and less reliable method had to be used for C licences.

An index (or list) of operators was compiled at the same time as the index of goods vehicles.

These two lists, which relate to Great Britain only, are now up-dated monthly.

The sample

A sample of 40,000* vehicles was decided on, about 10,000 being sampled in each of the weeks beginning 2 April, 2 July and 1 October 1962, and 7 January 1963. (The latter week was used owing to delays which prevented the survey starting in January 1962.) The 1963 figures were adjusted, by the use of supplementary information, to an estimated first quarter 1962 basis, so that the whole survey could be assumed to relate to the calendar year 1962.

Basically, the sample was a stratified random sample. In the case of the C licence list, which was in manuscript form at various Traffic Offices, the sample was taken by systematic selection with random starts. The public haulage vehicles A and B licences being recorded on punched cards, a fully random method was used for these. Stratification was by traffic areas (13), class of licence—A, contract A, B and C (4), and by 6 unladen-weight groups. There were thus 312 ($13 \times 4 \times 6$) classification cells. A variable sampling fraction was adopted, so that for each week the proportion of vehicles selected varied from 1 in 20 (A licence vehicles under 2½ tons) to 1 in 2,000 (C licence vehicles under 1 ton). Three types of questionnaire were used—one for public haulage vehicles, one for C licence vehicles of not over 1 ton unladen-weight, and one for heavier C licence vehicles. A separate questionnaire had to be completed for *each* vehicle.

The response was good; 70% of the questionnaires being returned by the date asked, a further 15% after one reminder, and all except 4% after a second reminder. Of the returned forms, about 5,000 were unusable for one reason or another, leaving, as mentioned in the footnote below just over 39,000 usable questionnaires.

On completion of the survey, the results (which refer to Great Britain only) were published in four volumes.

SURVEY OF ROAD GOODS TRANSPORT 1962

1. *Final results, Part I*

This first part reviewed the growth of road transport from 1952 to

* 40,000 usable responses were required, and to allow for wastage 46,500 vehicles were selected. In the event, just over 39,000 usable questionnaires were returned.

1962, giving details of the goods vehicle fleet and the work performed.

The tonnage carried increased from 847 million tons to 1,248 million tons, ton-mileage rising from 18·8 to 33·6 thousand million. The number of goods vehicles grew in the same period from 1·007 million to 1·524 million, there being a more than proportionate increase in the heavier vehicles. A comparison from 1952 to 1962 amongst road, rail, coastal shipping, inland waterways, and pipelines was also made. An extract from this table is given below (Table 7.1) revealing the preponderant influence of road transport.

The tables, which were preceded by a summary of the main results of the survey and a detailed commentary, were divided into two sections:

(*a*) characteristics of the goods vehicle fleet, giving tables on:
- (i) numbers of goods vehicles, by unladen-weight and by type of licence, 1952–62, and in more detail for 1962
- (ii) number of goods vehicles analysed by unladen-weight and type of fuel, by carrying capacity, type of body and licence category
- (iii) age distribution of vehicles, by licence and by unladen weight
- (iv) analyses of C licence vehicles, by use and industry of operator
- (v) numbers of articulated vehicles, by licence, unladen weight, type of body and industry of use.

(*b*) transport operations during 1962:
- (i) miles run, by type of journeys, and unladen-weight
- (ii) tonnage carried and ton-mileage, by unladen-weight and by length of haul
- (iii) number of journeys, classified by length and unladen-weight
- (iv) analyses of C licence vehicles, by industry or operator and use
- (v) use of trailers
- (vi) analyses of vehicles idle, and of use for purposes other than carriage of goods.

2. *Final results—commodity analysis*

This part gives the tonnage and ton-mileages of commodities carried by road in 1962, analysed by type of licence. Shares of various commodities carried, classified by licence-type, are also given, and

TABLE 7.1

Goods transport—Great Britain, 1952–1962

	tons (millions)						ton mileages (thousand million)					
	Road	*Rail**	*Coastal shipping*	*Inland water-ways*	*Pipe-lines†*	*Total*	*Road*	*Rail**	*Coastal shipping*	*Inland water-ways*	*Pipe-lines†*	*Total*
1952	847	285	39	10	2	1,183	18·8	22·4	9·0	0·2	0·1	50·5
1957	969	274	44	10	2	1,299	22·9	20·9	9·8	0·2	0·1	53·9
1962	1,248	228	49	9	7	1,541	33·6	16·1	10·8	0·2	0·4	61·1

* Excludes goods by passenger train (about 4 million tons yearly).
† Excludes pipelines of less than 10 miles in length; movements of gas also excluded.

Source: *Survey of Road Goods Transport 1962, Part I*

conversely, the proportions of each commodity carried by a particular licence-category. There is also a table showing the seasonal variation in commodities carried. Special attention is paid, as in Part I, to the C licence vehicles. Figures of tonnage and ton-mileage, analysed by industry of the operator and commodity, are given in considerable detail.

Comparative figures for tonnage and ton-mileage of various commodities carried by rail and coastal shipping are also supplied.

In practically all categories, the tonnage moved by road transport is much in excess of that moved by the other forms of surface transport. The only significant exception is in coal and coke, where by road 150·2 million tons were carried, compared with 145·0 million tons by rail. The rail hauls in this category tended to be longer than by road, on an average, 50 miles compared with less than 20 for road. In fact, in 1962 rail carried 7,300 million ton-miles of coal and coke to road's 2,134 ton-miles.

Finally, details of the commodity classification used in the survey are explained.

3. *Methodological report—*

This provides details of the construction of the sampling frame and the sample, the method of drawing the sample, the design of the questionnaire and the organization of the survey. Details of the response, the calculation of standard errors, and some problems encountered are also included.

4. *Final results—geographical analysis*

Here, for each of the eleven Standard Regions, a map showing the traffic flows by road is given and the following tabulations are provided:

Transport within region, out of region and into region
Transport in region, by length of haul
Tonnage moved in region, by commodity
Transport moved out of region, given region of destination
Tonnage moved outwards, by destination and length of haul
Tonnage outwards, by commodity
Transport inwards, by region and origin
Tonnage inwards, by origin and length of haul
Tonnage inwards, by commodity.

THE 1967–68 SURVEY

The most recent survey took place between July 1967 and May 1968, during which period the Ministry of Transport conducted its third survey of road goods transport.

The survey was designed to bring out the main changes which had taken place since the previous surveys, and to provide a new bench-mark for the continuous survey previously referred to.

The goods vehicle index (to which reference has been made earlier) was used as the sampling frame for all public haulage vehicles and for C licence vehicles of 3 tons and over. The traffic area lists provided the sampling frame for the smaller C licence vehicles. The selection of the sample followed lines similar to that of the 1962 survey, but the new survey was on a larger scale.

One week in each calendar month was selected for the survey, except where the week contained a Bank Holiday, when the second week of the month was chosen. The range of the variable sampling fraction employed was from 1/100 per week for the largest vehicles down to 1/26,000 per week for C licence vehicles of under 1½ tons unladen weight.

In this survey only two types of questionnaire were used—one for public haulage vehicles and one for the C licence operators, the provision of two types of forms for C licence operators in 1962 not having proved a success.

The survey covered about 79,000 vehicles—almost double the number covered in 1962. Once again, the overall response rate in respect of currently licenced vehicles was very good,—94%. The data is being analysed by computer, and the final results are expected to be published in 1972.

Although the final report is not yet published (early 1972) some information on journeys made and loads carried is already available, and covers such topics as origin, mileage, destination, tonnage and type of goods carried, analysed in various ways.

It is likely that the first volume of the final report will summarize the results as a whole, in more or less popular form. There will follow detailed tables for Great Britain as a whole, and a volume on methodology.

Analyses on a regional basis may be published if there seems to be sufficient demand. In any case, it is possible that much of the data will be micro-filmed in such a fashion as to make it possible to supply specific information on a regional basis to individual inquirers. If this is done the regional tables may not be published. In view of the very small demand from industry for the 1962 tables, this suggestion is not surprising. There is, in fact, little doubt that the results of such surveys are of main importance to government and regional bodies. A knowledge of the trends of traffic flow is most important for road planning and development, and indeed, in connexion with the statistics of rail and air traffic, to build up an overall picture of the inland freight pattern as well for estimates and forecasts of national income.

TRANSPORT FOR INDUSTRY SURVEY

A related but distinct survey on transport for industry was carried out in 1966–67. In contrast to the surveys of road goods transport, the transport for industry survey was conducted amongst manufacturing establishments, not transport firms. It was expected to be of immediate interest to all concerned with the goods transport industry in that it attempted to establish the qualities and types of service which are demanded by manufacturers, and which are offered by rail, road transport, postal, canals and coastal shipping services. The summary report points out that manufacturing industry spent some £600 million on transport services in 1963, £240 million on its own transport and £360 million with specialist transport firms, yet prior to the inquiry, very little had been known about the determinants of demand, and of the choice of mode of carriage of goods.

The survey was carried out in two parts. In both cases, a sample of manufacturing concerns was covered. Transport firms as such were not involved, the inquiry thus being user-orientated. There was a general survey of two major freight route areas—namely the catchment areas surrounding the London—Newcastle and the Liverpool—Glasgow routes. This survey identified thirteen broad commodity groups. However, in order to identify more closely problems associated with individual commodities it was decided to investigate a number of commodities in detail by means of a special commodity survey. The commodities were chosen from the following industry groups:

Industry chosen		*Reason*
Meat and vegetable processing.	—	products highly perishable; many requiring specialist transport
Iron and steel.	—	bulk commodities
Heavy chemicals.	—	bulk commodities needing specialist transport
Electronics.	—	fragile products
Paper etc.	—	homogeneous commodity demanded at two levels of demand,— *Final*—e.g. writing paper etc., *Intermediate*—e.g. newsprint.

The surveys were on a small scale—513 establishments being approached in the general survey and 502 in the commodity survey. Overall, only about 720 establishments returned satisfactory replies, giving details of over 13,600 consignments for the general survey and 16,600 for the commodity survey.* It is felt that, despite the small sample and the non-response rate of 30%, the data collected enabled a fair picture to be drawn of the allocation of demand between the different modes of transport.

The 720 manufacturing establishments supplied information on:

Numbers employed

Nature of the business

Transport facilities available (distinguishing amongst G.P.O., railways, outside road haulage, road vehicles, canals, coastal shipping) to the firm itself

Weight of goods despatched by the various transport facilities used

Expenditure on each mode of transport

For certain periods, each firm was also asked to give the following particulars of *each* consignment despatched:

Type of commodity

Weight, destination, method of transport used

Charges paid where an outside carrier was used

If the consignment had any special features e.g. was it of an 'urgent' nature, was it packed in a container, and so on.

In addition, a postcard was included with each such consignment, asking the consignee to say how quickly the goods had arrived and whether or not they were damaged.

---

* These were representative of a total of about 206,000 consignments dispatched by the establishments concerned in the survey period.

A 10% systematic sample of the consignments was selected, and in respect of these the firms were asked to give the charge they would have expected to pay for the cheapest alternative methods.

About 100,000 consignments were covered.

The *Transport for Industry (Summary Report)* was published in 1969. The main published analyses etc. in the Summary Report were classified by:

Mode of transport and distance sent
Mode of transport and weight of consignment
Mode of transport and different classes of goods
Mode of transport, tonnage, length of journey
Length of time taken for deliveries
Loss of, or damage to consignments
Number of consignments with special features
Distribution of commodities by consignment weight and by length of haul.

In addition to the more customary tabular approach, the report uses multiple regression analysis to estimate the probability of a consignment going by one mode of transport rather than another. Some of the comparisons made in this section are between:

Transport on own account / professional transport
Road haulier / transport on own account (general)
Road haulier / transport on own account (chemicals)
Rail / road haulier.

The twenty-five factors chosen as likely to have influence on the alternative choices investigated were:

Factors relating to consignment

1. length of haul (miles)
2. journey time (days)
3. charge (pence)
4. consignment weight (lb)
5. regularity of shipment
6. container used
7. special body required
8. inter-establishment move
9. consignment required more urgently than usual
10. ancillary service performed
11. type of commodity
12. destination

Factors relating to firm's circumstances

13. origin
14. size of firm
15. ownership of rail siding
16. ownership of C licence vehicles (or use of pool)
17. vehicles under A contract

Subjective assessments

18. knowledge of charge by alternative mode
19. charge by alternative mode
20. speed required to meet customers' requirements
21. speed required to ensure high utilization of vehicles
22. speed required to maintain low stock levels
23. ready availability of vehicles
24. freedom from loss
25. freedom from damage.

As can be seen, the factors have been divided into three categories. It is thus possible, in addition to assessing the influence of each factor independently, to compare the relative influences relating to the consignment itself, to the firm's circumstances and to the subjective assessments made by the shipper. The latter is of particular importance because subjective opinions are more susceptible to change, particularly when attention is drawn to their existence. Coefficients for the various factors were estimated for each of the comparisons mentioned. The sum of the significant factors, together with a constant value calculated using the multiple regression technique, estimates the probability of the consignment going by the one mode rather than that with which it is compared. Thus, for the comparison between rail and road haulage, let us suppose that the following coefficients were calculated and that they were the only ones of significance for this particular case.

Constant value	0·59
Length of haul (logarithm of miles)	0·17
Weight (logarithm of tons)	—0·15
Regular shipment	—0·04
Container used	0·09
Large firm	0·10
Freedom from loss	—0·26

Hence if a shipment of 10 tons were sent 200 miles in a container by a large firm which sent regular shipments and was anxious not to suffer loss, the probability equation would be:

$$\begin{aligned}\text{Probability} &= 0{\cdot}59+(0{\cdot}17 \times \log 200)\\ &\quad -(0{\cdot}15 \times \log 10)-0{\cdot}04+0{\cdot}09+0{\cdot}10-0{\cdot}26\\ &= 0{\cdot}59+0{\cdot}39-0{\cdot}15-0{\cdot}04+0{\cdot}09+0{\cdot}10-0{\cdot}26\\ &= 0{\cdot}72\end{aligned}$$

Thus the probability that this consignment would go by rail is 0·72 and the probability that it would go by road if that were the only alternative, 0·28 (1−0·72). These coefficients, being estimated from sample values, are subject to sampling errors, and the summary reports lists the standard errors against each estimated coefficient.

When the summary report was published in 1968 a more detailed publication was promised in the near future. It had not yet appeared when this book was in the press.

GOODS TRANSPORT OTHER THAN BY ROAD

In addition to the information on road goods transport published by the Ministry of Transport, the quarterly *British Railways Board Statistics* (in Northern Ireland—*Railway Statistics*) supplies similar data for the the railways. Air and sea transport statistics are published periodically by the Department of Trade and Industry, some initially in *Trade & Industry*, or the *Monthly Digest of Statistics*. Others appear in more specialist publications, such as the *Business Monitors* on civil aviation. In addition, special articles on air transport appear from time to time in *Economic Trends* (as in July 1963, November 1964, August 1969).

Some idea of the main classifications of goods transport statistics available by rail, air, and sea are given at the end of this chapter. Much of the data, whatever its source, is summarized in the *Monthly Digest* and the *Annual Abstract*.

PASSENGER TRANSPORT

In October 1961 the first of a series of sample surveys into private motoring was held. The surveys were intended to provide information on motor car usage, particularly in respect of vehicle and passenger mileage, and for road safety research purpose. Preliminary results were published in June 1963 (*Motor car ownership and use—Economic Trends*). Subsequently, a detailed report *Private*

Motoring in England and Wales was issued in 1964 by the Government Social Survey; reference is made to this on page 154.

The results of this survey were incorporated with other material in respect of rail, public service, road vehicles and domestic air transport in *Passenger Transport in Great Britain 1962*, published in 1963 (the first of a series of annual reports) which gave for the first time comprehensive information, extending over a ten-year period, on transport and travel within this country. More details of these annual reports are given on page 157.

PASSENGER MILEAGE ESTIMATES

Some of the methods adopted to estimate passenger mileage are given in an article in *Economic Trends* dated November 1963 and later republished in *New Contributions to Economic Statistics* (3rd Series, page 159 et seq.)

Prior to the motoring survey just mentioned, an average car-occupancy figure, throughout the week, of 1·5 persons had been used to enable estimates of private car passenger-mileage to be made. The new survey revealed an average occupancy of almost 2 persons per car—varying from 1·61 on Mondays to 2·63 on Sundays.* By employing automatic counting devices at various points on roads throughout the country, together with personal enumeration at selected times of the year, estimates of vehicle mileage are made, by day of week, month, and year. The figures thus obtained are combined with the car-occupancy figures just mentioned, to provide estimates of total passenger-mileage by private car. Information on seasonal changes in car-occupancy and passenger mileage have also become possible as a result of quarterly repetitions of the survey. Estimates of passenger journeys for public service vehicles travel continue to be based upon the number of tickets issued, but allowances have to be made for situations where more than one ticket is issued for a single journey, for return tickets, weekly and monthly season tickets, and so on.

The information so collected is used to provide estimates for passenger journeys separately in relation to the main urban areas, and also for the rest of the country as a whole. Data on passenger

---

* The private motoring survey in England and Wales continued quarterly until January 1964. The overall occupancy averages for Monday were 1·7 and for Sunday 2·73.

mileage is, in addition, available from the London Passenger Transport Board, and the Transport Holdings Company, but from no other road operators. The way in which these estimates are arrived at is fully explained in the article referred to above, both in respect of public service vehicles and passenger rail transport.

PRIVATE MOTORING IN ENGLAND AND WALES

The full report on the quarterly surveys on private motoring in England and Wales which were held between October 1961 and January 1964 was published in 1969. The intention on each occasion was to obtain a sample of about 325 households, from which it was expected to obtain about 1,000 car owners and 1,800 licence holders. For one month in each quarter a two-stage, stratified and effectively random sample of 7,000 electors was chosen from the Electoral Registers for England and Wales. The conventional stratification by area (four divisions of England and Wales, the Greater London conurbation, other conurbations, other urban areas, and rural areas) and the Jurors' Index was used. The first- and second-stage units were selected so as to give an equal overall probability of selection for each elector on the register.

Most of the electors chosen lived in private dwellings where there were fewer than five electors listed. In these cases the elector's address was included in the sample if and only if the chosen elector was the person first listed at the address. This reduced the size of the sample considerably (to 3,072 in October 1961). All households at these chosen addresses were interviewed. The addresses of electors who did not appear to live at private dwellings, or who lived where there were five or more electors, were all included in the sample. There were, in fact, only 164 of these in the October 1961 survey. From this group, only the households of the selected electors were interviewed. Certain other minor adjustments were made to ensure that there was no over-representation amongst these special cases.

Overall the first sample consisted of 3,282 households which yielded 1,039 household cars and 1,851 licenceholders—very close to what had been expected. For the remaining quarters of the survey the number of household cars varied from 1,006 to 1,241 and the number of licence holders from 1,780 to 2,080.

Each selected household was involved in the inquiry for one week, the dates of starting for the various households being spread through the month. An interviewer conducted a first interview, in which, if the household included a car- or a licence-holder, questions regarding sex, age, type of licence held and other related particulars were asked. In the case of co-operating households, a Mileage Book was left for each car. In this the types of journey, mileages, the number of occupants and drivers were to be recorded over a period of one week. At the end of the week, the interviewer returned with a second questionnaire. This asked for more details of journeys on a selected sample day, in the week, that day being divided into forty-eight half-hours. Information on age and sex of passenger, and whether front or back seat, were required for each half-hour period. Further questions on the use of the car for work, if any part of running costs were paid by employer, on holiday use, and on safety belts were also asked at the second interview.

The first part of the report gives full information on the conduct of the survey, including the method of dealing with non-response, the processing of the data and the sampling errors.

The report gives information on:

1. CARS AND THE MILEAGE THEY DO

Distributions of weekly and annual mileages,
Analysis of mileage; according to area of household,
according to cylinder capacity,
according to year of original registration.

2. PURPOSES AND TIMES OF JOURNEYS

Journeys and mileages for three different purposes (going to and from work, travelling in the course of employment, and journeys unconnected with work)

The purpose of journeys analysed by administrative area, by cylinder capacity and by number of years since first registration

An analysis by regularity of journeys to work and of journeys in the course of employment for each administrative area

The sample day figures gave the times of the day at which journeys were made, and these were classified according to purpose of journey. A similar analysis was made for journeys and mileage on each day of the week.

3. DRIVERS AND THE MILEAGE DRIVEN

Figures of the type of licence held, analysed by age, sex and year of passing test

Distribution of mileage driven, by age and sex, and average weekly and annual mileage by age, sex and driving experience

Age and sex of main driver classified by length of time since first registration of car driven

4. PASSENGER DETAILS

There was a problem in handling the data here. Only if a passenger was in the car for half or more of the journey was he recorded in the mileage book, being shown as there all the journey. However, as the sample day was split into half-hour periods, a passenger journey, which fell mainly in only one half-hour interval, might be recorded as of greater mileage in the mileage book than in the sample day questionnaire. Some of the tables given in this part of the report use mileages derived from the mileage book, others that from the sample day investigation. The source is indicated below by M.B. (mileage book) or S.D. (sample day). The main tabulations given relate to:

Number of persons in car in respect of journeys, and mileages for different purpose (M.B.)

Proportion of occupant-mileage on any given day (M.B.)

Occupancy rates for different days (M.B.)

Front seat/other passenger mileage as a proportion of car mileage (S.D.)

Proportion of passenger mileage done in front seat (S.D.)

Passenger mileage by age and sex (S.D.)

Interesting facts revealed by the report which have not already been commented on include the following.

Most car journeys tended to be short. Half were of five miles or less, and only about 8% of journeys exceeded twenty-five miles.

About two-fifths of cars made journeys to work on five or more days weekly.

More than 50% of the mileage was by people aged from 30–49 years. Males drove about 91% of all private car mileage. Men also had weekly car mileage averaging about three times that of women.

In general, the older the car the more likely it was to be driven by a male.

The average number of car occupants varied as follows:

For journeys to work; 1·4 to 1·5
For journeys in course of employment; 1·3 to 1·4
For journeys unconnected with work; 2·1 to 2·6
For all types of journeys; 1·9 to 2·2.

From 1964 onwards, the private vehicle surveys have been replaced by a series of national travel surveys which in addition to providing basic data on the use of private cars, cover other forms of inland passenger transport as well. The 1965 survey covered some 34,000 persons, 7,000 vehicles, and obtained details of about 400,000 journeys.

Some of the results of the national travel surveys have since 1965 been incorporated in the Ministry of Transport's annual *Passenger Transport in Great Britain* which is usually published in February, relating to the year ending fourteen months previously.

'PASSENGER TRANSPORT IN GREAT BRITAIN'

Passenger Transport in Great Britain is divided into five main sections. The first section consists of summary tables, giving total estimated passenger mileage by air, rail, public service vehicles, and private transport within Great Britain (for air also to Northern Ireland and the Channel Islands). Percentages of the mileage covered by each form of the transport are also given. Figures for *United Kingdom* consumers expenditure on passenger transport, and index numbers of the prices of the various forms of passenger transport (base 1963), taken or derived from the *National Income Blue Book*, are also given. Finally in this section, the number of passengers, journeys and the receipts from such journeys are analysed for the various forms of land passenger transport.

The remaining four sections deal with passenger transport by each of the four categories; rail, public service road vehicles, private road vehicles and domestic air services. The series usually cover an eleven year period unless stated to the contrary.

1. *Rail*

The information is obtained from the British Railways Board and London Passenger Transport Board. In addition to statistics of route mileage, rolling stock, number of passenger stations and seats available, detailed passenger data is given.

2. *Public service road vehicles*
All operators supply annually, on a calendar-year basis, details of number of passengers carried, vehicle-miles run and passenger receipts. In addition, firms with twenty-five or more vehicles supply further information for their own accounting year. Returns from the bigger undertakings are also obtained for each of the first three quarters of the calendar year. (Information from these latter returns are published quarterly in the *Monthly Digest of Statistics.*)

The statistics consist of information for the most recent year on number of fleets and number of vehicles, classified by size. A table gives number of passenger journeys by type of service, total mileage, and passenger receipts classified by size of fleet. There are also financial tables.

Vehicle miles run, passenger journeys and passenger receipts are all analysed separately by type of vehicle, type of undertaking, type of service and by two area-types. (The latter distinguish between main urban areas and other areas.)

3. *Private road passenger transport.*
A small amount of information is reproduced here from the more detailed *Highway Statistics.*

4. *Domestic air services.*
Department of Trade & Industry sources provide a single table showing aircraft miles flown, passengers carried, and passenger miles flown.

INTERNATIONAL PASSENGER SURVEY

In addition to surveys by the Ministry of Transport (Department of Environment) of inland passenger transport, the Board of Trade (now Department of Trade and Industry) has carried out since 1964 a continuing random-sample survey by personal interview of the movement of passengers into and out of the United Kingdom by air, short sea routes and long sea routes.

'HIGHWAY STATISTICS'*

This, the Ministry of Transport's third regular publication, was first issued in 1963. It incorporates, inter-alia, information from the

* *Highway Statistics* succeeded *Road Motor Vehicles,* first published in 1951.

surveys of road goods transport for 1962 and 1967–68, and the national traffic survey, and is published annually about nine months after the end of the year to which it refers.

Highway Statistics is divided into the following parts. Figures relate to Great Britain, unless otherwise stated.

PART I—ROAD MOTOR VEHICLES

The information in this section is obtained from the registration/licensing authorities.

1 (*a*) *Detailed tables on vehicles currently licensed;*

1 (*b*) *New registration of road motor vehicles.*

PART II—ROAD TRAFFIC

Information largely obtained from continuous automatic traffic-counts at over 200 sites, supplemented by manual counts at week-ends at monthly intervals at each site. In addition occasional large censuses are held to provide suitable bases for the continuing survey just mentioned.

PART III—ROAD MILEAGE AND ROAD EXPENDITURE

Information is obtained directly from the various Highway Authorities and the Local and Central Government Departments.

The method of classification was changed on 1 April 1967, so that figures before and after that date are not directly compatible.

PART IV—ROAD TRANSPORT

Goods data comes from traffic counts and the periodical surveys of road goods transport. The passenger figures come from the returns of public service vehicle operators from traffic counts, and from various special surveys such as the nation travel survey. The national travel survey, the family expenditure survey, the population censuses and the 1962 survey *Private Motoring in England and Wales* are used for car-ownership data.

'BUSINESS MONITOR FOR MOTOR VEHICLES'

In April 1969 the *Business Monitor* series (see page 103) was extended to include a monthly monitor (*M1*) on motor-vehicle registrations. (This superseded a previous series issued by the then Ministry of Transport.) The *Monitor* gives data for Great Britain and Northern Ireland, for all types of vehicles, engine sizes, and class of fuel used. Incorporated in the monitor is a quarterly supplement giving registrations in individual licensing areas. Seasonally-adjusted figures for registrations as well as actual are given. Recently changes in the seasonal pattern have occurred, and reference has been made to these in *Statistical News,* number 11.

Motor-vehicle registrations are taken as forward indications of the economic situation, and as such the statistics are used by government forecasters as well as by the motor industry.

'ROAD ACCIDENTS'

This, the oldest (date of birth 1951) of the four main publications of the Ministry of Transport, is published roughly eighteen months after the end of the year to which it refers. It deals, in the main, with casualties in road accidents, classified by type of vehicle/passengers/pedestrians involved and age of victim, divided into the categories,—death, serious injury, and slight injury. It is normally published in December, twelve months after the close of the year to which it refers.

TRANSPORT BY RAIL AND SEA

The basic statistics relating to these two modes of transport are summarized in the *Monthly Digest of Statistics* and the *Annual Abstract*. The main analyses are given below. Some of the rail figures also appear in *Passenger Transport in Great Britain.* Available statistics are

FOR RAIL: (BRITISH RAILWAYS (GREAT BRITAIN) AND LONDON TRANSPORT)

Figures are annual ones except where otherwise indicated (M=monthly).

Traffic receipts —for passengers, by type of fare
—for freight, by category of goods

Amount of traffic —number of passenger journeys, by type of fare, (M)
—number of passenger miles by type of fare
—weight of freight by category of goods, (M)
—net ton-miles by category of goods, (M)

Number of rolling Stock—in various categories,
Mileage of routes—in various categories,
Number of stations—in various categories,
Number of loaded train-miles and loaded-wagon-miles,

An analysis of rail accidents is also given.

Similar but rather more restricted information is given, separately, for Northern Ireland.

The main original sources are *British Railways Board Statistics,* and the *Annual Reports* of the British Railways Board and the London Passenger Transport Board.

FOR SEA

Number of merchant vessels registered

Analyses by tonnage, type and age, (M) and speed for those over 500 gross tons

Number of vessels entering and leaving United Kingdom ports, analysed as with cargo or in ballast, carrying passengers, mail, or other cargo (M)

Nationality of vessels

The main original sources are the *Registry of Ships,* and the *Digest of Port Statistics,* both published by H.M.S.O. for the Department of Trade & Industry.

CIVIL AVIATION TRANSPORT

Civil aviation statistics come from:

Licence returns made each month by U.K. airlines, giving number of flights made, total mileage, type of aircraft used and traffic carried,

Voluntary airport returns giving time of movement, type of movement, operator, type of aircraft, traffic carried, the next and previous stop, ultimate destination and origin.

Accounting information also comes from the British Airports Authority and the Air Corporation.

The main primary sources of statistics are the seven *Civil Aviation Business Monitors* referred to below.

For information on United Kingdom and Overseas operators we have:

MONITOR

CA1— airport activity (monthly): aircraft movements analysed by category (e.g. commercial, non-commercial, scheduled services, charter flights, U.K. operators, overseas operators),

CA2— air passenger (monthly:) passenger figures by type of service (scheduled or charter), type of operator (U.K. or overseas), and whether starting, or completing journeys or in transit,

CA3— air freight and mail (monthly): analyses freight by direction of movement, if by charter or scheduled service, and if by U.K. or overseas operators,

CA4— airlines (monthly): analyses of passenger, freight and mail carried, aircraft miles flown, capacity offered and taken up; for U.K. operators only in three groups,— BEA, BOAC and the independents,

CA5— airlines (quarterly): analyses information on the operation of each U.K. airline according to type of licence; information on fleet utilization by operator and aircraft type is also given,

CA6— domestic passenger traffic,

CA7— passengers international and cabotage (quarterly): statistics for international routes only, showing the geographical pattern with figures for important routes shown separately; figures for scheduled and charter services are shown separately,

CA8— an annual monitor on airline financial statistics is also published, usually two years in arrears.

In addition to the detailed *Business Monitors, Trade and Industry* publishes three regular sets of civil aviation statistics under the headings:

Trade by air (half yearly)
Mileage and traffic (half yearly)
Airport noise at Heathrow and Gatwick (quarterly)

The *Monthly Digest of Statistics* and the *Annual Abstract* summarize the more important civil aviation statistics in the following categories. Most of these statistics have previously been published in the sources mentioned earlier.

Breakdown of operations into number and length of stage flights, aircraft miles flown, passengers carried, passenger miles flown, and weight of freight and mail carried. The number of short-ton-miles flown for passengers, freight and mail is also given. The figures are given for domestic services, for international services, and for both combined. In addition, the operations of private companies are tabulated separately.

Accidents on scheduled flights, together with various ratios.

Number of aircraft flights and passengers carried between United Kingdom and abroad: Passenger origin and destination.

Traffic at civil aerodromes: number of aircraft, number of passengers and weight of freight and mail handled.

Trade by air: exports, re-exports and imports by commodity type and country (twice-yearly).

Aircraft noise at Heathrow and Gatwick (quarterly).

QUESTIONS

1. Discuss, using examples from the transport industry, the use of sampling in the collection of statistical data.
2. How far are passenger-mile statistics a more useful index of traffic trends than figures of either passenger-journeys or traffic receipts? Outline the problems involved in estimating passenger-miles for a public service operator.
3. Explain carefully the method of collecting and publishing any set of statistics in the transport industry with which you are acquainted.
4. Discuss the statistics available on road passenger transport, and indicate some of the problems associated with their interpretation.
5. Outline the development of statistics of road passenger transport since the Second World War. Explain carefully how the most recent survey of road goods transport was carried out, and comment on its limitations.
6. 'The *Transport for Industry Survey 1962* is the only user-orientated survey carried out in Great Britain this Century.' Comment on this statement, explaining the coverage of, and methods employed in, this survey. Do you think that regular surveys on these lines would be desirable and practicable?
7. Despite the overwhelming importance of road goods transport in this country, it is still the most poorly documented of the major forms of inland transport. Do you agree? Justify your answer.
8. Discuss the statistics available in this country on civil aviation.
9. In the transport industries, as in many other service industries, the problem of estimating net output is bedevilled by the difficulties of selecting appropriate units of measurement, and by the fact that the output of transport services is not confined to the narrowly defined transport industry. Comment.

8 National income and expenditure (G.N.P.)

'The National income is a measure of the money value of goods and services becoming available to the nation from economic activity' (*National Accounts Statistics—Sources and Methods,* H.M.S.O. 1968). The national income can be looked at in three ways:

As the total of all income received by the factors of production—*national income,*

As the total expenditure by the nation—*national expenditure,*

As the total money-value of the output of the various industries in the national economy—*national product.*

The national accounts not only provide us with information on the growth of the economy as a whole, but show us the way in which the various sectors of the economy are related. Information of this nature is essential for economic planning. It must, however, be realized that only items which are money-valued enter into the accounts. The value of the output of the engineering industry is included—because it depends upon monetary costs, but the contribution the housewife or the do-it-yourself handyman makes to the national economy is not, as their contribution is not measured in money. If the home handyman refused to do it himself but employed a paid decorator, carpenter or what have you, the national income and output, in money terms, would increase, but this would not represent any *real* increase. Because non-paid services such as the foregoing play a relatively unimportant part in our economy it is not considered worth while to impute a monetary value to them for the sake of giving a true picture. However in the less developed countries in which a large proportion of total output is on a subsistence basis—with peasants both producing and consuming their own crops—it would be necessary to make an estimate of the money value which would be attributed to such production in order to avoid grossly underestimating the national income.

Although a number of private individuals (notably Josiah Stamp and Colin Clark) have attempted in the past, to estimate the national income and output, their efforts, whilst helping to clarify some of the concepts involved, were incomplete and not particularly accurate. The first official estimates of national income and expenditure (relating to 1938 and 1940) were published in 1941. A White Paper giving such estimates has been published every year since, in March or April, immediately before the Budget. From 1952 onwards, a much more detailed and comprehensive set of tables has been published in the autumn of each year in the form of a Blue Book, some of the main tables from which are also reproduced in the *Annual Abstract of Statistics.*

We have spoken of these estimates as relating to the national income. In fact, however, prior to 1955 no attempt had been made to estimate the effect of depreciation on capital consumption and thus the final figures were given gross in the sense that they represented the value of the total output without taking into account the fact that some of this output was merely going, for example, to replace capital equipment which had worn out or become obsolete. Estimates of capital appreciation and consumption were first made available by Redfern of the Central Statistical Office (see page 186) in 1955, and since that time it has been possible to provide estimates of the net national income using a modification of Redfern's methods.

An article by Dean in 1964 (see page 186) showed the way towards making estimates of the capital stock of the United Kingdom, and official estimates of gross and net capital stock (see page 187) were first published respectively in the 1964 and 1966 *Blue Books.* In 1957, quarterly estimates of consumer expenditure were published, and since that date an increasing amount of information has become available on a quarterly basis, so that now a comprehensive set of tables on national income & expenditure extending to some thirty pages and dealing with the main divisions of gross domestic product and expenditure is published quarterly, in *Economic Trends.* (January, April, July and October issues). Rather more restricted quarterly information is also published in the *Monthly Digest of Statistics.* Further details on the quarterly capital accounts and all the financial accounts are also published in the monthly *Financial Statistics.*

It must be understood that substantial errors may be associated with the components of the national income tables. The quarterly figures tend to be less accurate than the annual ones, and both may be subject to revision in subsequent periods. Although it has not proved possible to calculate statistical limits of error such as might be derived from random samples, some indication of the extent of the accuracy of the estimates is given in *National Accounts Statistics —Sources and Methods* by grading each of the main components as follows:

Grade	*Margin of error*
A	± less than 3%
B	± 3% to 10%
C	± more than 10%

More importance may be attached to, say, year-to-year changes in the various estimates than in the absolute figures for any one year, and it is suggested that the errors in such *changes* are likely to be less than the amount indicated by the grading attached to the absolute values.

The fact that the national income is estimated in three separate ways does provide some sort of a check on the accuracy of the overall aggregate estimates. It is true that the three estimates are not entirely independent, but to a very large extent they are so. The extent of the discrepancy between the income and the expenditure estimates is usually no more than ± (0.5–1.5%) and since 1953 this has been shown as a 'residual error' entry in the income table. This is merely for convenience, and does not imply that the estimates of expenditure are more correct than those for income. Even though the residual error is small, relatively speaking, the fact that it may fluctuate markedly from year to year makes it difficult to reach any satisfactory estimate of the annual rate of growth of national income and output. More accurate estimates of growth rate must obviously await improvement in the accuracy of the component statistics.

The *Annual Blue Book on National Income and Expenditure,* in addition to presenting tables for the economy as a whole, provides balanced tables or accounts for a number of branches or sections into which the economy can be divided. These are referred to in some detail from page 174. The main sectors are personal, companies, public corporations, central government, local authorities, and overseas.

The advantage of this division is that it brings out the relationships between the different parts of the economy in a way which helps understanding and facilitates economic planning. Indeed it can be said that the national income and expenditure accounts form the most important economic document prepared by the central authority. Medium-term national economic planning leans largely upon these accounts and the data behind them, whilst they also provide the basis for short-term economic forecasts and for deciding budgetary policy.

The national Income and Expenditure estimates are derived largely from the following sources; Inland Revenue data on tax assessments, the censuses of distribution and production together with associated Department of Trade and Industry inquiries, and the accounts of the central government. In all, there are upwards of

TABLE 8.1

The gross national product (expenditure)

Expenditure	**(1969 figures)** £*m*
1. Consumers' expenditure	28,618
2. Public authorities' current expenditure on goods and services	8,118
3. Gross domestic fixed capital formation	7,927
4. Value of physical increase in stocks and work in progress	294
5. Total domestic expenditure at market prices	44,957
6. Exports and property income from abroad	11,986
7. *Less* imports and property income paid abroad	−11,318
8. *Less* taxes on expenditure	−7,868
9. Subsidies	844
10. Gross national product at factor cost (expenditure)	38,601

Source: *National Income and Expenditure 1970* (H.M.S.O.)

TABLE 8.2

The gross national product (income)

	(1969 figures) £*m*
1. Income from employment	27,174
2. Income from self-employment	3,009
3. Gross trading profits of companies	4,948
4. Gross trading surplus of public corporations	1,461
5. Gross trading surplus of other public enterprises	114
6. Rent	2,601
7. Total domestic income before providing for depreciation and stock appreciation	39,307
8. *Less* stock appreciation	−815
9. *Less* residual error	−342
10. Gross domestic product at factor cost	38,150
11. Net property income from abroad	451
12. Gross national product (income) at factor cost	38,601

Source: *National Income and Expenditure 1970* (H.M.S.O.)

eighty tables in the current *National Income and Expenditure Blue Book*. They range from the summary tables dealing with the national income, output, and expenditure aggregate, to those dealing with the analysis of income expenditure and saving by persons, with capital formation, with the current and capital accounts of the central government and so on. We give below the basic summary tables showing the break-down of the national income in the three different ways referred to at the beginning of this section, and in doing so introduce a number of basic concepts which are necessary for understanding the *Blue Book* as a whole.

TABLE 8.3

The gross national product (industry)

	(1969 figures) £m
1. Agriculture, forestry and fishing	1,197
2. Mining and quarrying	678
3. Manufacturing	13,346
4. Construction	2,559
5. Gas, electricity and water	1,364
6. Transport	2,348
7. Communication	930
8. Distributive trades	4,193
9. Insurance, banking and finance (including real estate)	1,250
10. Ownership of dwellings	1,991
11. Public administration and defence	2,391
12. Public health	834
13. Local authority educational services	1,153
14. Other services	5,073
15. *Less* stock appreciation	−815
16. Residual error	−342
17. Gross domestic product at factor cost	38,150
18. Net property income from abroad	451
19. Gross national product at factor cost	38,601

Source: *National Income and Expenditure 1970* (H.M.S.O.)

THE GROSS NATIONAL PRODUCT BY EXPENDITURE (Table 8.1, page 168)

The first two categories in the table are self-explanatory. They represent total home current expenditure. Items 3 and 4 likewise represent expenditure on capital goods (e.g. buildings, machinery and so on) together with any net *additions* to the stocks of goods or work in progress in the hands of producers, traders or as strategic stocks of the central government.

The total of the first four categories is the total domestic (home) expenditure at market prices. The next category—exports and property income from abroad—represent either goods which have been produced in this country, the value of which will accrue to residents of this country, or income from abroad which also accrues to residents of this country. This item is added to the total domestic expenditure at market prices, and the value of imports representing items which will have to be paid for abroad, and the property income which also has to be paid abroad, is deducted. The result is a sum of £45,625 millions, which represents the gross national product or gross national value of output at market prices.

The term 'gross' means that no deduction has been made for any of the (capital) expenditure which has gone merely to replace previously created capital goods which have worn out, depreciated, or become obsolete. The reference to market price means that the total includes any taxes on expenditure which have increased the price of goods, and also includes any subsidies which have been used to decrease the price of goods sold. The final two items in the table before the total are those necessary to convert the gross national product at market prices (G.N.P.M.) to the gross national product at factor cost (G.N.P.F.) In the first place, we deduct the taxes on expenditure, because the G.N.P.M. includes in its total any taxes which have been levied in this manner. We also add the subsidies, because the G.N.P.M. includes the value of goods which have been reduced in price because of subsidies which have been paid on them. The final total of £38,601 millions is the gross national product at factor cost (G.N.P.F.) i.e. the value of national output measured by the expenditure on what has been produced by the factors of production.

Now all expenditure must be income to someone else, and hence an alternative way of estimating this same gross national product is to total all incomes.

THE GROSS NATIONAL PRODUCT BY INCOME

(Table 8.2, page 168)

The first six items are fairly self-explanatory. They represent in sum the total incomes received by the various factors of production, i.e. the agencies providing the productive services. The total domestic income is £39,307 millions. Part of this income occurs because stocks and work in progress during the year may have appreciated in value since they were made. This must be deducted from the total domestic income. Ignoring for one moment the residual error, we require to add the net property income from abroad, which is really the difference between income that is received from abroad and income which is paid out to payees abroad.

This should give us the gross national product at factor cost. In fact, the total so far obtained is £35,249 millions, £342 millions more than the G.N.P.F. calculated by the expenditure method. The two methods of deriving the gross national product are essentially independent, and the difference between the two estimates is due to errors in the estimates of one or other of the sets of figures. We have no means of knowing where the errors lie and it is, therefore, conventional to insert, in the incomes table, an item 'residual error' to make up the difference. This does not imply that the incomes table is in error and the expenditure one correct, it is merely that the error has to be placed somewhere.

THE GROSS NATIONAL PRODUCT BY INDUSTRY

Estimates of the net output of each industry group are added together, stock appreciation being deducted and net property income from abroad added, with an appropriate adjustment for the residual error to give a gross national product at factor cost equal to those in the other two tables. *See* Table 8.3, page 169.

THE NET NATIONAL INCOME

Finally, an estimate of capital consumption, i.e. the cost of replacing capital goods which have worn out, depreciated or become obsolete, is made, and this is deducted from the gross national product to give the net national income. Thus:

	£m
Gross national product (1969) at factor cost	38,601
Gross capital consumption	3,694
	£34,907
Net national income—a measure of the net additional economic resources created during the year.	

It must be clearly understood that these tables form only a very small part of the whole.

In the remainder of this chapter we set out the main characteristics of the national accounts, and deal in some detail with some of the major concepts.

DEFINITIONS OF NATIONAL INCOME TERMS

Formal definitions of the main technical terms used in the accounts are given below.

GROSS DOMESTIC PRODUCT AT FACTOR COST

This is the total value, at the prices paid to the factors of production, of the goods and services produced by residents of the United Kingdom before allowing for capital consumption. Alternatively, it may be considered as the sum of all factor incomes, less stock appreciation.

GROSS NATIONAL PRODUCT AT FACTOR COST

This equals the gross domestic product at factor cost, plus net property income from abroad. It is equal to the total income of United Kingdom residents prior to allowing for depreciation or capital consumption. It may also be called the gross national income at factor cost.

NATIONAL INCOME

This is equal to the gross national product at factor cost, minus capital consumption.

GROSS DOMESTIC PRODUCT AT MARKET PRICES

This is the total value of goods and services produced by residents of the United Kingdom at the prices paid to the factors of production, plus the amount of taxes on expenditure, and less subsidies, all before providing for capital consumption. This aggregate, as generally defined, includes the taxes on expenditure on both home-produced and imported goods and services. Strictly speaking, the taxes on expenditure on imported goods and services should be excluded, as imported goods and services are not part of domestic production. It is, however, difficult in most cases to determine accurately the taxes on expenditure levied on imports, although a rough estimate is shown in the *Blue Book*.

TOTAL DOMESTIC EXPENDITURE AT MARKET PRICES

This is the total value of expenditure by residents of the United Kingdom on consumption and investment. It is equal to the gross domestic product at market prices, less exports and plus imports of goods and services.

Total final expenditure at market prices equals total domestic expenditure at market prices, plus the value of exports of goods and services. It is equivalent to total final output at market prices. Any estimates in terms of factor cost are converted to market price estimates by adding taxes on expenditure and deducting the cost of subsidies. The reverse procedure converts estimates at market prices into those at factor cost.

It is important to distinguish between *stock appreciation*, (i.e. the part of the change in the value of stocks and work in progress which arises from increases in prices at which the stocks and work in progress are valued), and the category, *value of the physical increase in stocks and work in progress.*

THE NATIONAL ACCOUNTS

As mentioned earlier, the Central Statistical Office published in 1968 a very detailed account of how the national accounts are compiled. This publication, *National Accounts Statistics—Sources and Methods* (H.M.S.O.—1968) superseded an earlier (1956) version. The first four chapters are essential reading for any student who wishes to obtain a basic grasp of the principles behind the construction of the national accounts.

National Accounts Statistics has an introductory chapter explaining the concepts underlying the national income computations. The second and fourth chapter describe the structure of the published accounts, whilst the third chapter deals in general terms with the estimates of the overall national income aggregates.

The main classification of the accounts in the *Blue Book on National Income & Expenditure* is by sector:

(*a*) *The personal sector,* showing the transaction of members of the community as final consumers. It covers:

final consumers
unincorporated businesses
non profit-making bodies such as charities, social clubs and churches
life funds of insurance companies treated as personal savings.

(*b*) *The production sector,* which for convenience is split into companies and public corporations. The term 'company' covers incorporated productive enterprises which can be identified separately from those who control and own them.

So far as financial transactions are concerned, it is desirable to distinguish between those companies which act as financial intermediaries and those which do not. We therefore have the industrial and commercial companies on the one hand, and the financial intermediaries, namely banks, insurance companies and other financial institutions, on the other. Public corporations are productive enterprises which are controlled by the government, but which are relatively speaking financially independent, and are free from direct government control. They include the Electricity and Gas Boards, the National Coal Board and the Post Office.

(*c*) *The government sector*, in which are shown the transactions of the central government and the local authorities, with the rest of the economy and with one another. As well as showing these two sectors separately, a combined set of accounts for the combined public authorities is provided, which eliminates transactions between local and central government, showing only their transactions with the outside sectors. Furthermore, for certain purposes it is desirable to treat the public sector as a whole, and prepare a combined set of accounts for the central government, local authorities and the public corporations together.

For 'central government', apart from the Civil Service Departments proper, this includes various funds for which accounts are kept separately, such as the National Insurance Funds. Public boards such as the Regional Hospital Boards, the Atomic Energy

Authority, etc., are included, as are such government trading enterprises as the Royal Ordnance Factories.

'Local authorities' includes the local government authorities, and the river and water boards.

(*d*) *The international or overseas sector*, records of transactions between United Kingdom residents and non-residents. Detailed definitions of 'residents' are given in *National Accounts Statistics—Sources and Methods*. Although the definitions dealing with marginal cases are rather complex, 'residents' can be broadly defined as:

Private individuals living in the United Kingdom or who have a residence in the United Kingdom which they visit during the year, or who stay in the United Kingdom for more than six months in any year

All public authorities in the U.K.

Business enterprises and non profit-making organizations located in the United Kingdom. This includes branches and subsidiaries of overseas companies, but excludes overseas branches and subsidiaries of United Kingdom companies

Any sections or offices of the United Kingdom government operating abroad are classed as residents of the United Kingdom, whilst similar offices of foreign Governments in the United Kingdom are classed as non-residents. There is a minor discrepancy in view of the fact that the Channel Islands and the Isle of Man are classed as being part of the United Kingdom for balance of payments purposes, but not included in the domestic accounts.

The information published in the *Blue Book on International Transactions* is consistent with that published in the *Balance of Payments Pink Book*.

FOUR TYPES OF SECTOR ACCOUNTS

Within the accounts for each sector, four types of account may be constructed. These are:

A production account, analogous to the trading account of a firm

An income and expenditure account, showing the source of current income and how it is appropriated. This account is sometimes called a current account or an appropriation account

A capital account, giving the allocation of savings to investment

A financial account, showing in detail that part of the capital account which involves transactions in financial assets and liabilities, as distinct from physical assets.

In practice, a production (or operating) account is only given for the Public Corporations. The information needed to produce a production account of the companies or the personal sector is not available. Even if it were, it would not perhaps be of very great value. It is more important to consider the production accounts of individual industries, or industry groups, which may be expected to be more homogeneous and more meaningful. Indeed the input-output tables (see page 104) produced periodically consist largely of the production accounts of individual industries brought together in a meaningful manner.

All the domestic sectors of the economy have an income and expenditure account. In the case of corporate enterprises (i.e. the company sector and the public corporation sector) this account is called an appropriation account. Separate appropriation accounts for the two sectors are produced as well as a combined one. The combined corporate appropriation account for 1969 is given below. The income and expenditure account of persons (final consumers),

TABLE 8.4

Corporate income appropriation account (1969)

	£m.		£m.
Income		*Allocation of income*	
U.K. income		Dividends and interest	
Gross trading profits of companies and trading surplus of public corporations*	6,409	Payments	4,140
Rent and non-trading income	2,019	Additions to reserves	44
	8,428	Current transfers to charities from companies	35
Income from abroad†	1,956	Profits due abroad† (net of U.K. tax and taxes paid abroad)	1,060
		U.K. taxes on income	
		Payments	1,124
		Additions to tax reserves	591
		Undistributed income (after taxation)*	3,390
	10,384		10,384

* Before providing for stock appreciation and for depreciation.
† After deducting depreciation allowances, but before providing for stock appreciation.
Source: *National Income and Expenditure 1970* (H.M.S.O.)

also illustrated below, shows the various sources of individual income i.e. employment income, income from self employment including the trading profits of unincorporated businesses, rent, dividends and net interest, payments to charities by companies, (which are considered as someone's personal income), and national insurance, and other benefits. This income is spent on consumers' expenditure, payments abroad, United Kingdom taxes, and National Insurance contributions.

TABLE 8.5

Personal income and expenditure (1969)

	£m.		£m.
Income before tax		*Expenditure*	
Income from employment	27,174	Consumers' expenditure	28,618
Income from self-employment*	3,009	Transfers abroad (net) and taxes paid abroad	99
Rent, dividends and net interest	4,423	U.K. taxes on income	
Current transfers to charities from companies	35	Payments	5,206
National insurance		Additions to tax reserves	94
Benefits and other current grants from public authorities	3,930	National insurance and related contributions	2,243
		Balance (savings*)	2,311
Total personal income*	38,571	Total expenditure and savings*	38,571

* Before allowing for depreciation and stock appreciation.

Source: *National Income and Expenditure 1970* (H.M.S.O.)

For the two public authority sectors the main income is from taxes, plus, in the case of the central government, national insurance contributions. Expenditure is largely made up of current expenditure on goods and services and transfer payments or grants, mainly to the personal sector. In the overseas (or international) sector there is an income and expenditure account which divides the international transactions, both credit and debit, into goods and services, property income, tax payments and transfer payments. The balance in this account represents net investment abroad, and is essentially the same as the current balance of payments with sign reversed.

CAPITAL ACCOUNTS

The difference between the income and the expenditure in each sector represents savings. The total savings of all sectors is the sum available for adding to the wealth of the community. For the nation as a whole the combined capital account shows the total savings, less stock appreciation, plus any net capital transfer or grants from abroad. It shows also how those savings are held, in the form of physical assets (either fixed assets or stocks) or as net investment abroad.

The capital accounts for each sector roughly parallel the foregoing except that, in addition, capital transfers to and from other sectors and financial claims on and obligations to other sectors, which cancel out in the combined account, are shown. The net results of these inter-sector financial transactions are shown, each as one figure, in the personal and companies capital accounts, the details of the financial transactions in these cases being shown in separate financial accounts. For the public sector, however, the individual capital accounts show details of the financial transactions. For the overseas sector there is no capital account as such, as the balance of the income and expenditure account is represented by financial assets, or liabilities. Particulars of the transactions involved therefore appear in the financial accounts to which we now turn.

FINANCIAL ACCOUNTS

These show in some detail the changes in the various financial liabilities and assets for each of the following sectors; personal, industrial and commercial companies, banks, insurance companies and superannuation funds, other financial organizations, the public sector and the overseas sector. The three new financial sectors mentioned are split off from the company sector so that their financial transactions, which would otherwise be cancelled out as internal to the company sector, may be shown.

The main items are:

Liabilities	*Assets*
Borrowing	Loans made
Issue of securities	Bank deposits
Business debts	Stock and shareholdings
	Amount owing to the sector

When one considers the nation as a whole, the financial transactions between residents cancel out, leaving only the net change in financial assets or liabilities in relation to the rest of the world. The transactions giving rise to this balance are shown, classified according to the types of assets and liabilities transferred, in the international transactions table. This consists, essentially, of the financial transactions giving rise to the current balance of payments.

The balance, namely the net acquisition of financial assets by the overseas sector, corresponds (with sign reversed) to net investment abroad in the income and expenditure account on page 177.

The main object of the national income and expenditure statistics is to show how the various forms of economic activity are inter-related e.g. between company savings and capital formation, between balance of payments and consumers' expenditure, between taxation on income and personal savings, and so on. A further object is to show how the main aggregates change over time. How, for example, has the gross national product and its constituent parts changed over the past ten years?

SOURCES OF NATIONAL INCOME STATISTICS

ESTIMATES OF INCOME

Inland Revenue Tax statistics provide information on company profits, income from self employment, part of rent income, and total wages and salaries. In all, about three-quarters of the income data comes from this source. Industrial analyses of wages and salaries come largely, however, from the censuses of production and the Department of Employment's earnings surveys. Census of population figures are also used, along with the foregoing, in assessing wages and salaries separately.

The Inland Revenue's P.A.Y.E. returns and the Department of Employment's quarterly earnings surveys enable estimates of wages and salaries to be made quarterly. The quarterly estimates of profit income are less soundly based, being mainly derived from the Inland Revenue's quarterly sample-survey of company profits. Only a very small amount of quarterly information is available on self-employment.

Information on income in the public sector is available annually through the accounts of the central government, the local authorities, and the public corporations. Quarterly estimates are made from returns from the central government and the public corporations, whilst for the local authorities, quarterly changes in line with observed trends are assumed.

Rent (outside the public sector) is estimated partly from the family expenditure survey, and partly from Inland Revenue Tax assessments. Farm rent is estimated from Agricultural Departmental returns. Quarterly figures are obtained by interpolation and extrapolation.

The balance of payments figures yield data on income from abroad.

Full information on transfer incomes, such as grants accruing to persons or to companies from public authorities, is available from the accounts of the public authorities themselves. So far as receipts of dividends and interest are concerned, those which involve the public sector are fully known, whilst receipts from other sources by companies are, in the main, built up from estimates of those companies' holdings and knowledge of interest rates. The receipts by persons are finally estimated as a residual figure, after taking into account the receipts and payments of all the other sectors.

ESTIMATES OF EXPENDITURE

A very wide range of sources is used for estimates on the expenditure side. Because of this, the results are probably rather less reliable than on the income side, and less consistent internally.

Information on consumers' expenditure comes from the following sources:

Food—the national food survey and other statistics from the Ministry of Agriculture, Fisheries and Food, and from the corresponding Scottish and Northern Ireland Departments

Alcoholic drink—mainly from H.M. Customs and Excise

Tobacco—information from tobacco manufacturers and distributors

Clothing, household goods and related commodities—retail sales statistics from the Department of Trade and Industry

Catering and motor vehicles—the regular Trade and Industry Department inquiries.

For most other aspects of consumer expenditure, information comes either from regular departmental inquiries, or from the family expenditure survey.

There are three main problems involved in the preparation of these estimates. Some of the data is estimated at the stage where the goods pass from the producer to the distributor, and not directly into the consumer's hands. Hence any changes in the level of stocks held, say at the distributive stage, will affect the figures, but this will not reflect genuine changes in consumer expenditure.

Another problem is that some consumers goods and services are purchased by businesses or by public authorities for business use.

An attempt is made to allow for this, but it is impossible to achieve accuracy.

A third difficulty is that as a variety of sources may be used to arrive at composite estimates in individual categories of expenditure, there is always the risk there may be omissions or double-counting.

Provided that the interfering factors in the second and third categories above remain constant, their presence should not interfere with year-to-year changes in the estimates, even if they lead to over or under-estimates of the absolute level of consumer expenditure.

The annual census of production and inquiries into the distributive and service trades carried out by the Department of Trade and Industry provide the majority of information for estimates of fixed capital formation and changes in stocks and working progress for private businesses. Shorter-term statistics provide the quarterly estimates in these categories, and now that the Business Statistics Office is rapidly developing its new system of business statistics more comprehensive information than has hitherto been provided can be expected to be available. For the public sector, as mentioned in connection with the income estimates, the sources of expenditure information, are the accounts of the bodies concerned. Estimates of fixed capital formation in the form of house dwellings are somewhat less satisfactory than are those for most other forms of production. The estimates are largely based on the number of houses currently under construction, their average price, and on estimates of building output obtained from regular sample-surveys of construction.

As so many of the estimates of fixed capital formation are obtained from accounting data, reliance has to be placed on the accountant's definition of what are and what are not capital goods; this definition is not necessarily what the economist would consider most appropriate.

The balance of payments statistics are used for estimates of expenditure on imports of goods, whilst corresponding information as regards services comes from a wide variety of sources including the Bank of England, the international travel survey and regular inquiries conducted by the Department of Trade and Industry into overseas activities of United Kingdom companies.

The Inland Revenue Department supplies information on dividend payments by companies, and interest payments are estimated largely from the same sources as are interest receipts. Transfer payments by the public sector are fully documented, and can be obtained from the accounts of the various organizations within that sector.

One of the big problems in handling the whole of these data relates to the exact time at which the transactions are recorded. Is it when the order is placed, the article or services delivered, the account sent by the seller, the actual payment made by the buyer; or at some other point? In the United Kingdom national income accounts an attempt is made, so far as possible, to ensure that transactions are recorded *at the time when the expenditure is incurred,* not when the payment is made. The main difficulty in achieving this occurs in connection with the central government's current expenditure on goods and services, which to facilitate Treasury control is recorded mainly on a cash basis. This gives rise to discrepancies due to timing differences. Adjustments are made to the figures of recording between the Government and the other sector accounts to effect a suitable reconciliation where possible.

The recording of capital expenditure on fixed assets which take a long time in production, for example, buildings and ships, also involves adjustments. An attempt is made to ensure that the value of the work done in a given period is included in the national income figures on the expenditure side in order to ensure that it balances with the factor-incomes generated during that time. Dividends and government transfers are recorded on a cash payments basis, this being the only feasible procedure here. However, other interest payments such as those on bank and building society deposits are recorded on a payable or accruals basis, it being assumed that the interest is earned continuously during the period of the deposit.

Finally, there is always the problem of adjusting figures which may be related to a year other than a calendar year, (e.g. to the income tax year from April to April), to the calendar-year basis of the national income and accounts.

Where difficulties such as those referred to in the foregoing arise, they are usually more acute in the quarterly than in the annual national income estimates.

MEASUREMENTS AT CONSTANT PRICES

The gross national product, the gross domestic product and indeed any of the constituents of the national income are measured in terms of money. The value of money—in terms of goods and services it may buy is not constant, and hence real changes in income, output, and expenditure may be obscured by changes in the money measuring rod, i.e. by changes in prices. It is often therefore convenient to measure changes in income, output and expenditure, after first eliminating the effect of price changes. This is done by revaluing the particular category concerned—say the gross domestic product—at the average prices of a selected base year. At the present time (1971) this base year is 1963. In the national income accounts, both in the quarterly and the annual series, the following categories are shown in terms of constant 1963 prices, as well as at current prices.

Gross domestic product in terms of expenditure,
Consumers' expenditure, classified by type of expenditure,
Gross domestic fixed capital formation classified by sector, by type of asset and by industry group.

In addition, index numbers of the gross domestic product in terms of the output of the various industry groups (based upon 1963) are given.

The base-year of 1963 was introduced in the *White Paper, Preliminary Estimates of National Income,* published in 1969, and of course in the subsequent *Blue Book* of that year. The change is commented upon in the April 1969 issue of *Economic Trends.* Earlier series were based on previous detailed census of production years—1948, 1954 and 1958.

THE PROCESS OF REVALUATION

The revaluation procedure, to obtain constant-price estimates, can be based on either the expenditure, the income or the output figures. An outline of the expenditure and the output estimates is given below.

EXPENDITURE AT CONSTANT PRICES

Several different methods are employed in adjusting the estimates in terms of current expenditure to those at base-year prices. The most used method is to divide the expenditure estimates by a suitable price index. Two-thirds of the current expenditure estimates, three-quarters of the public authorities' expenditure on goods and services (including wages and salaries), practically all the estimates relating to physical increase in stocks and work in progress, about half of the exports of goods and services and two-fifths of the imports of goods and services are adjusted by dividing by an appropriate price index. In some cases, it is more convenient to estimate the actual quantities of goods purchased in the current year, and multiply each category by weights proportionate to the base-year prices. This is done in the case of almost half consumer expenditure, and practically the whole of the remainer of the exports and imports of goods and services, and of stocks.

So far as services are concerned, the methods of adjustment are not so clear-cut, nor so satisfactory. In the case of services supplied by public authorities, the majority of which are free, the numbers employed are used as indicators. In principle, this means that base-year expenditure on these services is multiplied by the ratio of the numbers employed currently to those employed in the base-year. This procedure implies that there has been no change in productivity which, in view of modern developments in data-processing procedures and the like, is unlikely to be true. Nevertheless, it has not yet proved feasible to measure productivity changes in such circumstances, and this is why the conservative 'no change' assumption has been adopted. In the case of expenditure on other services where there is no obvious physical unit, we use indicators the movements of which are assumed to reflect changes in the volume of the particular services provided.

At present, these methods are applied to the various categories of final expenditure valued at market prices, so as to give the gross domestic product, classified by various categories of final expenditure, valued at market prices in the base-year. The gross domestic product, at factor-cost and at constant prices, is obtained by subtracting the total taxes on expenditure, and adding subsidies, also valued at base-year rates, from the market-price estimates. The adjustment of the indirect taxes is fairly simple. So far as *ad valorem* duties and taxes are concerned, the proportion of the tax to market-price in the base-year is multiplied by the expenditure at constant-prices for each of the other years on the items concerned. For the other indirect taxes, tax is estimated by multiplying the physical quantity of the taxable goods in the year in question by the rates of tax which applied in the base-year. The sum of these two estimates gives the estimate, at constant prices, of indirect taxes for each of the years concerned. So far as subsidies are concerned, the general procedure is to multiply the subsidy for each unit of the product in the base-year by the quantities marketed in other years. Public authorities subsidies on housing are revalued by taking the subsidy per house in the base-year, and multiplying it by the stock of houses in the current year.

Constant price estimates for the gross national product are obtained by adding net property income from abroad deflated by a suitable price index to place it on a 1963 constant-price level.

OUTPUT OR PRODUCTION AT CONSTANT PRICES

The contribution of each industry to the gross domestic product is its net output, i.e. the value of its total output, less the value of any goods or services it has obtained from outside the industry. Net output includes provision for depreciation and excludes stock appreciation, hence it is not *net* in the same sense as is the net national income.* The total of the net outputs of all industries is the *gross* domestic product.

Thus, in measuring the gross domestic product at constant prices, we should ideally revalue at constant prices the total (gross) output of each industry, and deduct therefrom that industry's inputs of goods (including fuels) and services. Apart from agriculture, where this method is applied because the necessary information is available, other methods are employed in practice. For all other industries, an attempt is made to find some indicator which will reflect changes in net output as closely as possible. Gross output alone is the most common indicator used. If there is a constant ratio between net output and gross output, changes in gross output at constant prices will reflect changes in net output at constant prices.

Such a constant ratio rarely exists, of course, and thus gross output is never a completely accurate indicator of net output. In other cases, net output is estimated from inputs, usually of materials, and here too one cannot expect complete correspondence between the indicator and the net output it is supposed to measure. However, in so few cases is it practicable to measure net output in the ideal way that these indicators must be used for want of any-

* Net output in this sense differs from the Census of Production 'Net output' in which inputs of certain services are included.

thing better. Because the estimates of output at constant prices are derived largely from indicators which represent changes in physical net output, and not in terms of value series, the results are presented in the form of index numbers and not in terms of estimated values, as in the case of the expenditure approach. For the Standard Industrial Classification (1968) Orders II to XXI the index numbers form the familiar Index of Industrial Production. For the other industries various indicators in percentage form are used. The whole are combined, using weights based on the relative net output of each industry in the base-year (i.e. the year for which the latest full census of production is available). A more detailed explanation of how this index of total output is constructed is given in Chapter 12.

CAPITAL CONSUMPTION AND CAPITAL STOCK

Although there has been for many years general agreement amongst economists that the national income ought to be measured after a deduction had been made from total output to represent capital assets which had been used up in the process of production, the problem of estimating the amount of capital consumption had, prior to 1955 been considered to be too difficult to tackle effectively. However, in 1955 an article, *Net Investment in Fixed Assets in the United Kingdom 1938–1953* by P. Redfern (*Royal Statistical Society Journal* series A, vol. 118, pt. 2, 1955) was published. This set out a procedure whereby reasonable estimates of capital consumption might be made. From 1956 onward, the procedure outlined by Redfern, with subsequent modification, has been used to calculate the annual consumption of capital in the United Kingdom. A subsequent article by G. A. Deans, *The Stock of fixed Capital in the United Kingdom in 1961* (*R.S.S.J.* series A, vol. 127, pt. 3, 1964) carried the principles still further, and led to the current methods employed for estimating capital stock.

It should be emphasized that the provision made by companies and public authorities, for example, for depreciation in their accounts, is not a satisfactory measure of capital consumption, primarily because these provisions are generally based on original cost. They normally take no account of changes in the cost of replacement as time passes.

A procedure advocated by Redfern is the perpetual inventory method. It involves the following.

Consider estimates in respect of a given year (say, Year A).

1. estimates are made of the gross fixed capital formation in Year A separately for each type of asset
2. estimates are also made, (often just broad assumptions) of the average length of life (L) separately for each class of asset
3. gross fixed capital formation for each class of asset is now estimated for L years prior to Year A. L is taken to be the average life of each class of asset treated individually. Thus L for industrial buildings might be 50 years, for houses 100 years, for certain machinery 25 years, and so on
4. price indices using a convenient base-year (currently 1963) are constructed for the various classes of assets. By dividing these into the various figures for gross fixed capital formation referred to above, estimates of gross fixed capital formation at constant prices in the base year can be derived.
5. the aforementioned information being available, final calculations are made as illustrated in the following (very simplified) example.

Example of the perpetual inventory method calculation
(see Table 8.6)

We begin with fixed investment for £8m. The asset so purchased has an assumed length of life of eight years and represents an increase in gross capital stock of +£8m. (Column 6). Thus at the end of the first year the gross capital stock is £8m. (Column 7). The length of the life of the asset is 8 years, and we are assuming straight line depreciation, so £1m. of capital has been consumed and this is entered in Column 8. The net capital formation during that year is, therefore, £7m. and the net stock of capital is also £7m. (columns 9 and 10).

At the beginning of the second year, a capital asset worth £10m. is purchased; it is expected to last for ten years. Thus there is an increase in the gross capital stock of £10m. in the second year, and the gross capital stock at the end of the year is £10m. plus £8m., i.e. £18 m. Capital consumption during the second year is £2m.; £1m. in relation to the first asset, and £1m. in relation to the second

TABLE 8.6

Year	Gross fixed capital formation (£m.)	Length of life of asset (years)	Annual decline in value (£m.)	Gross value of assets withdrawn (£m.)	Change in gross capital stock (£m.)	Gross capital stock (end year) (£m.)	Capital con-sumption (£m.)	Net capital formation (£m.)	Net stock of capital (£m.)
(1)	(2)	(3)	(4)	(5)	(6)	(7)	(8)	(9)	(10)
1	8	8	1	—	+ 8	8	1	7	7
2	10	10	1	—	+10	18	2	8	15
3	20	10	2	—	+20	38	4	16	31
4	18	6	3	—	+18	56	7	11	42
5	24	8	3	—	+24	80	10	14	56
6	12	6	2	—	+12	92	12	—	56
7	8	8	1	—	+ 8	100	13	− 5	51
8	—	—	—	—	—	100	13	−13	38
9	—	—	—	8	− 8	92	12	−12	26
10	10	10	1	18	− 8	84	10	—	26
11	—	—	—	—	—	84	10	−10	16
12	—	—	—	22	−22	62	7	− 7	9
13	—	—	—	44	−44	18	2	− 2	7
14	—	—	—	—	—	18	2	− 2	5

asset, and the net capital formation is £8m., i.e. the change in the gross capital stock less the capital consumption. At the end of the year, the net stock of capital is £15m. (the sum of the two items in Column 9).

The beginning of the third year sees the purchase of capital assets to the value of £20m. These assets are expected to last for ten years only; the change in gross capital stock, and the gross capital stock at the end of the year are obtained, as previously, being £20m. and £38m. respectively. The capital consumption during the third year is £1m. in respect of the asset installed in Year 1, £1m. in respect of the asset installed in Year 2, but £2m. in respect of the asset installed in Year 3 because this latter asset depreciates at the rate of £2m. per year. The net capital formation is, therefore, £20m. less £4m., namely £16m. which is inserted in Column 9, and the net stock of capital becomes £31m.

The figures in respect of years 4 and 5 are obtained in a similar manner. The asset installed in year 4 has an annual decline in value of £3m., and the same applies to the asset installed in year 5. In year 6 it will be seen that the increase in the gross capital stock is just offset by the amount of capital consumption so that there is no increase in the net capital stock, whilst in year 7 the capital consumption exceeds the addition to the gross capital stock.

In year 8 no assets are added, but the existing assets are still deteriorating, hence there is a decline in the net capital stock to £38 At the beginning of year 9, the asset purchased in year 1 has declined in value to zero and is thus withdrawn from the gross capital stock. We have, therefore, a decline of £8m. in gross capital stock, to £92m. Capital consumption during year 9 is £12m., not £13m., because, as the asset installed in the first year now no longer 'exists', we cannot include a decline of £1m. per annum in respect of this.

In year 10, a new asset to the value of £10m. with an estimated life of ten years is installed, but at the end of year 9, the asset purchased for £18m. in the year 4 went out of existence. This is noted in Column 5, and results in a decline in the gross capital stock of £8m., i.e. £10m. for the new asset minus the £18m. referred to. Ignoring the assets purchased in the first and fourth years, which now no longer exist, the capital consumption is £10m., which just offsets the value of fixed capital formation in year 10, so that there is no net fixed capital formation in this year and the net stock of capital remains at £26m. If the reader cares to carry on the computations the figures for years 11, 12 and 13 of the table can be obtained. Assuming no further capital investment takes place, the net stock of capital becomes zero at the end of year 19.

In real life, of course, we do not know at all exactly the length of life of each individual asset, and the estimates of length of life of the various asset-groups within the several broad industrial classifications can only be very rough. However, it can be shown that errors in assumed length of life have only a limited effect on the final estimates of capital consumption, because if length of life is under-estimated the capital consumption in respect of each particular asset for a given year will tend to be over-stated. Any net error will probably be offset by the allowance for capital consumption being made in regard to too few assets.

There are problems also in measuring the current cost of replacing assets, and it has only proved possible so far to introduce the estimated cost of replacing existing fixed assets with other identical assets. Thus the estimates of capital consumption will not allow for technological change, whereby existing assets are replaced with assets which may, in some cases, be substantially different from them. Net fixed-capital formation is estimated by deducting the capital consumption estimates from those for gross fixed-capital formation for each year. There are also the problems of allowing for a fall in the productivity of assets over time, as distinct from their decline in value. These problems have, so far, not been solved.

In general, no allowance is made for obsolescence, when fixed assets become valueless other than at the expiry of their normal life, e.g. when they are superseded unexpectedly by a new type of equipment, or when they are no longer needed for the productive purpose for which they were originally intended. Furthermore, the value of an asset depends not only on its replacement cost and age, but also on the extent to which it has been maintained. Up to now, it has not proved practicable to make any allowance for the addition to capital stock, or the reduction in capital consumption which might result from what Redfern terms 'excess maintenance'.

Neither has it been possible to make any specific allowance for destruction of fixed assets by fire, war, accident, or similar circumstances, except in a very few special cases. Nevertheless, it is suggested that some allowance here can be made for these events by perhaps slightly under-estimating the average life of assets.

THE NATIONAL INCOME AND EXPENDITURE TABLES

The main constituents of the national income and expenditure accounts have already been indicated. Below we give an outline of the make-up of the *Annual Blue Book* itself, and of the quarterly tables published in *Economic Trends*:

THE BLUE BOOK MAKE-UP: (A) GENERAL SECTIONS

I. *Summary tables*; containing the basic accounts showing the gross national product (analysed in various ways), personal income and expenditure, corporate appropriation accounts, public authorities' current accounts, the national capital accounts and international transactions,

II. *Expenditure and output at constant prices;* containing

i. Analysis of expenditure at constant market prices and constant factor cost,
ii. index numbers of output, analysed by industry at constant factor cost,
iii. index numbers of cost per unit of output and prices indices for broad categories of expenditure,

III. *Industrial input and output;* detailed analysis of the make-up of the gross domestic product by industry and by type of income. Breakdown of total wages and total salaries by industry group,

THE BLUE BOOK MAKE-UP: (B) SECTOR ACCOUNTS

IV. *Personal sector;* income and expenditure account, capital account, consumer expenditure by type at both current and constant prices, breakdown of personal income by type, analysis of taxes on expenditure by type of goods etc. and analyses of subsidies,

V. *Company sector*; appropriation and capital accounts of industrial commercial and financial companies, analysis of trading profits by industry group,

VI. *Public corporations*; operating and appropriation accounts, capital accounts, (analysed by industry group),

VII. *Central government (including the national insurance fund)*; current and capital accounts, together with separate current account for the national insurance funds,

VIII. *Local authorities*; current and capital accounts.

IX. *Combined public authorities;* capital and current accounts for VII and VIII combined, breakdown of current expenditure on goods and services by type, taxes on expenditure and subsidies, a separate table on housing subsidies. Analysis, by type and source, of taxes on income and capital,

X. *The public sector*; combined capital and current accounts for VI, VII and VIII, together with a detailed analysis of public expenditure and capital formation by the service involved,

THE BLUE BOOK MAKE-UP: (C) INTEGRATED ACCOUNTS

XI. *Capital formation;* gross domestic capital formation by sector and type of asset, by industry group, by industry and type of asset,

capital consumption and net domestic fixed capital formation by type asset and by sector,

net capital stock by sector and by type of asset, gross capital stock by industry and type of asset—all at replacement cost in terms of 1963 prices,

value of physical increase in stocks and work in progress, analysed by industry and by sector,

XII. Financial accounts; net acquisition of financial assets analysed by sector,

transactions in financial assets, by sector and by type of asset.

A list of definitions of the main terms is given, together with comments on the various tables. A set of tables showing how H.M. Treasury analyses public expenditure, which may be compared with the public sector accounts in Section X, is also provided. Apart from the fact that the Treasury accounts are on an April/March basis whilst the national income accounts are for calendar years there are a number of differences of treatment which are referred to in notes, and also in *National Accounts Statistics—Sources and Methods.*

'ECONOMIC TRENDS'

The quarterly tables in *Economic Trends* follow the pattern of those in the *Blue Book,* the main aggregate being the gross domestic product. Many of the quarterly series are published on a seasonally-adjusted basis, the method used usually being some variation of the ratio to moving average method. The general procedure is to produce seasonally-adjusted estimates for detailed sectors within each of the categories, and then to combine them, using suitable weights. The seasonally-adjusted estimates of consumer expenditure at constant prices, for example, are constructed from thirty-eight separate sections. In general, seasonal adjustments for the expenditure categories involve much more detail, and are less straightforward than are those on the income or output side.

The October issue of *Economic Trends* contains longer series of quarterly figures than the other three quarterly issues. Figures going back up to ten or twelve years are currently published, in order to cover the main periods given in the *Annual Blue Book* which comes out in the previous month. In addition, various tables from the main *Blue Book,* converted to percentages, are given, along with others showing annual rates of change in the gross domestic product over a period of years.

The basic tables published each quarter are (1971):

(*a*) Expenditure making up the gross domestic product
(*b*) Gross national product as the sum of factor incomes
(*c*) Seasonally adjusted index numbers of output (base, currently, 1963)
(*d*) Comparisons of gross domestic product
(*e*) Personal income and expenditure
(*f*) Appropriation accounts of companies
(*g*) Appropriation accounts of public corporations
(*h*) Current account, central government
(*i*) Current accounts, local authorities
(*j*) Combined capital accounts, all sectors
(*k*) International transactions
(*l*) Consumers' expenditure
(*m*) Fixed capital formation, by industry group
(*n*) Fixed capital formation, by sector and type of asset
(*o*) Value of physical increase in stocks and work in progress.

Articles on aspects of the national income appear regularly in *Economic Trends.*

In *Economic Trends,* November 1970, for example, an article appeared explaining in detail the way in which taxes and subsidies are allocated to the various items of final expenditure. Such information, showing as it does the impact of taxes and subsidies on the various categories of spending, is valuable for economic and social purposes. Some taxes and subsidies can fairly easily be allocated to specific types of final expenditure e.g. duties on final consumer goods such as alcoholic drink and tobacco. Others, which fall on intermediate products, (products used by businesses to produce other goods or services) or on employment (Selective Employment Tax and Selective Employment Premium, S.E.T. and S.E.P.) can only be allocated by some indirect form of assessment, to particular categories of final expenditure. It is largely with the problems posed by the latter group with which the article referred to above is concerned. Other articles which have appeared during the last few years are referred to on pages 9 and 10.

QUESTIONS

1. Discuss the problem of measuring the contribution of housewives, as such, to the national income.
2. What are the main statistics used for estimating fixed capital formation in the United Kingdom, and what are their limitations?
3. Discuss the problem of estimating capital consumption in the national income statistics.
4. Distinguish between the physical increase in stocks and work-in-progress and stock appreciation, in the national income statistics. What are the problems posed in estimating these two categories?
5. Outline and contrast the three ways in which the national income may be measured.
6. What problems arise in attempting to measure the national income by adding together the total expenditure of the nation?
7. What are the problems involved in measuring the national income of the community using the output method?
8. Describe how constant-price estimates of national expenditure and output are obtained.
9. What are the problems involved in using price index numbers to deflate national income and expenditure aggregates in order to obtain estimates at constant prices?
10. Explain briefly how estimates of the capital stock of the community are made, and discuss some of the difficulties associated with making these estimates.
11. For certain purposes, the national-income statisticians distinguish between financial intermediaries and other corporate businesses. Explain the reason for this and, at the same time, comment on the contents of the tables dealing with financial transactions in the *National Income and Expenditure Blue Book.*
12. For the purposes of the national income account, the nation is divided into sectors. State what these sectors are and outline briefly the types of accounts provided for each.
13. The gross domestic product may be estimated in terms of market prices or of factor cost. Explain the differences between the two types of estimates, indicating the economic significance of each.

14. Compare and contrast the problems associated with estimating the national income of Great Britain and of Sierra Leone.
15. Explain why measures of depreciation and stock appreciation are used in national income statistics, and comment on the problems involved in obtaining them.
16. Explain why the national income is calculated at constant prices, and comment on the implications of such calculations for comparisons of productivity over a period of time.

9 Overseas trade and the balance of payments

Some details of merchandise trade have been recorded officially for many years; non-merchandise figures have only been collected since the beginning of the twentieth century. It is only since the Second World War, however, that a comprehensive breakdown of the 'invisible' category of transactions (see page 211) has become possible, Exchange Control records providing the information for the original statistics.

MERCHANDISE TRADE STATISTICS

Some figures were collected as early as the thirteenth century. Comprehensive figures date back to the mid-nineteenth century. The present authority for collection is the *Customs Consolidation Act 1876*, as subsequently amended.

The key to the methods of classifying oversea trade statistics is currently found in the *Guide to the classification of Overseas Trade Statistics,* which in 1970 superseded the publications, *Statistical Classification for Imports and re-exported Goods* and the Export List. The *Guide* is revised annually on 1 January.

The statistics themselves are published in the *Overseas Trade Statistics of the U.K.*, previously known as the *Overseas Trade Accounts.*

Since January 1954 the commodity categories used in these statistics have been based on standard international trade classific-ations, as laid down by the United Nations Statistics Commission. This facilitates international comparisons, but the continuity of the British series was broken because the United Kingdom statistics had been based previously on a substantially different arrangement. The break affects the arrangement of the tables, and the grouping of commodities in the classified list. The figures of trade for individual commodities were affected by the more detailed classification introduced in 1962.

The figures are first published, two or three weeks after the end of the month, by press release and in *Trade & Industry*. Main totals, in seasonally adjusted form, are given. Originally, the difference between exports and re-exports plus imports (that is, the crude 'Trade Gap') was shown, but for a number of years a figure called the Visible Trade Balance has been given. This figure, which is fully explained on page 206, is obtained by making adjustments to the trade figures so as to eliminate certain inconsistencies in the recording of imports and exports, and to place both sets of figures on a comparable basis. A week or two later, the monthly *Overseas Trade Statistics of the United Kingdom* (previously called *Accounts relating to the Trade and Navigation of the United Kingdom*) is published, giving very detailed figures.

The main figures relate to

a. commodities and groups of commodities,
b. total figures of United Kingdom imports, exports and re-exports with each country in the world, and analyses by groups of countries.

The figures given in the monthly accounts are for the current month, the corresponding months for the two preceding years, cumulative figures for the year to date, and comparative figures for the two preceding years. The December accounts therefore show the year's total.

In 1950 the Board of Trade (now the Department of Trade & Industry) introduced the monthly *Report on Overseas Trade*.* This is issued about seven weeks after the month to which the figures relate. It gives a summary of figures of trade by commodities, countries and trading areas for the current month, with comparative figures. This publication is more useful for economic analysis than *Overseas Trade Statistics*. Indices of the volume and unit value of British exports and imports are also given here, as well as in *Trade & Industry*.

More detailed breakdown of overseas trade statistics for individual

* This publication was discontinued after February 1971. Its discontinuance not only reflects the relative lack of demand for it in recent years, but also foreshadows changes in the form of the other publications.

industries may be obtained by subscribing to the Customs and Excise 'Bill of Entry' Service. This service provides very cheaply computer-produced figures not immediately available in detail in the regular publications.

Both the *Monthly Digest of Statistics* and *Economic Trends* publish summary figures of overseas trade from the *Report on Overseas Trade*. Periodically also there are articles relating to overseas trade statistics in *Economic Trends*. In addition, *Trade & Industry* publishes a quarterly summary article on overseas trade, and a separate regular analysis of Sterling Area trade.

The *Annual Statement of the Trade of the United Kingdom with Commonwealth Countries and Foreign Countries is* published by H.M. Customs & Excise (H.M.S.O.), usually about a year in arrears. It is in five volumes, the contents of which are summarized below.

Vol. I The value and volume of trade by commodity and by country in summary form

Vol. II The value and volume of imports and re-exports by type/commodity, with details for principal countries of origin. A supplement gives the amount of duties collected under each Act concerned and there are also tables on the import and export of gold and coin

Vol. III Export figures analysed by value and volume, commodities, and country of destination

Vol. IV The value and volume of trade with each country, analysed by main commodities

Vol. V Imports into and exports from each U.K. port.

The figures of Volumes I to IV are revised, and may differ from those in *Overseas Trade Statistics*. They are given, moreover, in greater detail.

Comparative figures are given for the past four years. The *Annual Abstract of Statistics* gives yearly figures of some of the more important items, so providing comparable figures over a number of years.

Improvements in the layout and coverage of *Overseas Trade Statistics* were introduced in 1970 and as a result of this H.M. Customs & Excise were considering, when this book was in the press, what changes might be desirable in the form of the Annual Statement of Trade (*see* article in *Trade & Industry* 26 August 1971).

COVERAGE OF THE FIGURES

The returns include particulars of all goods crossing our national frontiers with the following exceptions:

Movements of gold and silver bullion and coin (accounts for these are published in a separate section of *Overseas Trade Statistics*),

Trans-shipment of goods under bond (separately recorded)

Ship's stores and bunkers (consumed on the ships themselves), loaded at United Kingdom ports by vessels engaged in foreign trade

Second-hand ships and aircraft (sold or purchased)

Diplomatic goods e.g. goods imported directly by Ambassadors and Ministers accredited to the United Kingdom, or by certain international bodies

Extra-territorial goods, i.e.

a. fresh fish landed by British ships direct from fishing grounds
b. exports of British Government stores for use of the British Government overseas
c. imports of stores for Forces use on Government ships
d. imports of captured enemy military equipment
e. import of military stores by the United States Government for use of United States troops in the United Kingdom

The above are not considered as imports and exports proper.

Newly-built ships, bought by United Kingdom firms from abroad and delivered at ports abroad

Commercial aircraft entering this country other than for major repairs

Certain materials used in the production of atomic energy. Details are recorded, but for security reasons are not published

Personal and household goods purchased abroad and brought in by passengers. (Prior to 1 May 1947 *dutiable* goods of this nature were recorded) similarly personal effects, purchased in United Kingdom and taken out by foreigners

Exports by letter post

Smuggled goods

Figures for the import and re-export of unset precious stones and pearls (excluding unmounted diamonds drilled for dies) were excluded from 1949 to 1964 because of the difficulty of recording the movements completely. From 1965 onwards however this trade has once again been included.

With the foregoing qualifications, all import and export trade is included. Until the end of 1969 distinction was made between *exports* and *re-exports*. *Re-exports* are goods which come into the country and are exported with *little or no change*. The dividing line, between exports and re-exports proved difficult to draw, and this led to the somewhat belated decision to eliminate the distinction, from the beginning of 1970.

TRADE BY COUNTRIES

There are four main systems in use for classifying trade by country.

Imports	*Exports*
By country of,	
1. Original production	Ultimate consumption
2. Purchase	Sale
3. Shipment	Shipment
4. Consignment	Consignment

The United Kingdom returns use the consignment method (4) for classifying for both imports and exports. The main reason for this is its simplicity. The trader always knows the country of consignment; he may not know the country of origin or other data. The country of consignment is defined as 'the country from which (or to which) the goods were originally despatched, with or without breaking bulk in the course of transport, but without any commercial transaction in the intermediate country'.

Comparison is a matter needing extreme care, as not all countries adopt the same basis for their statistics. Indeed, the comparison of United Kingdom overseas trade figures with those of other countries is a very difficult and complicated task, despite the rationalization introduced by the adoption of the Standard International Trade Classifications previously referred to. The introduction of this classification, as we have seen, reduced the comparability of the United Kingdom figures over time. Another problem is that from the point of view of economic analysis the methods employed in the *valuation* of imports and exports are not by any means the most suitable. This is commented on below.

VALUATION OF IMPORTS AND EXPORTS

Valuation is based on 'declared' value. For imports, the finance

Act 1935 lays down that declared value should be the price in the open market at the time of importation; carriage, insurance, freight and landing charges included. This is known as a *c.i.f.* valuation and was originally introduced for Customs Duty purposes. The Import Duties Act 1932 introduced a general *ad valorem* tariff, and it was because this required a common method of valuation for imports that the *c.i.f.* procedure was standardized. Although nowadays less than 13% (by value) of our imports are subject to duty, the method of valuation has not been changed. Where goods are imported from associated companies they may be consigned at below their open market value, and in this case the Customs makes an addition called 'uplift' for tax purposes. It is the uplifted value which is included in the trade statistics.

For exports, valuation is on the basis of the cost of goods to the overseas purchaser, 'free on board' (*f.o.b.*). This means the cost of goods delivered to the ship or aircraft which is to take them out of the country.

Any comparison made between total values of imports and exports for a given period, using trade statistics, must have regard to the use of different bases of valuation, and it must be remembered that the figures relate to the physical movement of goods into and out of this country. This movement does not necessarily take place at the time when ownership changes, or when the goods are paid for.

RECORDING OF EXPORTS AND IMPORTS

The figures for imports and exports in each month are compiled from documents received by the Statistical Office of the Customs & Excise Department. Import documents are received promptly, as the goods cannot be cleared through Customs without them. Export documents however, are normally presented after despatch. There is an appreciable delay, perhaps a fortnight on the average, between the shipment of exports and their inclusion in the records.

Thus, the export figures do not relate to the same period as the import figures. This is perhaps not serious when quarterly figures, or monthly averages over three or more months are concerned, but it can disturb single-monthly results considerably. For instance, when a dock strike occurs, import documents (and hence import figures) are more quickly affected than are the export documents. This produces a false trade surplus. When the strike is over, the lag in export documentation coupled with the fact that exports may have to await the unloading of imports before they can be shipped, will tend to produce the reverse effect.

In addition to the foregoing, some net under-recording of exports was noted in 1969 and earlier years. This led to Customs checks, which were intended to have eliminated the problem. However, evidence of under-recording was again found in 1970, after the lapse of a few months, and it seems likely that continual checks for it will need to be made as a matter of routine. A new system for recording exports was introduced in August 1971 (*see Trade & Industry*, 19 August 1971). It is too early to know if it will be successful.

These points emphasize the danger of relying upon overseas trade figures, covering only limited periods of time, as indicators of the progress of the economy in the international field.

THE TRADE BALANCE

From what has been said earlier it will be apparent that a comparison of the crude figures for imports and exports of goods does not give us any idea of the real balance between the two. For some years, therefore, it has been the practice to publish in *Trade & Industry*, along with the totals of imports and exports, a figure for the 'visible trade balance'. More recently, an article, *New form of presentation for monthly trade figures* in *Trade & Industry* (4 November 1970), foreshadowed the introduction, in January 1971, of a modified form of presentation using the term 'visible balance', which is calculated to make it easier to relate the monthly figures to the current balance of payments account (see page 207). In what follows, we deal with the translation of the crude import and export figures into comparable totals, using change of ownership from resident to non-resident as the criterion.

The aim in each case is to measure the value of true imports and exports, free on board (*f.o.b.*), after making adjustments for discrepancies in coverage (such as those mentioned on page 200) and after making a seasonal adjustment to avoid misleading month-to-month comparisons.

IMPORTS

VALUATION ADJUSTMENTS

Imports are recorded with the inclusion of port charges carriage, insurance and freight. A deduction therefore needs to be made to eliminate these charges.

In certain cases goods involved in transactions between associated companies are sold at prices below the open market value. H.M. Customs 'uplift' these to estimated market values. However, it is the actual *transaction value* which affects the balance of trade, and hence this 'uplift' has to be deducted from the declared import figures.

COVERAGE ADJUSTMENTS

From page 200 we see that certain imports are not actually recorded as imports, e.g.

Purchases of secondhand ships and aircraft
Certain atomic energy materials
Ships purchased abroad and delivered abroad to United Kingdom owners.

Also, the following categories are recorded as imports, but as no change of ownership is involved when the goods move into this country they should not be so recorded:

Goods sent to United Kingdom for processing and repair
Returned goods.

Certain goods imported on consignment may initially have no value declared, in which case, H.M. Customs place a value on the consignments, usually in *excess* of market value. When the goods are sold, a correction will be made if *ad valorem* duty is charged. However, where the goods are duty-free or subject to specific (physical unit) duties, this correction may be neglected, in which event a deduction needs to be made to correct the overstatement of value.

There are also a number of other minor adjustments.

Thus we have:

	Value
Declared imports, *c.i.f.*	A
valuation adjustments,	
deduct freight insurance,	
port charges,	
'uplift' etc., ...	B
	A−B
coverage adjustments,	
add secondhand ships and aircraft,	
ships purchased and delivered abroad,	C
	A−B+C
deduct returned goods,	
goods for repair and processing,	
consignment adjustments, ...	D
Adjusted imports, *f.o.b.*	A−B+C−D

EXPORTS

As exports are recorded *f.o.b.*, and are not subject to 'uplift', no valuation adjustments are necessary.

COVERAGE ADJUSTMENTS

The following exports are not recorded in the overseas trade statistics:

Secondhand ships and aircraft
Certain atomic energy materials
Exports by letter post.

The following do not pass into foreign ownership and therefore, although included in the trade statistics as exports, are not exports proper:

Goods exported by N.A.A.F.I. for the use of British troops abroad
Returned goods
Goods for repair or processing
United Kingdom components sent to United States for inclusion in military aircraft which are to be supplied to the United Kingdom.

UNDER-RECORDING ADJUSTMENTS

An allowance has recently been made, for some of the years prior to 1970, in respect of under-recording of exports known to have occurred (see page 203). It is likely that such an adjustment will now be made regularly.

Certain other minor adjustments are also made.

Thus we have:

Declared exports, *f.o.b.,*	W
coverage adjustments,	
add secondhand ships and aircraft,	
certain atomic energy materials,	
exports by letter post, ...	X
	W+X
deduct returned goods,	
goods for repair and processing	
NAAFI exports,	
U.K. components for U.S. Aircraft	
to be sold to U.K.	Y
	W+X−Y
add under-recording adjustment before	
1970 only, ...	Z
Adjusted exports, *f.o.b.*	W+X−Y+Z

In the monthly press release and the monthly *Trade & Industry* article, the practice until the end of 1970 was to show *seasonally adjusted* the declared export figures (*f.o.b.*), and the declared import figures (*c.i.f.*). In addition, the import figures were shown after the deduction of the value of United States military aircraft imported in that month for government use. Moreover, payments made for these aircraft were not included. The idea behind this was that such aircraft were in a special category; statistics relating to them would, if included, tend to obscure regular trade comparisons. It should be emphasized that the statistics referred to above are the crude figures, before valuation and coverage adjustments. However, without showing any detail of the adjustments themselves figures were also published monthly for the visible trade balance, which equals adjusted exports (*f.o.b.*). Minus [adjusted imports (*f.o.b.*) less imports of United States military aircraft for United Kingdom Government].*

* The bracketed figures represent imports net of United States military aircraft for U.K.

This figure for the visible trade balance would seem to be a good measure of the extent to which our visible trade is enabling us to pay our way. Nevertheless, United States military aircraft have to be paid for, like everything else, and the view has prevailed amongst statisticians responsible for calculating the country's balance of payments figures, in which the visible trade results play a part, that the payments made to the U.S.A. for these aircraft should be allowed for when working out the visible balance. Thus in the balance of payments accounts (which appear quarterly and annually) in addition to the visible trade balance, a figure called the *visible balance* appears. This is the visible trade balance *plus* payments made for United States military aircraft, i.e. it is the adjusted exports (*f.o.b.*) figure, *less* [adjusted imports (*f.o.b.*) minus U.S. military aircraft delivery *plus* payments for U.S. military aircraft]

or more simply,

Visible balance = exports (*f.o.b.*), fully adjusted, *less* imports (*f.o.b.*), fully adjusted.

With effect from January 1971, the monthly press release and the subsequent *Trade & Industry* article, when dealing with trends of trade as a whole, has quoted only the fully adjusted figures and the visible balance. This has gone some way to reducing the confusion that previously existed over the two 'balances' and makes it easier for the layman to reconcile either of these balances with the difference between the quoted values of declared exports and imports.

The analyses of trade by area and by commodity continue to be in terms of declared values because of the impracticability of making the necessary adjustments to all the detailed categories.

THE BALANCE OF PAYMENTS

As they stand, the overseas trade statistics cannot supply us with a record on a consistent basis of all transactions between residents of the United Kingdom (including the Government) and overseas residents. Some of the reasons why this is so have been indicated in the previous section. Even more important however, is the fact that the overseas trade accounts include reference to physical goods only. They make no allowance for the value of services provided by residents of this country to overseas residents nor vice versa. Moreover no references is made in the trade accounts to investment income nor to gifts moving across our borders. These invisible items (see page 211) are as important in determining whether or not this country is paying its way as are transactions involving physical trade. It is the overall effect of all these transactions and their interrelationships, together with the flows of investment capital, which is significant from the point of view of our economy, and the balance of payments accounts which provide this information are amongst the most important statistical data produced in this country.

From 1923 to 1938 the Board of Trade published balance of payments figures based on the trade accounts, with the addition of some (incomplete) information on invisible items and monetary transactions. An adjustment was made to the import figures, intended to convert the figures from a *c.i.f.* to an *f.o.b.* basis. In 1939 the introduction of exchange control provided a new and more efficient basis on which the balance of payments accounts, a record of all external transactions as mentioned above, could be constructed. From the end of the Second World War, the Bank of England, largely using the exchange control records, but also by reference to the trade accounts and ancillary sources, compiled balance of payments accounts, which from 1948 to 1963 were published half-yearly in April and October.

These accounts, because they arose from the applications which importers made for foreign currency and the returns which exporters were required to make of their overseas earnings, were constructed on a 'cash payments' basis rather than on a 'shipment of goods' basis. This arrangement, although convenient when a tight exchange control was in existence, proved less satisfactory when restrictions were relaxed, and by the late 1950s it became necessary to consider the use of other sources of information if satisfactory balance of payments accounts were to be produced. Additionally it was felt desirable to move more completely from a 'cash payments' basis to a 'change of ownership' basis, so that as far as possible the timing of the entries in the accounts relate to the dates on which ownership of the imports and exports is deemed to change. This conforms with the payable-receivable basis used generally in the national income accounts.

In 1960, during the period in which the new inquiries were being developed to fill the gap left by the reduction in exchange control coverage, the responsibility for preparing the balance of payments accounts was transferred to the Central Statistical Office. Already in 1958 quarterly balance of payment figures were being issued to the Press by the Treasury. In March 1959 the *United Kingdom Balance of Payments 1946–1957*, giving comprehensive and detailed tabulations of the accounts under the newly revised system, was issued. This was the precursor of a change in the method of publication. In place of the half-yearly *White Papers* and the quarterly press notices, we have had since 1963 an *Annual Pink Book*, running up to some ninety or so pages of notes and tables, giving comparable figures over a period of years, together with much improved quarterly figures in *Economic Trends*, and with a single *White Paper* just before the Budget relating to both the balance of payments and the national income.

The quarterly figures published in *Economic Trends* include seasonally adjusted estimates. In as much as a great deal of publicity is currently given to balance of payments figures in view of their implications for the stability of the economy, it is highly desirable that the markedly seasonal nature of the data should not give rise in the public mind to unduly pessimistic or optimistic interpretations. Seasonal adjustment helps to avoid this. An article on these seasonal adjustments appeared in the January 1968 issue of *Economic Trends*. Furthermore although it has not yet proved possible to produce monthly overall balance of payments figures, seasonally adjusted figures of the visible trade figures on a balance of payments basis, together with a rather crude estimate of the invisible balance, have been issued monthly for some time by the Board of Trade and, latterly, by the Department of Trade and Industry.

THE GENERAL BALANCE OF PAYMENTS

From 1965 until the issue of the 1970 *Pink Book* the General Balance of Payments Account (Table 9.1) was divided into three sections; the current account, the long-term capital account, and the monetary movements account. Very superficially, the current account shows the relationship between our current earnings and expenditure, and the long-term capital account the balance of our borrowing and lending on a long-term basis. Thus to take one example, if the United Kingdom has a deficit on the current account, this means that as a country we are spending more on goods and services and interest payments than we are earning.

If this deficit is offset by our borrowing on *long term* the situation is satisfactory because we are not suffering the risk of running down

TABLE 9.1

U.K. balance of payments (1968)

	(£ million)
CURRENT ACCOUNT	
Exports and re-exports (f.o.b.) (1)	6,103
Imports (f.o.b.) (2)	6,801
Visible trade balance (1) (2)	−698
Net under-recording of exports	+130
Payments for U.S. military aircraft	−109
Visible balance	−677
Invisibles	
Government services and transfers (net)	−462
Other invisibles	
Private (3) services and transfers (net)	+455
Interest, profits and dividends (net)	
Private sector	+654
Public sector	−235
Invisible balance	+412
Current balance	**−265**
LONG-TERM CAPITAL ACCOUNT (4)	
Inter-government loans (net)	− 6
Other U.K. official long-term capital (net)	+ 27
Private investment	
Abroad	−736
In the United Kingdom	+573
Balance of long-term capital	**−142**
Balance of current and long-term capital transactions	**−407**
BALANCING ITEM	−130
MONETARY MOVEMENTS (4)	
E.E.A. loss on forwards	−251
Miscellaneous capital (net)	− 24
Change in liabilities in non-sterling currencies (net)	+ 53
Change in liabilities in overseas sterling area currencies (net)	− 46
Change in external liabilities in sterling (net)	+166
Change in account with I.M.F.	+525
Change in gold and convertible currency reserves	+114
Balance of monetary movements	**+537**

(1) Excluding allowance for net under-recording of exports.
(2) Excluding deliveries of U.S. military aircraft and missiles.
(3) Including public corporations.
(4) Assets: increase −/decrease +. Liabilities: increase +/decrease −.

Source: *U.K. Balance of Payments* 1969

our monetary assets (e.g. gold and convertible currency reserves). If, however our net long-term borrowing does not offset the current account deficit there will be a deficit on the combined current and long-term accounts (sometimes called the basic balance) which must give rise to adverse monetary movements. The latter essentially means that we must either increase our short-term debt, with the risk that our creditors may demand payment at any time, or transfer gold or other currencies from our reserves to the creditor countries. Thus in very general terms the monetary movements account may be said to represent the changes in our gold reserves or short-term assets and liabilities resulting from current and long-term capital transactions.

The current account includes the visible balance i.e. the difference between the value of our imports and exports of goods—both *f.o.b.* as mentioned earlier. The invisible balance includes all receipts and payments for services such as insurance, transport, banking and travel. It includes also dividends, interest and profit accruing to the United Kingdom from overseas and similar items payable by United Kingdom residents (including the government) to persons overseas. Military expenditure overseas, grants to under-developed countries, and royalties due to or payable by United Kingdom residents also enter into the 'invisibles' account and are obviously just as relevant a part of the current account as are the physical or visible items of trade.

The increasing attention paid to the analysis of invisible transactions was reflected in the introduction of periodical articles in the Board of Trade *Journal* dealing with trends in invisible transactions, the first of which appeared on 17 September 1969. A recent article dealing with the revision of some of the sources and methods of classification of our invisible earning appeared in *Statistical News 3, Invisible earnings and payments,* (J.W.S. Walton) (C.S.O.).

The sum of the visible and invisible balances form the balance of payments on current account.

The long-term capital account basically includes government and private long-term borrowing or lending overseas.

The balance of current and long-term capital transactions, or basic balance *should* be exactly offset by the necessary changes in the monetary movements account. A glance at the table will see that this was not so in 1968, and indeed it has never been the case. There has and always been an unexplained difference which is referred to as the balancing item.

The amount of this item can vary astonishingly. In the 1968 *Pink Book* the figure for 1967 was +£176m, and for 1964 it was −£13m. The existence of this balancing item is one indication of the imperfection in the data as a whole. In the first place, as the information to make up the current account comes from so many sources there are very great problems in obtaining complete and consistent coverage, and indeed in ensuring that the timing of each component of the accounts is reconcilable. It is true that the Board of Trade's special inquiries into capital movements and the introduction of regular investigations into export and import trade credit removed some sources of error, but there are still many gaps in the coverage of the invisible items. Recent inquiries aimed at improving coverage of services include the international passenger survey (estimates of expenditure on travel), and an inquiry into payments and receipts of royalties.

The balance of monetary movements must, allowing for the unknown balancing item, just offset the combined current and long-term capital balances. A positive sign for the monetary movement balance reflects an adverse change in the overall position of the United Kingdom, as might be expected as this must offset any deficit in the current and long-term accounts which is shown as a negative. Whether we should place more emphasis, from the point of view of measuring the performance of the economy, on the balance of monetary movements than on the current plus capital balance is a debatable point.

In the Balance of Payments *Pink Book* 1968 we had for the year 1967:

	£ million
1. Combining current and long-term capital balance	−490
2. Balancing item	+175
3. Monetary movements	+315

If the balancing item consisted largely of under-recording of invisible earnings, then the current and capital deficit was really much less than was shown and the monetary movement of £315m was a better measure of our performance than was the former. Where the balancing item consists mainly of unrecorded short-term lending it really ought to form part of (3), implying that the combined capital and current balance is realistic. On the whole it is fair to say that where the balancing item is large and positive, the combined current and capital balance almost certainly gives too pessimistic a view of the country's position.

Finally we should add that, as with most official statistical data dealing with large aggregates, extensive revision often occurs over the years as more accurate data comes to light, and hence it is, perhaps, only after some years have passed that a proper interpretation of the figures can be made. This is, in fact, examplified by the figures for 1967 as published in the 1969 and 1970 *Pink Books* when as a result of extensive revisions we have:

	From 1969 £million	From 1970 £million
Combined current and long-term capital balance	−417	−451
Balancing item	+176	+201
Monetary movements	+241	+250

Special efforts have indeed been made since 1969 to allow for what appears to have been a slight but regular under-recording of exports over the years. An article in the *Board of Trade Journal* of 10 September 1969 dealt with this topic, revealing inter-alia that in the previous year exports appeared to have been underestimated by about 2%.

THE BASIC BALANCE

The idea of using the basic balance as an indicator of the stability of our balance of payments situation has been increasingly questioned in recent years. The problem is that the distinction between long-term capital movements as included in the basic balance and other flows of funds cannot be made in a clear cut way. Conventionally the movements included in the traditional long-term capital category have been those which refer to the purchase or sale of assets with an original maturity of more than one year, or which take place across the United Kingdom boundary between associates or subsidiaries and their parent companies.

With a few exceptions other capital movements have been classed as short-term. There are three main reasons why this distinction is not very satisfactory.

Short-term influences, i.e. alterations in interest rates, expectations of changes in exchange rates or of the future movement of share prices may lead to transactions of a volatile nature in long-term securities. Thus a decline in industrial activity leading to a fall in the stock market in one country may encourage funds to move into United Kingdom securities. These movements may be of a temporary nature but will be recorded as long-term for basic balance purposes.

Secondly, funds may be borrowed on long-term from overseas, being ultimately intended for long-term investment overseas. However, if the time is not ripe for long-term investment, the funds may be temporarily held on short-term deposit in London.

These transactions represent an addition to the long-term capital account (+), having a favourable influence on the basic balance whilst at the same time adding to the United Kingdom's short-term assets (−) (see Table 9.1). If next year these funds are used for their original intended purpose, they will be recorded as an outflow of long-term funds (−) adversely affecting the Basic balance. At the same time, there is a reduction in the short-term assets (+) as recorded under monetary movements. If however our attention is directed to the basic balance, the impression may be given that the United Kingdom is over-lending on long-term in the second year at the expense of short-term assets, when, in fact those assets would not have existed had we not borrowed on long-term a year earlier.

These and other related circumstances in which concentration on

TABLE 9.2

U.K. summary balance of payments (new presentation)

(£ million)

	1967	1968	1969
CURRENT ACCOUNT			
Visible Trade	−552	−643	−141
Invisibles	+240	+324	+557
Current balance	−312	−319	+416
CURRENCY FLOW AND OFFICIAL FINANCING			
Current balance	−312	−319	+416
Investment and other capital flows	−560[1]	−1,010[1]	+ 48
Balancing item	+201	− 81	+279
Total currency flow	−671	−1,410	+743
OFFICIAL FINANCING OFFSETTING TOTAL CURRENCY FLOW			
Official borrowing (drawn+) (repaid−)	+556	+1,296	−699
Official reserve changes (drawn on +) (additions to −)	+115	+114	− 44

1 Includes losses on the Exchange Equalization Account arising out of devaluation.

Source: *Economic Trends*, September 1970

the basic balance may mislead are dealt with more fully in the 1970 *Pink Book.*

A third difficulty is that nowadays export and import credits may stretch over a period of years; they are coming more and more into the category of long-term loans. Such credits, nevertheless, are not normally included in the long-term capital account.

NEW FORM OF ACCOUNT

For the reasons dealt with above the importance attached to the basic balance has been very much reduced.

Commencing with the 1970 *Balance of Payments Pink Book* and the September 1970 issue of *Economic Trends* the form of the main balance of payment accounts has been altered so as to emphasize three figures of particular importance (Table 9.2).

The current balance of payments. This measures the degree to which the nation has added to or reduced its external assets.

The total currency flow. This gives the current balance together with investment and other capital flows (i.e. official long-term capital transactions, private investment, trade credit, changes in short-term balances held by other countries in London). It shows the net effect on the nations reserves of *all* external transactions which give rise to *official financing* movements.

Official financing. This covers those movements of funds necessary to bring the balance of payments into balance i.e. changes in our official reserves, net borrowing from the International Monetary Fund, net official borrowing from overseas monetary authorities. Whilst figures of the basic balance continue to be given in a separate table, the use of the total currency flow recognizes the fact that the distinction between 'long-term capital account' and 'monetary movements' is no longer significant, and that to concentrate attention on these aggregates can be misleading.

The amount of the total currency flow is known exactly, but it can only be interpreted properly by reference to the transactions contributing to it. Short-term influences (e.g. flows of 'hot money' moving in response to interest rate changes or anticipated devaluation or revaluation of a currency) may have a major effect on the total currency flow, and obviously such relatively ephemeral movements may have a different implication than long-term investment transactions, or payments for goods and services. We know the total currency flow at the end of any period, whilst the details of the transactions giving rise to it are published quarterly, two months after the end of the quarter to which they relate.

It must not be forgotten, however, that the values of the component items in the total currency flow are estimates, and subject to error. The current balance is itself also an estimate, although it is not affected by short-term influences such as the movement of funds referred to above. Over continuing periods of time the current balance is a reliable indicator of the extent to which the nation is paying its way. The same cannot always be said of each individual quarterly current balance. Strikes here or abroad affecting the production or movement of goods across our frontiers can cause 'bunching' of transactions from one quarter to another, thus giving rise to current balance estimates which are misleading in the short run. The dock strike of 1970 and its aftermath is a case in point. Other short-term disturbing influences on the current balance of payment may be sudden fluctuation in ship charter rates, the timing of government aid expenditure or temporary restrictions on certain types of expenditure.

The monthly figures of the visible balance, even when seasonally adjusted, are affected to an even greater extent by such disturbances. Moreover, the monthly figures for invisible earnings cannot without a disproportionate expenditure of time and effort be obtained at all accurately. Currently they are obtained by smoothing quarterly data, which themselves may be subject to significant errors of estimation. In no sense can they be said to provide a forecast of invisible earnings in the current period. Thus, monthly estimates of the current balance of payments obtained by adding the visible and invisible balances can be very misleading. Whilst the monthly articles in *Trade & Industry* quote the two estimates separately, it is tempting to add them together, but it is doubtful, in view of what has been said, if any real service is performed by the publication of the total.

There is an interesting discussion of some of the points raised in this chapter, and on the question of the margin of error in the balance of payments current account, in an article in *Statistical News 11, Towards a better understanding of the Balance of Payments Figures,* by J. Hibbert, and in the 1970 issue of the *Balance of Payments Pink Book.*

THE CONTENTS OF THE PUBLICATIONS

The *Annual Pink Book,* in addition to containing a summary or general balance of payments account, (illustrated and explained earlier) also contains detailed tables showing how each of the components of the general table is arrived at. Thus there are detailed tables for visible trade, analysed by commodity and by area, and an account showing the make-up of the invisible items; government overseas current expenditure, travel, interest, profit and dividends, direct investment earnings and investment overseas by area and by type, overseas investment in the United Kingdom public sector, assets and liabilities of the United Kingdom, investment and capital flows overseas, United Kingdom external assets and liabilities, aid and private investment in developing countries, trade credits extended and received, analyses of direct investment abroad, overseas earnings of United Kingdom financial institutions, and several others.

A reconciliation of the visible trade figures as given in the trade and navigation accounts, and the balance of payments visible trade figures is given annually in the *Pink Book* in a table entitled *Visible Trade in the Balance of Payments.* In addition to the tables, the *Pink Book* contains detailed notes and definitions of the categories used in the accounts, as well as a set of references to related publications.

Economic Trends gives quarterly figures of the main components of the United Kingdom balance of payments one quarter in arrears in the March, June, September and December issues. Separate articles and tabulations appear in the same issues, but in arrears by two quarters, for the balance of payments of the overseas sterling area. Annual figures for upward of six years with quarterly values for three or more years are provided in most cases. The figures for the latter are of no less importance to the United Kingdom than its own balance of payments because, as the name implies, the Sterling Area countries hold their reserves largely in sterling.

QUESTIONS

1. Discuss the adequacy of the returns of United Kingdom imports and exports classified by countries as a means of assessing the trading relations between the United Kingdom and the rest of the world.
2. What do you understand by the *current balance of payments*? How is it arrived at? How far does this give an indication of the extent to which the United Kingdom is paying its way in the world?
3. Comment on the extent to which published data on overseas trade and on the balance of payments are adequate for assessing the external economic position of the United Kingdom.
4. 'Unfortunately the true current balance of payments position has never yet been accurately estimated by any country.' Discuss the truth or otherwise of this statement, in relation to the United Kingdom.
5. The frequent changes which it is necessary to make to balance of payments estimates for any given period in the past makes them most unreliable as a guide to current policy. Discuss this statement and its implications.
6. Discuss the nature of the *balancing item* in the *United Kingdom Balance of Payments Pink Book*, and comment on its relevance to the assessment of our international capital position.
7. Discuss the difference in coverage of the figures in the *Balance of Payments Pink Book* and in the statistics of overseas trade.
8. Briefly outline the structure of the official tables summarizing the balance of payments on current and capital account. Also define the main components.
9. 'Dock strikes and postal strikes have an entirely spurious influence on our balance of overseas trade.' How far do you consider this comment to be justified?
10. The overseas trade statistics include information on all merchandise trade passing across the United Kingdom frontiers, with certain exceptions. What are these exceptions, and why do they arise?
11. Discuss the various conceptual systems used for classifying trade by country. Which system is used by the United Kingdom, and why?
12. Comment on the methods of valuation employed by the

Customs Authorities for United Kingdom imports and exports.

13. 'The figures for our exports and imports published monthly do not in fact relate to exactly the same time period.' Comment on this statement and indicate some of the problems to which this may give rise.
14. Why is it considered dangerous to rely on overseas trades figures covering only limited periods of time as indicators of the progress of the economy in the international field?
15. Distinguish between the visible balance and the visible trade balance in our overseas trade figures. How is the visible balance arrived at?
16. What adjustments have to be made to the figures of declared imports and exports to put them on a comparable basis?
17. In January 1971, the form of presentation of the visible trade figures in the journal *Trade and Industry* was altered. What were these changes, and why were they made?
18. Discuss the use of the 'basic balance' as an indicator of the United Kingdom's international financial situation.
19. Recently, emphasis in the balance of payments accounts has been transferred from the 'balance of monetary movements' to the 'total currency flow'. Suggest reasons for this development, indicating quite clearly in your answer what you understand by the two terms mentioned above.
20. Each month, in addition to giving the figures of imports and exports, and the visible balance, an estimate of invisible transactions is also given in *Trade and Industry*. How is this estimate of invisible transactions obtained, and how accurate do you consider it to be? Why is no figure for the current balance of payments published at the same time?
21. To what extent do you consider the published data on trade and on the balance of payments adequate for assessing the external economic position of the United Kingdom?

10 The family expenditure survey

As we remark in the section dealing with the index of retail prices (page 225), large-scale official inquiries into household expenditure were carried out by the Ministry of Labour in 1937–38 and 1953–54. These were primarily aimed at establishing a weighting system for the retail price index. The smaller-scale continuous inquiry called the family expenditure survey was introduced in 1957, and from the beginning was planned not only to provide up-to-date weighting for the retail price index, but also for a variety of other purposes. Indeed it can be said that this survey provides a unique fund of economic and social data essential for planning purposes.

The survey has been conducted since 1957 by the Government Social Survey, now incorporated in the office of Population Censuses and Surveys. Currently it is used to assist the Central Statistical Office in providing estimates of consumer expenditure for the national income and expenditure statistics, to provide data on the re-distribution of income, on the incidence of taxation and on the relationship between income and expenditure for various types of households. It is the only source of information on earnings for the economy as a whole. It provides information on holiday expenditure for the Department of Trade & Industry, on housing expenditure for the Ministry of the Environment, and so on.

Originally, a sample of 5,000 households a year was aproached. From 1967, the sample has been increased to some 10,000. Rather less than three-quarters of households co-operate. The purposes of the increased coverage are to provide more precise information, particularly about income and expenditure patterns, and also to permit of an extension of the scope of the survey. It is proposed that ultimately about 20,000 households will be included annually, divided into two groups one of which is involved in the conventional survey. The other group of about 10,000 will be approached on a series of special topics, changing from year to year, as well as being asked some basic questions in common with those addressed to the first group.

Though the analysis of the data is the responsibility of the Department of Employment, the Government Social Survey* is responsible for conducting the survey. A three-stage stratified random sample, with probability proportional to size, covering the whole of Great Britain is used. Prior to 1967, the Northern Ireland family expenditure survey was really an integral part of the survey for the whole United Kingdom. From 1967 onwards, the sample of households in Northern Ireland has been increased from 130 to 900, and the results, besides being incorporated with the Great Britain figures, are likely to be published separately. Private households only are covered—a household being defined as including all those who normally live at the same address and who are catered for by the same person. The survey is spread evenly throughout the year. Each person of the age of sixteen or over in a co-operating household (under sixteen, if working) keeps a record of expenditure over two seven-day periods.

In addition to expenditure records kept by the respondents, three questionnaires completed by the interviewers are used. One questionnaire calls for general information on each member of the household—age, sex, marital status occupation and so on. It also asks for information on certain items of regular expenditure e.g. gas, electricity and telephone charges, and also on any receipts in kind or of a concessionary nature. This questionnaire is completed with the co-operation of the head of household or the housewife.

Questionnaire number two is completed, one for each individual member of the household, and deals with income, employment, status, occupation and industry. The third questionnaire deals with expenditure recurring at fairly long intervals of time e.g. licences for T.V., car etc., season tickets, hire-purchase commitments, insurance and education payments.

On the successful conclusion of the survey for a particular household, each member is paid £1 for his trouble. The various documents are checked, edited and coded by Social Survey officials and are then passed, with all means of personal identification removed, to the Department of Employment for tabulation and analysis. An article on the expansion of the family expenditure survey appeared in the *Employment & Productivity Gazette* in January 1967.

The reports are published annually about nine months after the close of the calendar year to which they relate. Some preliminary

* Now incorporated in the office of Population Censuses and Surveys.

information is published in the *Department of Employment Gazette* in January and in June, each covering a twelve-month period terminating six months earlier.

The sampling design of the 1967 and subsequent family expenditure surveys was explained in an article by W. T. F. Kemsley in *Statistical News* 1. A simplified outline is given below.

The sampling frame consists of 1,800 areas comprising London Boroughs, municipal boroughs, urban and rural districts in England and Wales, the four Scottish cities and large burghs, the small burghs and landward areas in Scotland.

> The frame is stratified as follows:
> Fifteen standard regions and sub-regions
> Four types of area—provincial conurbations, other urban areas, semi-rural, and rural areas, and
> by economic criteria usually related to rateable value.

This eventually gives 168 strata of roughly equal size.

The selection of areas from the sampling frame is with probability proportional to size, one area being chosen from each stratum.

Each selected primary sampling unit (i.e. each area) is divided into wards or groups of parishes, and four such secondary units are selected by systematic sampling at intervals with a random start. In each selected ward or parish group, a similar procedure is adopted to selected sixteen addresses from the register of electors.

There are now four sets of sixteen addresses for each of the 168 primary sampling unit areas. In each period of three months the sixteen addresses from one of the wards is used, so that over a year each primary area will be included four times, with sixteen different households each quarter. The sample is a rotating one, so that after the first three months, forty-two of the selected areas drop out to be replaced by new areas, selected one each from the strata from which the dropped areas came. This means that ultimately each area stays in the sample for four quarters, but that at any given time the sample will include 42 'new' and 126 'old' areas.

Each quarter, $16 \times 168 = 2{,}688$ addresses are included, and to further space the sampling, interviews are conducted at a third of them each month during the quarter.

Many other points taken into account when selecting the sample are explained in the article referred to earlier, and in the references contained therein.

A handbook on the sampling fieldwork, editing and coding procedures involved in the survey, by W. T. F. Kemsley, was published in 1969 (*Family Expenditure Survey—Handbook on Sample, Field-work and Coding Procedures—H.M.S.O.).* This book is very comprehensive, and in addition to its obvious value for students of the survey itself provides a very useful object lesson on procedures for all concerned with large-scale sample surveys of human populations.

THE FAMILY EXPENDITURE SURVEY REPORTS

The reports published annually commence with a general description of the survey. There follows the main statistical tables which currently (1970 *Report*) give for various weekly income groups:

Average number of persons per household in various age categories,
Sources of the income and the average amount of each source,
Type of housing accommodation,
Average weekly household expenditure, on some 100 categories of goods.

Further tables are given for the categories referred to above, but relating to households of particular composition. For example, the foregoing analyses are shown separately for households containing one adult only; one man and one woman; one man, one woman and one child, and so on.

The income and expenditure of households by type of administrative area (Greater London, provincial conurbation, other urban areas, and rural areas) are also given, once again analysed separately by households of varying composition.

Additional tables analysing income and expenditure by occupation of the head of the household (in three categories) and by age of head of household are also given.

There are also summary tables, cross-classifying number of households by:

Classes of weekly income — administrative area
" " " — tenure of dwelling
" " " — size of household
" " " — composition of household
" " " — number of workers in household

Classes of weekly income — number of children of working married women

" " " — income of head of household

" " " — occupation of head of household

" " " — age of head of household

Distributions of weekly earnings in various orders of the standard industrial classification for all male employees, for manual employees, for all women employees, for women manual employees and for full-time and certain part-time employees in selected occupations are given.

There is also a regional supplement which breaks down much of the income data previously mentioned on a regional basis.

A set of appendixes, listing the standard errors to which the data are subject, and including detailed definitions of the categories employed in the report, is also provided.

Questions on Chapter 10 will be found with those on Chapter 11, on page 240.

11 The index of retail prices

Since 1914 information about retail prices has been collected continuously. The 'Cost of Living Index' was based on 1914 = 100, and its weights were based on the consumption pattern of a sample of 1,944 working-class households in 1904.

The original aim of the index was to enable a check to be made on the living standards of the poor, and over the years it had become progressively inappropriate for this or, indeed, any other purpose. In 1937–38 an 'inquiry' into the spending habits of over 10,000 working-class households were carried out, and these results were to provide the weights for a more up-to-date and realistic index of retail prices. The Second World War, however intervened, and it was not until 1947 that the new index—'Interim Index of Retail Prices' based on 17 June 1947—was introduced. The weights were already out of date, but in view of the continuance of rationing and shortages of various products it was not thought desirable immediately to conduct a new survey. The need for revision just as soon as a normal peacetime situation returned was, however recognized by designating the new 1947 Index an interim index.

The Cost of Living Advisory Committee appointed in 1946 recommended in 1951 that the time was ripe for a new inquiry into household expenditure; in the meantime, they said that the interim index should be modified so as to bring its weighting more up-to-date. This revised index was now rebased on January 1952, and plans were made to start a comprehensive survey at the end of January 1953 to provide information for the weighting of the new index.

THE 1953 INQUIRY

This inquiry was conducted by the Ministry of Labour and National Service.

A multi-stage stratified random sample of 20,000 addresses was drawn from local rating records, to be representative of all types of households in the United Kingdom.

Interviewing began in January 1953, and the survey continued over the ensuing twelve months, different households being visited at different periods. Thirteen thousand households co-operated fully by supplying detailed records of their expenditure over three consecutive weeks, plus other information. The information had been analysed sufficiently for assessment during the latter half of 1955.

Much discussion on the purposes and value of indices purporting to measure the cost of living had been engendered in the post-war years. It had been widely thought, for example, that

An index of the existing type could not be considered a true measure of the cost of living as many categories of expenditure—notably income taxes, insurance premiums, medical and dental fees, betting payments, club and union subscriptions—were not included. Moreover the existence of rent controls for example may keep down the contribution of certain rents to any overall price change, but they do not measure the effect on the cost of living for those who have to live outside the controlled sector.
The foregoing led many to the conclusion that no single index could adequately measure the retail price changes for all classes of persons, and that separate indices for significantly different economic groups are necessary.

Whilst at the the time there was no indication that these suggestions would be put into practice the Cost of Living Advisory Committee did take a step in the right direction when in 1955 it recommended that certain of the budgets collected should be omitted from those to be used for weighting, so as to allow the index to refer to a more homogeneous group than would otherwise have been the case.

SELECTION OF BUDGETS TO BE USED FOR WEIGHTING

The classes of households whose expenditure pattern was used are given below. Two limits were finally selected.

UPPER LIMIT

The Committee believed that the pattern of household spending in the higher income groups is likely to be determined more by the income of the head of the household than by its total income.

'If the object is to exclude households whose expenditure pattern differs substantially from that of the bulk of households we believe that at the upper income level this object is more likely to be achieved by excluding households by reference to the income of the head, rather than to the total income of the household.' *Report on Proposals for a New Index of Retail Prices*—March 1956.

Of the 12,911 households providing useable budgets it was found that 58 households had heads with gross income of £50 per week or more, 11 with heads having £30 but under £50 and 291 where it was £20 but under £30. i.e. 460 households out of the 12,911 ($3\frac{1}{2}$%) were in the 'head of household £20 and upwards' group.

It was believed that response from households in this class was somewhat less than for the lower income groups. If included in the scheme they might therefore be somewhat unrepresentative as a class.

The most important point, however, was that these 460 households had a consumption pattern different from that of the bulk of households of the same size, and hence they were excluded from the weighting scheme.

LOWER LIMIT

Of the total of 12,911 households, 1,843 (or about 14%) were households where the head had less than £3 per week. Of these only 747 were households where the total income was less than £3 per week. In many cases it was discovered that the income of the person classed as the head was only a small part of the total income of the households. *It was therefore decided that at the lower end of the scale the income of the head of the household was unlikely to determine the spending pattern of the household.* A proposal that the lower line of demarcation should be the aggregate income of the household was considered, but rejected.

It was ultimately decided that income should not be the sole criterion at lower end of scale, but that the line of demarcation should be set so as to exclude those whose chief source of income was a national insurance retirement or similar pension.

It was found that there were 813 households in which at least three-quarters of the total income came from National Assistance, National Insurance, or similar sources. These households contained 1,216 persons (only ten of whom were working for gain.) Nearly

60% of the households contained only one person. The budgets of these households were excluded from those used for weighting.

NUMBER OF BUDGETS USED

The excluded groups comprised about 10% of households considered, and left a group of 11,638 households to supply budgets for the weighting.

DEFICIENCIES IN THE SURVEY

One major deficiency in the accuracy of the information supplied by the survey was observed—the amounts given as spent on alcohol and tobacco. Comparison of the results with estimates based on Customs and Excise figures showed that there had been a substantial under-recording of this type of expenditure and that the figures in question were unacceptable. Adjustments were made to take account of this. There was also some under-recording of expenditure on meals consumed outside the home, and on sweets and chocolates, ice cream and soft drinks. For all other categories the budget figures were well in accord with data obtained from other sources.

Households were asked to supply some information about their incomes in addition to keeping full records of their expenditure. Of the co-operating households 96% agreed to supply information about income (in income ranges only) but it is clear that in many cases there was considerable understatement. Nevertheless the information supplied was sufficient to enable the households to be adequately grouped in order of magnitude of their incomes.

TYPES OF EXPENDITURE INCLUDED AND EXCLUDED FROM WEIGHTING

Suggestions that the index of retail prices should take account only of basic necessities (e.g. by exclusion of alcoholic drink, tobacco, entertainments, books, etc.) were rejected, and the index aims to measure price changes over the whole range of goods and services over which households distribute their income except:

income tax
national insurance contributions
life insurance premiums and payments to pension funds

premiums for household insurance, other than insurance of buildings

subscriptions to trade unions, friendly societies, hospital funds, etc.

church collections, other cash gifts

pool and other betting payments

doctors and dentists fees, etc.

capital sums or instalment, mortgage payments, etc. for house purchase, and expenditure on major structural enlargements and additions.

With regard to housing, however, an attempt was made to include in the index a net rental equivalent of the dwelling house of an owner-occupier.

The weights finally calculated were based on the 1953–54 *consumption* pattern as revealed by the survey, but at January 1956 prices. The index was introduced in the March 1956 issue of the Ministry of Labour *Gazette* with 17 January 1956 as 100. The index may be expressed symbolically as

$$P_{56,c} = \frac{\Sigma p_c q_{53/54}}{\Sigma p_{Jan.\ 1956} q_{53/54}}$$

In this expression Σ means 'the sum of', p means prices, and q means quantities; the suffixes relate to the year or period of time with which we are concerned. The whole equation may be expressed in words as follows:

'The numerator is obtained by multiplying the price of each selected commodity in the current month by the quantity bought in 1953–54 and summing the products. This gives the cost of a given basket of goods at current prices. The denominator of the expression is obtained in a similar manner but this time using the prices for January 1956. The whole is a price index which compares the cost of a particular basket of goods in a given current period with its cost in January 1956.'

More detailed information on this index number is contained in the *Report on the Proposals for a New Index of Retail Prices* (March 1956) H.M.S.O.

A CONTINUING SURVEY

It had been realized for some time that with rapidly changing consumption patterns, weighting systems drawn from large-scale inquiries carried out several years prior to the commencement of a newly based index series were likely to be out of date before the index had actually started. An alternative method of approach was required and the information needed was fortuitously at hand. Since 1957, what was originally a small scale continuous inquiry called the family expenditure survey has been carried out (see Chapter 10). Until 1967, a sample of some 5,000 households were taken each year, and asked to keep detailed records of expenditure over a fortnight, and to supply certain other long-term information. In 1967, the survey was expanded to cover 10,000 households annually and since then this number has been increased to 20,000.

Throughout, about three-quarters of the sampled households have produced useable budgets. The data collected is comparable with that obtained in the full-scale surveys previously mentioned. By 1961, the results of the first three years of the family expenditure survey was published. The information, of course, is of considerable social importance, and of value to the Central Statistical Office for its national income and expenditure computations as well as in other fields. However, the use of the results of the family expenditure survey for re-weighting the index of retail prices was announced in the *Report on the Revision of the Index of Retail Prices* (Cmd 1657), published in February 1962. It recommended that the information from the family expenditure survey over a period of three consecutive years should form the basis of the new weighting system for the index. Each January, commencing with January 1962, the weighting pattern was to be changed, the weights being used based on the results of the family expenditure survey for three consecutive years up to the previous June.

The six-month gap is the time required to process the information. Even so, the continual updating of the weights each January has been a fundamental improvement, which has provided this country with probably the most efficient index of its type in the world. As is usual on such occasions, steps were taken during 1962 to overcome the difficulties of transition from one index base to another, and throughout that year indices using both 1962 and 1956 as base were published.

The index for any given month in a particular year is calculated in two stages. Firstly an index is calculated for a particular month using the *preceding* January as 100. This index for a particular commodity group, for say March 1971 can be symbolically given as:

$$P_{\text{Jan 71/Mar 71}} = \frac{\Sigma\left[p_{\text{Jan 71}}q_{68/70} \times \dfrac{p_{\text{Mar 71}}}{p_{\text{Jan 71}}}\right]}{\Sigma p_{\text{Jan 71}}\, q_{68/70}}$$

This is a simple fixed-weight index number, the weights being the cost of goods bought in the three-year weighting period, multiplied by prices in the base (January) month.

The next step is to link the index for March 1971 back to January 1962. This is done by multiplying the March 1971 index based on January 1971 by the index for January 1971 based on January 1962. The latter index is obtained by multiplying together a series of indices for each January, based on the preceding January—right back to January 1962.

The current index of retail prices is thus a chain-based index with weights changing annually. It is published monthly as eleven separate indices, one for each of the commodity groups in Table 11.1. These group indices are combined, by multiplying each by its weight, summing and dividing by the total of the weights, into a single 'all items' index called the 'general index of retail prices'.

TABLE 11.1

Index of retail prices—weighting

	Commodities	*Weighting for* 1962	*Weighting for* 1971
I	Food	319	250
II	Alcoholic drink	64	65
III	Tobacco	79	59
IV	Housing	102	119
V	Fuel and light	62	60
VI	Durable household goods	64	61
VII	Clothing and footwear	98	87
VIII	Transport and vehicles	92	136
IX	Miscellaneous goods	64	65
X	Services	56	54
XI	Meals bought and consumed outside the home	—	44
		1,000	1,000

The principles involved in the selection of budgets to be used for weighting continue to be the same as in the 1956 based index. Due however, to the rise in incomes, the upper limit which originally excluded households the head of which had a gross income of £20 per week in 1953, has been progressively raised so that in 1970 the exclusion level was £55 per week.

As in 1956, under-recording of certain types of expenditure (see page 228) continues and the weighting for these items is obtained from sources other than the family expenditure survey.

THE COMMODITIES AND THEIR PRICING

The index covers ten main commodity groups (*see* Table 11.1, page 231). The two weighting columns give some indications of changing consumption habits. Within each main group there are sub-groups bearing an appropriate proportion of the weight, and within each sub-group are allocated the actual items for which prices have to be regularly obtained. The following table relating to main group VIII illustrates:

TABLE 11.2

Transport and vehicles	*Items priced**
Purchase of motor vehicles	Specified models of second-hand cars Motor scooters
Maintenance of motor vehicles	Charge for specified maintenance jobs Car and motor cycle tyres Car battery
Petrol and oil	Petrol Engine oil
Motor licences	Annual licence for car Annual licence for motor-cycle
Motor insurance	Third party insurance for specified car and motorcycle

* The priced items are representative—not comprehensive. So long as their general movement reflects that of the commodities as a whole in that particular section all is well, and they are in fact chosen with this in mind.

PRICING

The collection of prices is dealt with fully in *Method of Construction and Calculation of the Index of Retail Prices.* (H.M.S.O. 1964). A brief outline only of the procedure is given below:

Food. Information is collected locally by Department of Employment and Productivity officials in a sample of some 200 areas, the areas being stratified by population. Where possible the price of each item is collected from five retailers—including a co-operative store, a multiple and a self service store. Prices of certain foodstuffs, particularly milk, fruit, potatoes and other vegetables are treated specially either because of the seasonal factors or, in the case of milk, because of price variations not shown up by normal retail outlets.

Alcoholic Drinks. Prices are obtained from a large sample of public houses involving a geographical coverage similar to the food inquiries. Because of variations in the strength of beer an adjustment is made, but it is not possible to make a complete allowance.

Tobacco. Prices are collected direct from manufacturers, and since the end of retail price maintenance locally on lines similar to the food inquiries.

Housing. Local authorities supply information on rent and rates. This is supplemented by sample inquiries from time to time of tenants of privately owned unfurnished accommodation. Repairs and similar costs are estimated largely from information supplied by local authorities.

Fuel and Light. Information on the prices of coal and coke is obtained from retailers in a manner similar to that used for food. The prices for gas and electricity are obtained from the appropriate area authorities, using a national level of consumption. Paraffin prices are collected by postal inquiry from retailers throughout the United Kingdom.

Durable household goods. The furniture, floor coverings and domestic appliances in this group tend to be purchased in the larger towns, and prices are obtained by personal visits to big stores in twenty-three large urban areas. An important part of the work here is the assessment of quality changes in the very varied group. Prices for drapery, hardware and ceramics are obtained by post from a very large fixed sample of retailers. The procedure adopted is similar to that for clothing and footwear mentioned below.

Clothing and Footwear. Several hundreds of retailers, classified into multiple store, department store, co-operative society and 'other' categories, supply information by post on a continuing basis. The items included are very broadly defined and each retailer is required to select and quote prices for a representative item or item within each definition. Regular personal visits are made by officials of the Department of Employment and Productivity Statistics Department to ensure that comparability from month to month can be maintained, and to ensure that proper allowance is made for changes in quality.

Transport and Vehicles. The prices of certain classes of used cars are considered to provide a better indication of price movements than those of new cars. In addition to second-hand car prices, prices of car accessories and fuel are obtained postally from manufacturers. Insurance companies supply information on car and motor cycle insurance costs. Public transport fares are also included in this section, being obtained from British Railways, the London Passenger Transport Board, and the Ministry of Transport and corresponding authorities in Northern Ireland.

Miscellaneous Goods. These include a very wide range of items from books to toilet preparations, toys to cameras, and detergents to suitcases. The methods of pricing employed vary from a postal approach to manufacturers or publishers (e.g. books, toys, toilet requisites), to retailers (soaps, detergents, suitcases and clocks).

Services. Much information is available centrally (postal and telephone charges) whilst the majority of the remainder—hairdressing, shoe repairing, laundry work is obtained from personal inquiries of firms in the 200 chosen areas referred to previously. A postal inquiry is made of representative dry cleaning firms.

PUBLICATION

Publication. The index is normally calculated in respect of prices on the Tuesday nearest the 15th of the month and the 'all items' index is itself issued during the third week of the following month, fuller figures with commentary appearing in the Department of Employment *Gazette* shortly thereafter.

RETAIL PRICE INDICES FOR SPECIAL SOCIAL GROUPS

Whilst the present index is by no means a complete 'Cost of Living' index it has a certain validity for a large proportion of the working population, and as such is frequently quoted in wage negotiations. It is however in no way suitable as a measure of such changes as they affect, for example, the older retired person, whose consumption pattern, as has been remarked, differs markedly from that of the general population. Moreover it is becoming more and more evident that there are marked regional differences in the prices of the items included in the retail price index.

A retail price index for the whole country may ill reflect regional price changes. As long ago as 1951 the Cost of Living Advisory Committee considered and rejected proposals for more than one index of retail prices. However, the matter was raised again in December 1966 in the report entitled *Government Statistical Services (4th Report)* (Estimates Committee of the House of Commons) which recommended that the Cost of Living Advisory Committee be asked to re-examine the desirability of publishing retail price indices for special social and income groups and by region. The Cost of Living Advisory Committee reported (Cmnd 3677) in June 1968. Its major recommendations, all of which are in process of implementation are summarized below.

(1) A study of the technical problems involved in providing regional retail price indices should be initiated as soon as possible.

The Committee pointed out that regional price indices could be of two distinct types:

(i) to show changes, over time, of prices in each region, and
(ii) to enable comparisons to be made between 'the cost of living' (or at least that part of the cost of living which a retail price index measures) in different regions at given points in time.

If the latter type of index were to be introduced several technical and social problems would arise. These would include,

(*a*) The choice of the pattern of consumption or 'basket of goods' on which the inter-regional comparisons should be based

(*b*) The problem of allowing for differences of quality between the goods and services consumed in the various regions (This is particularly important in the case of housing) (*c*) The problem of allowing for the cost of travelling to work, which varies considerably from region to region even where there is no difference in the price of transport in terms of pence per mile. (Associated with this is the imputed cost of time spent in travelling.)

(*d*) The choice of regions for which the inter-regional comparisons should be made, e.g. planning regions (or groups of planning regions) on the one hand, or conurbations, urban areas and rural areas on the other

(*e*) The margin of error which should be regarded as tolerable in inter-regional comparisons

(*f*) The frequency with which inter-regional comparisons should be made.

The Department of Employment has been charged with the task of examining the feasibility of providing such indices and will report back to the Cost of Living Advisory Committee in due course.

(2) Special indices of retail prices for one person and two person pensioner households should be published.

Indices for pensioner households were first published in June 1969 in the *Employment and Productivity Gazette*, and, for the time being will exclude housing costs, which are the subject of a special inquiry. The indices are constructed and published on lines parallel to those for main index, using of course weighting data available from the family expenditure survey, but excluded from the main index calculations. They are now published quarterly in August, November, February and May.

The weighting for the year 1969 for one person pensioner households and two person pensioner households compared with those for the general index of retail prices (the latter adjusted for the omission of the housing group) is given below. Food, fuel and light and services have much greater weight in the pensioner households budgets, whilst alcoholic drink, tobacco, transport and vehicles, and meals outside the home have lower weighting than in the general index.

The pensioner indices have been calculated back to 1962. Despite the marked difference between their weighting systems and those of the general index throughout this time, the change in the group indices in each case have been very similar, the

1968 index one person pensioner households being 124·5, two person pensioner households 124·6, and the general index (excluding housing) being 123·1.

After some experience with the new 'pensioner indices' further consideration is to be given to the practicability of compiling a special index for low income households with children.

TABLE 11.3

1971 weighting of the three retail price indices

	1-person pensioner	*2-person pensioner*	*General (excluding housing)*
Food	414	435	284
Alcoholic drink	19	35	74
Tobacco	32	69	67
Fuel and light	200	150	68
Durable household goods	45	45	69
Clothing and footwear	65	60	99
Transport and vehicles	32	47	154
Miscellaneous goods	83	79	74
Services	91	73	61
Meals bought and consumed outside home	19	7	50
Total all items	1,000	1,000	1,000

Source: *Department of Employment Gazette*, March and April 1971

(3) Meals bought and consumed outside the home should be included amongst the priced items to be used in the index of retail prices. They should be included in the index as a separate major group. (This recommendation has now been carried into effect).
(4) No change should be made in the current methods of treating the housing costs of owner-occupiers.
(5) That three sub-groups indices should in future be published for housing (rent, rates and water charges and maintenance repair charges) for gas and electricity separately and for medicines and total requisites and for soaps, polishes etc.
(6) That the name of the Committee should be changed to the Retail Prices Advisory Committee.

(This long-delayed but welcome change was made at once.)

RETAIL PRICE QUOTATIONS

A further recommendation of the Government Statistical Services report was that data on actual price quotations for individual commodities be published regularly. This latter recommendation was implemented in the March 1968 edition of the *Ministry of Labour Gazette*, average prices figures for eighty important items of food being published in respect of figures obtained for 200 areas of U.K. for November and December 1967 and January 1968. Since then, figures have been published monthly, two months in arrears. A typical extract is given in Table 11.4.

TABLE 11.4

Average retail prices
(per lb unless otherwise stated) of certain foods

Item	*Number of quotations 20 May 1969*	*Average price 20 May 1969*	*Price range within which 80% of quotations fell*
		d.	*d.*
BEEF: HOME-KILLED			
Chuck	851	71·7	66– 78
Sirloin (without bone)	860	96·6	84–108
Silverside (without bone)	909	91·2	84–102
Back ribs (with bone)	762	62·9	54– 72
Fore ribs (with bone)	793	61·7	54– 72
Brisket (with bone)	776	39·9	32– 48
Rump steak	906	121·8	100–144
BREAD			
White, 1¾ lb wrapped and sliced loaf	842	19·9	19–21
White, 1¾ lb unwrapped loaf	729	19·3	18½–20½
White, 14 oz. loaf	785	11·3	10 –12½
Brown, 14 oz. loaf	707	13·3	12½–14

Source: *Employment and Productivity Gazette*, July 1969

Each year, in March, standard errors for the January averages are published.

The new series provides a valuable adjunct to the retail price index, particularly in view of the estimates of the price ranges given.

CONSUMER PRICE INDEX

The index of retail prices covers only the prices of commodities with respect to a certain section of the population.

Indices of price changes for consumers as a whole are given in the *National Income Blue Book*, and can also be calculated from the quarterly estimates of personal expenditure in Economic Trends and the *Monthly Digest*. (The *Blue Book* publishes annual figures only.)

The current indices are based upon 1963. An all-items index is obtained by dividing the total expenditure in the current period at current prices by the total expenditure on all items in the current period at 1963 prices.

Symbolically we have

$$\text{Index based on 1963 for year 1971} = \frac{\Sigma p_{71}q_{71}}{\Sigma p_{63}q_{71}}$$

The resulting price indices are, in formal terms, current-weighted arithmetic averages.

They are therefore influenced by current changes in the pattern of consumption, but as well as this they reflect the 'average' experience of all consumers.

Thus the consumer price index may differ significantly from the index of retail prices.

For many years consumer price indices for individual commodity groupings were published, as in the case of the commodity headings of the index of retail prices. Nowadays however, only an 'all items' consumer price index is published.

At present the consumer price indices, based on 1963, are carried back to 1948. Previously the indices were carried back to 1946.

QUESTIONS (Chapters 10 and 11)

1. Trace the development of the Family Expenditure Survey since its introduction in 1957.
2. Outline the sampling procedure and the methods of collection employed in connection with the Family Expenditure Survey.
3. What is the purpose of conducting a regular Family Expenditure Survey and what information is obtained as a result of this survey?
4. Outline the difference between the Index of Retail Prices, and the price index used to measure changes in consumer-expenditure published in the *National Income and Expenditure Blue Book*.
5. Using the Index of Retail Prices as a model, explain the main problems arising in the construction of an index number of prices.
6. It has been suggested that an index of retail prices chained on an annual basis provides an accurate measurement of changes over short periods of time in the prices of goods and services which consumers are currently purchasing, as well as maintaining a suitable basis for long-term comparisons. To what extent do you agree with this statement?
7. To what extent do you consider the United Kingdom Index of Retail prices to be a measure of changes in the 'cost of living'?
8. Explain the problems involved in measuring changes in the cost of living, making reference in your answer to any price index number which you consider appropriate.
9. Discuss the developments of the indices of retail prices in this country since the beginning of the First World War.
10. Explain in some detail how the weighting system for the current index of retail prices is obtained, and comment on any limitations or deficiencies it might have.
11. Discuss the desirability of, and the problems involved in, producing retail price indices for special social groups.
12. Outline the recommendations of the Cost of Living Advisory Committee (published in June 1968). Indicate the problems involved in implementing these recommendations, and indicate to what extent the recommended changes have been made.
13. Discuss the conceptual and methodological problems involved in preparing an index of retail prices, and explain how these problems are tackled in this country.

12 Two indices of output

In the chapter on national income statistics it was mentioned that the gross domestic product at constant prices in terms of output data was measured by an index number. The base year for this index number is currently (in 1971) the census of production year, 1963. This 'total output' index number covers all the industries included in the 1968 Standard Industrial Classification. For many years prior to the introduction of a total output index, an index of industrial production, in the narrow sense, currently covering Orders II to XXI of the Standard Industrial Classification 1968, had been established. This index covers basically the census of production industries, and is of particular significance in relation to those industries—apart from agriculture, forestry and fishing—which are involved in the production of physical goods rather than services.

The problems associated with measuring the output of the service industries (e.g. transport, distribution, finance etc.) are very much greater. Moreover the data for the index of industrial production is available sufficiently frequently for the index to be published monthly. For the other industries it has only proved practicable to produce quarterly figures. Hence, the index of total output is currently available only quarterly.

Because of differences in the problems met in dealing with the data, it is convenient to deal separately with the index of industrial production, and with the additional information necessary to arrive at an index of total output. However, the general principles on which the total output index is based, and certain of the problems of measurement can conveniently be dealt with first of all.

GENERAL PRINCIPLES

In principle the index is a base-weighted (Laspeyre type) arithmetic mean of quantity relatives, i.e.

$$\frac{\Sigma\left(w_i \cdot \frac{q_{ci}}{q_{63_i}}\right)}{\underset{i}{\Sigma}(w_i)} \times 100$$

The (w_i) are proportional to the value of net output for each industry in the base year (1963).

Each q_c ideally is the net output of a given industry in the period (quarter, or year) to which the index relates and q_{63} is the net output of the corresponding industry in the base year. The ratio q_c/q_{63} for each industry is the proportionate change in output (*not* value) from the base year to the current period.

Two basic problems then are involved in constructing the index number.

1. We require to estimate the value of net output for each industry in fact for each 'minimum list heading' of the standard industrial classification) in the base year. These estimated net outputs provide the weighting system. Conventionally they are adjusted proportionately so that they sum to 1,000.
2. Measures of the physical net output for the base year and for the current period are required for each industry. It is only rarely that physical net output (or 'value added') for each industry, i.e. the value of total output less any goods or services acquired from outwith the industry, can be measured. In other cases some other measure called an 'indicator'—which is assumed to move more or less in line with net output—has to be used.

INDICATORS OF NET OUTPUT

Where no direct measure of net output is available—i.e. in all industries excepting agriculture—other series must be used as 'indicators' of net output.

The indicators used are changes in:

(1) GROSS OUTPUT

Provided the ratio of gross to net output remains constant, this is an accurate measure. However, if there is an increasing economy in the use of materials for a given output or if the given materials are subjected to more processing than hitherto, gross output will underestimate the true increase in net output.

(2) INPUTS

These are usually inputs of materials used or received, and are subject to the same type of limitations as are the gross output measures. Occasionally where all else fails, the input of labour (i.e. numbers employed) may be used but as employment takes no account of productivity changes this indicator is used as little as possible.

Gross output indicators, either actual quantities or values of output, can be determined fairly easily so far as physical goods are concerned. Nevertheless, if an industry makes a large number of products it is not practicable to cover each individual one with a separate output series, and what usually happens is that several commodities are lumped together, or the output of one or two are taken as representative of the others. This can lead to errors if the 'product mix' of the industry varies substantially from time to time. With values of course, division by a suitable price index is needed in order to eliminate the effect of general changes in prices, leaving a series representing changes in quantities which is what is required (but see page 246).

Where services rather than physical quantities are produced, measures indicating output are more difficult to find. The road haulage output indicator is the number of ton-miles for all road goods transport—a fairly direct indicator. For some other services, the indicators are more difficult to choose and almost certainly less directly linked to the immeasurable net output. Thus the output indicators for professional accountancy services are the number of Schedule D tax assessments and the number of tax assessments on companies; for legal services, a weighted average of kinds of cases tried and the numbers of grants of probate are used.

The main input indicator, materials used, is used where physical output cannot conveniently be measured. The main difficulty here is analogous to that referred to in respect of quantity indicators of gross output. Many materials may be used by an industry. It is impracticable to measure all of them, therefore one or two are selected as representative. If there is a change in the proportions of the various materials used this may not be indicated by the *selected* ones and hence the index may be distorted.

Employment data—usually weighted in some way by type of job —is used only where no other indicator is feasible. It is used in the case of some public services which, because they are not provided at market prices, have no satisfactory unit of output. Because the 'number employed' gives no measure of productivity changes, this indicator is not very sound.

The types of indicator and the extent to which they are used in the weighting of the total output index is given below.

Type of indicator	*Percentage of total weight*
Net output at constant prices	3
Output indicators	
quantity of output of goods	19
quantity indicators for services rendered	12
value of output of goods revalued at constant prices	19
value indicators for services rendered at constant prices	27
Input indicators	
quantity of material inputs	5
employment	15
	100

INDEX OF INDUSTRIAL PRODUCTION

The purpose of this index is to reflect changes in the volume of industrial production in the United Kingdom. Up to 1968 it covered Orders II to XVIII (Standard Industrial Classification). With the revision of the Standard Industrial Classification in 1968 it now covers Orders II to XXI. It *excludes* agriculture, forestry and fishing, trade, transport, finance and public and private services.

All production other than that excluded above is (theoretically) covered (e.g., new work and repairs, capital and consumption goods and goods for home consumption or export). In all, 'industrial production' as thus defined constitutes about 44% of the total gross national product.

Up to the end of 1952 there were two indices. One was weighted on the census of production figures for 1935 projected to 1946—

$$\text{i.e. 1935 figures} \times \frac{\begin{array}{c}\text{industry's}\\ \text{1946 total wage bill}\end{array}}{\begin{array}{c}\text{1935 total wage bill}\\ \text{(of particular industry)}\end{array}}$$

—and called the interim index (this was the official index published by the Central Statistical Office). The other index was produced by the now defunct London and Cambridge Economic Service. In both cases, 1946 = 100.

The census of production 1948 was used to provide a new weighting system, and a new index—the one considered—was drawn up. Since then the index has been rebased on 1954 and 1958, and the current index introduced in 1969 is based on 1963 using weights derived from the 1963 census of production. The aim of the rebasing which hitherto has taken place every five years is to ensure that the weighting system is kept up to date.

The index is in effect a Laspeyre (base-weighted) arithmetic mean of quantity relatives. (1963 = 100)

$$\text{i.e.} \quad \frac{\Sigma(p_{63}q_c)}{\Sigma(p_{68}q_{63})} \times 100 \qquad \text{or} \qquad \frac{\Sigma\left(p_{63}q_{63} \times \dfrac{q_c}{q_{63}}\right)}{\Sigma(p_{63}q_{63})} \times 100$$

THE WEIGHTING SYSTEM

It must be understood that the formula is purely symbolic. It must not be thought that a series of prices are multiplied by given quantities of output, but rather that the weights (p_{63} q_{63}) are (proportional to) the value of net output in 1963 as defined below (A, B and C), whilst q_c/q_{63} *represents* the ratio of net output* in a given month and goods to that of the base period for each industry.

(A) *Index net output* is the net output according to the census of production 1963, minus payments to other industries etc. for services e.g. advertising, research, outside repairs, postage, insurance, rates (ex water rates) etc. in so far as they can be identified.

(B) *A correction* is made to uplift the net output figures so as to take account of the *small establishments* (with twenty-five or fewer employees) for whom only a limited amount of data was collected at the census.

(C) *Figures* are *estimated* for certain trades omitted from the 1963 Census.

THE MEASURE OF OUTPUT

Net physical production (net output) represents the difference between output of products and input of materials and services from

* The ratio should be of net output but, as explained earlier (page 98), it is not practicable to obtain such data other than at the time of a full census.

other industries, taking into account changes in stocks and partly finished goods.

The above is only ideally obtainable, so the quantities in the ratio q_c/q_{63} for the index are measured in terms of gross output or some indicator of gross output, i.e.

(i) industries having 43·2% of the weighting are covered by quantities delivered or produced (i.e., output),
(ii) in industries carrying 43·3% of total weighting, the value of deliveries (or sales suitably deflated) is used. In this group comes construction, where products take a long time to make, and where an attempt is made to measure the value of work done each quarter supplemented by an employment indicator each month,
(iii) in cases carrying 11·2% of weights, the quantities of major materials received are used,
(iv) in about 2·3% (by weighting) of the industries, the number of persons employed is used.

Note (A). Value series are the only practicable way of measuring 'unique' output, as in much engineering and building, repair work, replacement work, etc. Changes in quality can best be indicated in this way too. The difficulty lies in eliminating the *effect of changes in prices* due to causes other than physical changes (which include quality changes) in the goods, and for this purpose the value series have to be deflated by a suitable price index. In recent years the index of wholesale prices has been used for this purpose. To some extent this index makes some allowance for changes in types of goods produced, and of quality but only to a limited extent.

A change in quality is merely a change in the *quantity* of services yielded by the commodity in question, and we therefore need to include quality changes in our measure of output. The aim should be to define commodities (and services) in such detail that changes in quality can be detected and allowed for, before any attempt is made to adjust to a constant price base. Thus care must be taken when deflating a value series only to eliminate those price changes which are not due to quality changes. Also where quality changes occur without an increase in price, there must be some means of bringing the additional 'output' into the gross domestic product calculations. Where new products as distinct from improved old ones are concerned, it is unfortunately often impossible to distinguish between an increase in quantity and an increase in price level.

Note (*B*). Input of materials should ideally refer to actual *consumption*; often it refers merely to receipts which are not such a reliable indicator.
Note (*C*). 'Employment' usually refers to numbers on pay rolls towards the end of the month, adjusted to allow for loss of production due to holidays. Even then, these numbers do not reflect changes in actual hours worked, nor in productivity.

THE PUBLISHED FIGURES

The index is published monthly by press release and in *Trade & Industry*, the *Monthly Digest* and *Economic Trends*, about six weeks after the end of the month to which it relates, along with revised figures for the previous month. Percentage changes for the most recent three months (seasonally adjusted) compared with the figures for the preceding three months (seasonally adjusted) are also given. These are intended to give a sounder indication of recent production trends than can the comparison of monthly figures. Sub-indices are given for each order of the Standard Industrial Classification, for manufacturing industries together, for various other sub-divisions and for 'all-industries'. Table 12.1 shows the type of information provided. The 'all-industries' index is obtained from the indices for the individual industries in a manner exactly analogous to that illustrated for the index of retail prices on page 231.

The manufacturing and 'all-industries' aggregates have been shown both in unadjusted and seasonally adjusted form since 1956.

The indices for the individual industries and other sub-groups were given in the unadjusted form only, until July 1962, when seasonally adjusted figures were introduced for these also. Although not adjusted for seasonal variation as such, correction factors are applied to all the 'unadjusted' series to eliminate the effect of variation in the length of calendar months, and the varying number of Sundays and Saturdays therein.

NOT ALL INDUSTRIAL PRODUCTION IS ACCOUNTED FOR

Ninety-four per cent of total production, represented by 892 individual series, is included. The reason for exclusion of some output is due chiefly to the fact that in many cases data for the output of the main products only are available. Where the coverage

TABLE 12.1

Index of industrial production
(average 1963 = 100)

Industrial group	*Weights*	*1970*	*September 1970* *Unadjusted*	*Adjusted*
Total, all industries	1,000	124	125·4	125·7
Mining and quarrying	56	78·1	76	80
Total, all manufacturing industries	749	127·1	131	129·3
Food, drink, tobacco ...	84	121·4	130	127
(Two sub indices of this group... are also given) ...				
Coal and petroleum production	7	151·1	149	155
Chemical and allied industries	64	158·5	162	163
Engineering and allied industries...	313	128·2	130	129
(Six sub group indices also) ...				
Metal manufacture ...	60	114·2	114	110
(Two sub group indices also) ...				
Textiles, leather clothing ...	88	116·7	121	118
(Three sub group indices also)...				
Bricks, pottery, glass etc. ...	29	124·7	130	132
(Two sub group indices also) ...				
Timber, furniture etc.	21	114·0	131	124
Paper, printing, publishing	59	120·5	121	124
Other manufacturing industries	25	146·4	158	153
Construction	127	115·0	118*	116·1*
Gas, electricity, water	68	143·8	116	141

* The construction indices are for the quarter July/September.

Source: *Monthly Digest of Statistics*, October 1970

appears to be high, it may be because in certain cases, output figures had to be estimated from the input of materials or labour.

SEASONAL ADJUSTMENT

Seasonally adjusted indices were first introduced in 1956. The seasonal corrections are applied in two stages.

(1) The indices (already corrected for number of days in each month) are further adjusted to take account of annual holidays in different industries.

(2) The figures after correction as outlined in (1) are now seasonally corrected by using seasonal adjustment factors calculated by a ratio to moving-average method.

The first adjustments were based on 1950–55 monthly figures, it being assumed that the seasonal pattern for these years would tend to recur in 1956. At the end of 1956 the seasonal factors were re-determined by taking into account the actual (unadjusted) pattern for 1956, as well as that for the earlier years. This has been repeated for each subsequent year. Thus the seasonal adjustments are kept constantly under review and brought up-to-date each year. Where special circumstances give rise to obvious abnormalities in the figures for any given month (e.g. an influenza epidemic affecting output) these abnormal figures will be eliminated from the seasonal variation computations.

It must be emphasised that the seasonally adjusted series are in no way more accurate than the unadjusted series, the former merely being intended to make the trend of production clearer by eliminating regular month-to-month fluctuations.

We have already commented upon the fact that it is only rarely possible to measure the actual physical production in any industry. All methods, whether based on quantities produced (ignoring input), value of output, quantities of materials received, or number of persons employed are at best approximate. The employment criterion is likely to be particularly unreliable, for reasons already stated, and that is why it is used in only a small number of cases. However, in addition to such inaccuracies there are difficulties arising out of the timing of the production series used. Some of the information is collected on a weekly basis, others on a monthly or quarterly basis. Table 12.2 shows that currently 280 of the production series, carrying nearly 44% of the total weighting, are mainly available on a quarterly basis. Obviously all the series have to be adjusted to a common monthly base, and in addition some form of estimation for monthly figures has to be used in connection with the information available only on a quarterly basis.

TABLE 12.2

Intervals at which information is produced

	1963-based index		*1958-based index*	
	No. of series	*% of weight carried*	*No. of series*	*% of weight carried*
Weeks and weekly averages	92	19·3	110	28·1
Calendar months	520	36·8	600	34·0
Quarters	124	8·1	70	4·4
Quarters (with some alternative series for shorter intervals)	156	35·8	100	33·5
	892	100·0	880	100·0

Source: 'The index of industrial production and other output measures', *Studies in Official Statistics*, No. 17 (H.M.S.O., 1970)

The information available does not all relate to the same intervals of time, and it does not all take the same time to reach the Central Statistical Office. Tables were published in *Economic Trends* in March 1962 (in respect of the 1958 based index) and in *The Index of Industrial Production and other measures,* in respect of the 1963 based index, giving an indication of the rate of receipt of information for the index. The following table (12.3), modified from the latter publication, shows the position in October 1969 when the August index was being calculated.

TABLE 12.3

Rate of receipt of information for Index of Industrial Production

Information received by mid-October 1969	*Total available*	*1963 based index Percentage of weight covered: In provisional form*	*In final form*
1969 indices for:			
August	90	65%	25%
July	91	55%	36%
June	100	8%	92%
May	100	7%	93%
April	100	7%	93%

Source: 'The index of industrial production and other output measures', *Studies in Official Statistics*, No. 17 (H.M.S.O., 1970)

It can be seen that in mid-October 1969 only 25% of the weighting data for August was in final form, and even for the July index (published in mid-September) the majority of the information was still provisional and subject to revision as more information became available.

Thus for general use, too much reliance should not be placed upon individual monthly figures, regard being had rather to the general pattern over several—preferably not too recent—months.

THE INDEX OF TOTAL OUTPUT

For the industries not covered by the index of industrial production there is no census of production from which to derive estimates of net output in the base year for use as weights. Instead the analysis of gross domestic product by industry and type of income for 1963 (estimates as given in the *1969 Blue Book*) is used as the basis of the weighting scheme for these 'remaining' industries. Certain adjustments to the figures as given in Table 17 of the *Blue Book* are necessary.

(1) Stock appreciation is included in the *Blue Book* figures, and as it does not represent actual output it must be deducted from each industry total.

(2) The *1969 Blue Book* used the 1958 Standard Industrial Classification. Adjustments are therefore necessary to convert the figures onto the 1968 Standard Industrial Classification basis.

(3) 'C' Licence vehicles are those run by non-transport firms for the carriage of their own goods. As it was felt all goods transport should be included under the 'Transport industry' heading, appropriate transfers in respect of the operation of these vehicles were made from the other industry groups to the Transport category.

(4) The gross domestic product is calculated for each industry without regard to payments or receipts of interest, which are considered as transfer payments and not as payments for work done. This means that the insurance, banking and finance Sector total (Order XXV. Standard Industrial Classification 1968) does not include receipts of net income. However, for the purpose of estimating the output weight for that sector, it is highly desirable that its net interest receipts be included as a measure of the value of its services. This implies that appropriate deductions of net interest payments should be made from the output figures for all other industries. Unfortunately sufficient information is not available for this to be done accurately. For want of a better procedure what is done is to reduce the weighting figure for each of the other industries proportionately.

(5) Taking into account the adjustments referred to it was found that the proportion of the gross domestic product (less stock appreciation) attributable to the index of industrial production industries was 0·4383. In other words if the total weights for *all* industries was 1,000, the index of industrial production industries contribute a weight of 438·3, and the 'remaining' industries 561·7. The detailed weights within the 438·3 were compiled from the individual index of industrial production weights.

Thus in the index of industrial production the textile industry has a weight of 56·44. In the total output or gross domestic product index, the weight for textiles is: $56{\cdot}44 \times \frac{438{\cdot}3}{100} = 24{\cdot}74$.

INDICATORS OF OUTPUT

Reference has been made on page 246 to some of the problems associated with obtaining suitable indicators of net output to estimate the ratio q^c/q_{63} for each industry. Suffice it to say that for the 'remaining' industries it is frequently necessary to use a different indicator for the quarterly estimates than for the annual series. One or two examples of the indicators used are given below.

Industry	*Weight per 1000*	*Annual series*	*Quarterly series*
Agriculture and horticulture	32·3	Net output (before deducting depreciation) of agricultural and horticultural holdings and of agricultural contractors, at constant prices.	Interpolation and projection of the annual figures.
Road passenger transport	1·6	London Transport road services: number of passenger-miles.	All operators: total number of passenger journeys.
	1·8	Transport holding company road services: number of passenger journeys.	
	5·6	Other operators: number of passenger journeys.	
	2·1	Taxis and private hire cars: consumers' expenditure at constant prices.	
Retail distribution of food and drink	7·1	Volume of sales of multiple food shops.	
	15·9	Volume of sales of food shops (other than multiple retailers).	
Insurance	8·7	Consumers' expenditure on life assurance at constant prices.	
	0·4	Accident insurance: premiums paid less claims deflated by consumer price index (3 yr. average).	Number in employment in Order XXIV
	3·1	Fire insurance: premiums paid less claims deflated by price index for gross domestic capital formation (3 yr. average)	
	2·4	Marine, aviation and transit insurance: premiums paid less claims deflated by average of unit value indices for imports and exports (3 yr. average)	
	4·0	Motor vehicle insurance: premiums paid less claims deflated by price index of vehicles (3 yr. average).	
	4·3	Miscellaneous insurance: premiums paid less claims deflated by consumer price index (3 yr. average).	

The total output index is seasonally adjusted in a manner similar to that described for the index of industrial production.

A detailed explanation of the construction of both the index of industrial production and the gross domestic product total output index is contained in *Studies in Official Statistics, No. 17; The Index of Industrial production and other output measures* (H.M.S.O.) The following relevant articles also appeared in *Economic Trends: Index of Industrial Production—Rebasing on 1963, (Economic Trends* August 1969): and *Index Numbers of Output at 1963 Factor Cost,* (*Economic Trends,* October 1969.) For those who are interested, the construction of the earlier 1958 based index of industrial production was fully explained in *The Index of Industrial Production—Method of Compilation* (*Studies in Official Statistics No. 7*; H.M.S.O.) Earlier articles in *Economic Trends* regarding total output measures are *Index Numbers of output at 1954—Factor Cost; Economic Trends,* August 1960 (subsequently republished in *Studies in Official Statistics No. 2*) and *Quarterly estimates of Gross Domestic Product based on output data, and Economic Trends,* February 1966—(subsequently republished in *Studies in Official Statistics No. 205).*

INDEX OF INDUSTRIAL PRODUCTION FOR WALES

For the first time in the 1969 *Digest of Welsh Statistics* (published 1970) an index of industrial production for Wales was published. It is constructed on similar lines to that for the United Kingdom as a whole. The index is now published quarterly, in both unadjusted and seasonally adjusted form. The November 1970 issue of *Economic Trends* contained an article explaining the coverage of the index and its method of construction.

QUESTIONS

1. Explain how the current index number of industrial production is calculated.
2. What do you understand by the index of total output and what is its purpose and how is it arrived at?
3. Net output can only very rarely be measured directly. Explain how estimates of net output are made for the purpose of calculating the index of industrial production.
4. Discuss the problem of allowing for increases in productivity when measuring, at constant prices, the output of the service industries.
5. How are seasonal adjustments made in the index of industrial production? Distinguish between those adjustments, and those made to allow for variations in the number of working days in the month, holidays, etc.
6. 'The Index of Industrial Production is calculated monthly, yet by no means all the data required is available on a monthly basis.' Comment on this statement, and indicate what attempts are made to overcome this difficulty.
7. 'Industry would rather have quick, if somewhat inaccurate, data of industrial output rather than have to wait months for definitive figures.' Discuss this statement in relation to the flow of information available for the construction of the index of industrial production.
8. Where is the data obtained for providing the weighting system for the index of total output in respect of those industries whose output is not measured by the index of industrial production? Comment on any alterations or adjustments which will have to be made for this purpose on the basic data available.
9. What problems are involved in attempting to measure production other than industrial production? How can these problems be overcome?
10. Comment on the value of the United Kingdom Index of Industrial Production as a measure of changes in economic activity.
11. Describe the sources and the nature of the statistics published in the United Kingdom on industrial production.
12. What steps are taken in the calculation of the index of industrial production to allow for the effect of:

(*a*) holidays
(*b*) varying number of working days in each month
(*c*) seasonal movement

13. What steps are taken to allow, in the index of industrial production, for output which cannot be measured physically? Why is the concept of net output important in the calculation of an index of total output? Explain how this concept may be used in choosing weights and indicators of output for the index, and explain to what extent the data actually used compares with the ideal.
14. Compare and contrast the problems arising in the calculation of an index number of industrial production on a monthly basis, and on an annual basis.

13 The uses of economic statistics

Economic statistics, says Pyatt*, can be looked upon as an historical record of economic affairs, a guide in the formulation of economic policy, and as a guide to understanding the system within which we live.

In practice it is difficult to separate the two latter functions, for surely it is impossible to guide economic policy in any rational way without having some understanding of how the economy works. What Pyatt is saying, however, is that economic statistics may be used in a purely empirical rule of thumb fashion largely on the basis of past experience, or we may attempt to establish functional or stochastic relationships which can be used to build up models of the economy. In the former case—which embraces much of current official economic forecasting—it is suggested that whilst we may have some success in forecasting by observing the results of similar situations in the past, we are no nearer to understanding the system. Models can, however, be tested and their effectiveness compared with one another in the sense that the synthetic empirical forecasts cannot, and that is why many would agree that economic models could contribute much more to our understanding of the economy.

The actual type of economic statistics collected must depend on the uses to which they are to be put. Thus if economic statistics are to contribute to the greatest extent to our understanding of the system in which we live, they should be such as will enable us to construct quantitative testable models. Ideally also the collection of the basic data should be carried out in a manner that permits of the calculation of standard errors so that the limits of any estimates obtained can be expressed in probability terms. Unfortunately in many cases it is not practicable, or there may not be sufficient information available, to enable samples to be selected in a random fashion.

---

* *On Official Economic Statistics*, F. G. Pyatt, Journal of the Royal Statistical Society, *Symposium on British Official Statistics*.

We are thus restricted as mentioned in Chapter 8 (page 167) to giving limits of error, largely of a subjective nature, for components of national income. It may be that 'experience' gives such estimates some semblance of reality, just as the idea of 'taking a view' of future developments in the economy is successful more often than not in experience. Nevertheless we should be working away from such methods as far as possible, and towards those which are reproducible no matter which skilled person is doing the estimating. Unless we do so it cannot really be said that we are making much progress in discovering how the complex system works.

OFFICIAL STATISTICS AS A RECORD OF THE PAST

An important problem here is the provision of adequate documentation of the developments over time of the methods of calculating a particular series, so that those wishing to use the data understand the changes which have taken place in the definitions over the years and what changes there have been in the bases and weighting systems of indices used, when and how breaks in the continuity of the series have occurred, what additional material may have been introduced and at what stage, and so on. It is not so much that records of these changes do not exist, but that the information may be scattered over so many issues of the various government publications that far too much time has to be spent in searching for them. Five years after the report on Government Statistical Service only a little has been done officially to provide adequate integrated guidance to facilitate the interpretation of lengthy historical series.

GUIDES TO ECONOMIC POLICY

A fundamental purpose of the collection and analysis of economic statistics is to assist in the formation of government policy. In the previous chapters, particularly those referring to population, manpower, production, distribution and the national income, this has been brought out clearly. Of particular significance in this connection are the forecasting activities of the statistical services.

SHORT-TERM GOVERNMENT FORECASTING

Short-term forecasts are made three times a year, up to eighteen months ahead, of the gross domestic product and its components, of total demand, of import and exports, and of the balance of payments. They provide a basis for decisions influencing domestic activity and the balance of payments during the period of the forecast.

The forecasts are made on assumption of static fiscal and credit policies, and are based on constant prices, although current price estimates for rather different purposes are also made.

The aim is to provide forecasts of the level of activity at the end of a period by building up a series of quarterly forecasts. An outline of the basic procedure is given below.

The starting data consists of:

Current estimates of the gross domestic product which are issued on a quarterly basis and which are calculated in three different ways, i.e. as a sum of expenditure, of factor incomes, and of industrial outputs

Monthly and quarterly figures of industrial production or sales

Particulars relating to earnings (new earnings survey), employment and vacancies unfilled

Retail sales figures

Hire-purchase transactions

New car registration

Exports and imports

Housing starts and completions

Investment intentions and orders on hand, and new orders.

The available basic material in the form of seasonally adjusted series is smoothed and, as far as possible, inconsistences are removed from the series. For example, the three methods of measuring the gross domestic product are largely independent, and because of estimation and other errors will not necessarily be identical.

First of all, preliminary forecasts are made of the various components of expenditure.

So far as fixed investment is concerned, public investment is considered separately from private investment. The forecasts for the public corporations, public authority housing and other public services are in each case made from the investment plans submitted by the various nationalized industries, the Civil Service and Local Authority Departments, as agreed by the Treasury.

So far as private fixed investment is concerned, in manufacturing, distribution and other services, and shipping industries the Department of Trade and Industry conducts sample enquiries into investment intentions three times a year. On the whole, these investment intentions tend to over-estimate actual investment, but it has been found that a fair degree of reliance can be placed upon the changes between the estimates from one period to the next corresponding period and it is on these changes, together with longer period evidence which might show up any cyclical movement, that the forecasters work.

The forecasts of investment in stocks tend to be difficult. They are based on an analysis of how stocks have moved in the past in relation to changes in production. Apparently the ratio of total stocks to total output tends to fluctuate around a fairly stable level. Forecasts of the stock/output ratio are made, therefore, giving weight in the estimate to the particular position in the stock-building cycle at the time in question, whilst, at the same time, estimating the likely rates of stock-building which can be reconciled with the ideal of a fairly stable basic stock-output ratio in view of the output implied by the rest of the forecast.

Public authorities' current expenditure, like their investment in fixed capital, is the subject of forward estimates which the departments and authorities are required to submit to the Treasury. These estimates are made on an annual basis and, obviously, an attempt has to be made to interpolate their development over the various quarters.

Personal consumption forecasts are developed by forecasting for the various components of personal income, for direct taxes, for consumer prices, and for personal saving. Because changes in income, and therefore in consumption, depend on changes in the level of output, which in turn is largely affected by personal consumption (thus implying a recurrence relationship) it is necessary to employ an iterative approach in order to obtain forecasts of personal consumption which are consistent with those for total output. Forecasts are made of the total wage and salary bill for the period, which implies the need to estimate wage rates. These forecasts are considered in the light of past periods, where the level of demand for labour has been similar, and also on the basis of current information about wage negotiations, and on assessments of changes in prices of consumption goods. Income in the form of dividends is supposed to be related, with a time lag, to changes in profits. Other property income is usually estimated by extrapolation of recent trends. The central authority has, of course, a considerable amount of firm information at its disposal on income to persons, e.g., Civil Service and Forces pay.

Forecasting of consumer prices is primarily based upon the monthly index of retail prices. For this purpose the price index is divided into three groups:

foods which are subject to short-term fluctuations
rent and rates
other items.

For the first two groups, the basic principle is to extrapolate the general trend. The remaining group of items, which make up about 80% of the total, is assumed to move in price, after a time lag, in the same way as costs.

Estimates of personal saving are very complicated, and hard and fast rules have not been laid down. Changes in the proportion of disposable income saved appears to some extent to vary with change in net lending by banks, and on variations in hire purchase charges.

Initially a ratio of gross saving to personal disposable income averaged over a period of past years is obtained. This is applied to the forecast of personal disposable income already made. If the forecast of personal income shows a sudden change, however, from the previous trend the savings forecast requires to be modified. Such modifications are mainly on a rule-of-thumb basis influenced largely by forecast changes in direct taxes, consumer prices, and net lending to persons by the financial sector.

Exports and imports are brought into the forecast both directly, and from the point of view of the forecast of the balance of payments. The balance of payments itself is forecast initially by an assessment made of the development of output in the main industrial countries.

So far as exports are concerned, reports from official British representatives in the main countries which provide markets for United Kingdom goods are sought as to the likely future of United Kingdom exports. Different indicators are used in respect of different countries, for example, United Kingdom exports to the United States appear to be closely associated with the movements of the gross national product of that country, whilst the development of private investment in Western Europe is inclined to have a marked effect on United Kingdom exports of capital equipment to that area. The forecasts are considered from the point of view of (a) individual commodity information currently available (e.g. from statistics of orders) and (b) information on expected relative changes in United Kingdom costs and prices, compared with those for the world as a whole.

Imports have tended over the years to rise rather faster than the output of home-produced goods. Fluctuations in this movement occur due to changes in the rate of stock building, but in addition, changes in prices, and the current progressive liberalization of imports are also taken into account. Forecasts are made on a commodity basis, as well as by reference to forecasts made elsewhere of total sales and of stock building in the United Kingdom as a whole.

The various main invisible items are forecast separately, government current income and expenditure being derived largely from the budget estimate figures. Forecasts of shipping income and payments are obtained from forecasts of the volume of imports and exports and of freight rates, together with an estimate of the likely trend of the share of British shipping in world trade. Travel debits and credits for Western Europe, North America and the sterling area separately are largely extrapolations of recent trends, together with information drawn from forward bookings. Forecasts of interests, profits, and dividends are based on an assessment of prospects of company earnings in the United Kingdom and abroad, allowing for the industrial and area distribution of the investments. Estimates of oil company earnings are obtained from forecasts made by the major oil companies.

Forecasts of private long-term capital investment are very difficult and have not been particularly successful. They are largely influenced by an assessment of the economic prospects here and abroad, bearing in mind that it has been found that the proportion of profits invested by United Kingdom companies operating abroad tends to be fairly stable. Oil investment movements are again obtained from forecasts made by the major oil companies. Official long-term repayments of capital are, of course, accurately known, but the rate at which drawings are made on loans is difficult to forecast and some broad assessment in each individual case is made.

As in so many other cases, the need by government for detailed statistics to guide policy may conflict with the willingness of the suppliers to provide the information. Some mention was made in Chapter 2 of the ways in which the Central Statistical Office is by a process of rationalization attempting to overcome this problem.

These forecasts are very largely of the synthetic type and are subject to the limitations already discussed. Recently, however, more attention has been given to econometric model building in certain areas (*see* below) but it still does not play a major part. This is probably due more to the limitations of the basic statistical data than to any inertia on the part of the forecasters. For more detailed information refer to: 'Short term forecasting in the United Kingdom', *Economic Trends,* August 1964; 'Econometric research for short term forecasting', *Economic Trends,* February 1967; 'Short term forecasting of United Kingdom exports', *Economic Trends,* May 1967; 'Short term forecasts of income expenditure and saving', *Economic Trends,* February 1968.

For a constructive criticism of a recent example of medium-term planning (the abortive National Plan) reference may be made to 'Statistics of medium term economic planning' by Armstrong and Lecomber, *Journal of Royal Statistical Society*, vol. 131, pt. 1, 1968.

THE NEED FOR MORE DETAILED STATISTICAL DATA

The current attention which is being paid to regional and sub-regional planning, and to the needs of various groups within the community (such as persons living on social security, retirement payments or students' grants) demands more detailed statistical information than has been available in the past. It also calls for a high degree of compatibility between the statistics produced by the various departments, at a very detailed level. The standard classifications referred to in Chapter 3 do not solve this problem entirely by any means. For example, statistics of income from the Inland Revenue Department are not available in respect of the employment exchange travel-to-work areas used by the Department of Employment.

The providing of information from several sources which require to be linked at a given level raises the question of confidentiality as well as practicability. Are firms prepared to have such a breakdown of output—at a detailed sub-regional level—that their own individual sales will be revealed? Can income-distributions be prepared for towns without disclosing some of the larger individual incomes? The Statistics of Trade Act, in addition to requiring firms to disclose certain information in connexion with government inquiries, has strict rules regarding the confidentiality of the data to the government department collecting it. Although transfers of information from one department to another may take place in certain circumstances, there is nothing like the free flow that should exist if the authorities are to make the best use of the data which exists. We mentioned in Chapter 2 the reasons why a completely centralized system of statistics for this country had been rejected. The decision is probably a correct one, but only so if all obstacles to the transfer of information from department to department are removed.

As the measures for improvement outlined in Chapter 2 come to fruition we can expect a more rationally organized and informative system than we have had previously, but many of the problems referred to earlier in this chapter will continue to exist unless the attitude of the supplier of the data can be changed. One way of doing this is by convincing business firms—who are the major suppliers—that the processed statistics will be useful to them as a guide to their own policies. Considerable attention is being given to this at present, as the close attention to publicity and the consultations with industry referred to in other chapters indicates.

What statistical information then does industry require to help it formulate policy? This will of course vary in detail with each firm and industry. There is however a very general measure of agreement on what is basically required.*

OFFICIAL STATISTICS AND INDUSTRIAL REQUIREMENTS

Firms require information from the statistical services to enable them to plan their output, both so far as total capacity and its allocation between different products are concerned. They also require it in order to be able to monitor competition. They must

* See (1) *Statistics for Business Planning* (Zinker & Booer J.R.S.S., series A, vol. 131 No. 1, 1968); (2) *Proceedings of the Industrial Marketing Research Association*, February 1970; (3) *Evidence of the Economic Directorate, Confederation of British Industries*; and (4) *Providers & Users of Official Statistics*—Evidence by A. M. Alfred, Chief Economist, Courtaulds Ltd. Both (3) and (4) are in *Government Statistical Services* (4th Report of the Estimates Committee 1967–68).

endeavour to assess to what extent the demand for their products is likely to be sustained, both from the point of view of short term planning, and also to assist in the making of decisions about fixed capital investment. The Confederation of British Industries, in its evidence to the Estimates Committee (*Government Statistical service Report 1967–68*), indicated broadly the information which was likely to be useful to industrialists. Firstly, statistics of orders received, deliveries and outstanding orders at a given time are needed. The statistics of orders are expected to give an early indication of the trend of trade, whilst those for deliveries and outstanding orders will give a rather longer-term picture, with particular reference to the extent to which back-logs may be building-up, or to whether or not a decline in activity is in the offing.

Secondly, the importance of having information on the production of various commodities in terms of both value *and* quantity was emphasized in the C.B.I. evidence, and indeed has been the theme of the comments of many other industrialists subsequently. Without quantitative information, it is suggested that average values and costs, etc., cannot be computed, and that it is less easy to take into account the effect of price changes in an inflationary situation. Emphasis has also been laid on the need for production and sales statistics, classified by type of customer, and by the end-use of the product.

Industrialists who use the official sources of statistics frequently comment that the commodity groupings are too broad for their requirements. In general, they require breakdowns in greater detail, not only in connection with statistics of orders, production, sales, deliveries, etc., but also for stocks and work-in-progress. In particular, there are requests for the publication of the index of wholesale prices with much more detailed categorization of materials. Detailed price indices in respect of industrial plant and machinery would appear also to be welcomed.

Overall, there is a considerable emphasis on speed of publication. In general, industrialists seem to prefer figures as early as possible even if they have to be revised a great deal subsequently. Again, business users often call for monthly figures in the categories referred to, rather than quarterly ones.

Some criticism have been made of the suitability of official statistics for business purposes. There appears to be a continued feeling that the information on individual commodities may get out of date rapidly, and thus not give business the figures required. Moreover, business particularly needs information on new products and new areas of growth, and it is sometimes felt that it takes too long for new commodities to find their true place in the present system. Moreover, in the emphasis on quarterly rather than monthly data, and on value figures rather than quantity figures, the new system of industrial statistics appears, to some extent, to be moving away from suggestions on these matters made by industrial users.

Whilst there is some validity in these criticisms it must not be forgotten that industry speaks with two voices. There is on the one hand a demand for more detail, at more frequent intervals, of closely defined products, in respect of narrower market areas; on the other, there is a resistance by many firms to supplying even the more limited data which is needed for even the current statistical programme, and to any relaxation of the confidentiality rules—which themselves limit the amount of detail which can be provided. The problem is well stated in the following comment,

'... it must be remembered that the demand for information comes from a few hundred firms at most which are avid devourers of information, but the information they want to devour has to be supplied by thousands of small people. Maybe there should not be this disproportion, but it is a fact of life I am afraid. Incidentally, every firm has a certain number of people who want data and a certain number who supply the data which are the foundation of the statistics. These two sets of people are not the same. More than once we have found that we have had demands from one side of an organization and an absolute refusal to supply anything from the other. If the demanders could get in touch with their colleagues and educate them a little, it would help us no end.' (Source: H. E. Browning, Board of Trade, 'Discussion on the Papers on Economic and Business Statistics', *Journal of the Royal Statistical Society*, vol. 131, pt. 1, 1968.)

Index